Praise for Stephen Brunt and **GRETZKY'S TEARS**

NATIONAL BESTSELLER
A Chapters/Indigo Editors' Pick

"We thought we knew the story. With Brunt's account, we know that we only had the ugly half of it. His is the most detailed account yet, and it makes for an unforgettable set-piece that is at the centre of [the] book." *The Globe and Mail*

"Brunt gets into the meat of the story. A writer with a deep understanding of hockey's importance to Canada's national identity, he is nonetheless unafraid to explode many of the game's dearest myths. . . . In Brunt's telling, a story whose ending we all know still manages to take on the suspense of a tautly plotted novel, one whose scenes are set with skill and economy." *The Gazette*

"Fast-moving and totally enjoyable. . . . Required reading if you want to understand why our favourite game is the way it is." *The Georgia Straight*

"Brunt deftly connects the dots between the deal and the NHL's Sun Belt strategy to expand further into the U.S., and in the process revisits what was a seminal moment for the game. . . . Unlike many breathless sportswriters, Brunt has both a literary sense and a detachment from the story, allowing it to unfold unencumbered by the routine hyperbole of the nightly sports newsreel or the partisan newspaper scribe." *Quill & Quire*

"Brunt . . . is a remarkable talent, one of Canada's finest journalists. . . . The description of the game action is vivid and poetic, the off-ice drama enthralling and brutally frank." *The McGill Tribune*

"With *Gretzky's Tears*, Brunt reminds us that sports-writing can be eloquent. And with knowledge that extends beyond mastery of the sports world, he is able to seamlessly fill in social and political context, bringing gravitas to his topic." *The Tyee*

"One of the best sportswriters out there." *The Hamilton Spectator*

"Brilliant . . . research and writing by Brunt. . . . Brunt's account is amazing, spiked by detailed profiles of the business antics of two disgraced main characters in the Gretzky story—Pocklington and McNall. Business never read so well." *London Free Press*

ALSO BY STEPHEN BRUNT

Searching for Bobby Orr
The Way It Looks from Here: Contemporary Canadian Writing on Sports
Facing Ali: The Opposition Weighs In
Mean Business: The Rise and Fall of Shawn O'Sullivan
Second to None: The Roberto Alomar Story
Diamond Dreams: 20 Years of Blue Jays Baseball

GRETZKY'S TEARS

HOCKEY, CANADA, AND THE DAY EVERYTHING CHANGED

STEPHEN BRUNT

Vintage Canada

Published in Canada by Vintage Canada, a division of Random House of
Canada Limited, Toronto, in 2010. Originally published in hardcover in Canada
by Alfred A. Knopf Canada, a division of Random House of Canada Limited,
in 2009. Distributed by Random House of Canada Limited.

Vintage Canada with colophon is a registered trademark.

www.randomhouse.ca

"The Trade that Shook the Hockey World," on page 170, is from the collection
The Hockey Player Sonnets: Overtime by James B. Lee. Kind permission to reprint
the poem has been granted by the author and by Penumbra Press.

Library and Archives Canada Cataloguing in Publication

Brunt, Stephen
Gretzky's tears : hockey, Canada, and the day everything changed / Stephen
Brunt.

ISBN 978-0-307-39730-0

1. Gretzky, Wayne, 1961–. 2. Hockey—Canada—History. 3. National Hockey
League—History. 4. Hockey players—Canada—Biography.

GV848.5.G78B78 2010   796.962092   C2010-900840-5

Book design by Leah Springate

Printed and bound in the United States of America

2 4 6 8 9 7 5 3 1

For Jeanie MacFarlane

Contents

Chapter One

THE NEXT ONE

IT IS THE SAME STORY. It is a different story.

Small town, working folks, genius sprung straight from the land, honed on frozen slough or backyard rink. Twenty years on, the shinny creation myth hadn't really changed so much, even if so much else had. A new setting now, and Brantford wasn't Parry Sound. Not the near north, the cottager's idea of wilderness, not a prairie crossroads, a backwoods outpost, but the kind of place where most Canadians really lived. It was a city of modest proportions, industrial and gritty, the town that Massey Ferguson built, the country's capital of combine harvesters. The Grand River split it in two, but on Varadi Avenue most of the skating was done on dad-made ice. Walter Gretzky was a driven man, a hard man, who never made more than twenty-five grand working for the Bell (Alexander Graham had lived in Brantford too). He grew up on a farm, never drove a new car, and counted every nickel. He was a tough little guy who once cracked his skull in an accident on the job, was in a coma for awhile, was off work for eighteen months while the family struggled to live on disability payments. When he recovered, he was left deaf in one ear and his head hurt all the time.

There was nothing golden or glamorous about Wally. He didn't like the night life or want to charm the ladies or walk with the ex-athlete's swagger, though he certainly didn't mind a bit of attention. He had a big schnozz, a face right from the old country, and his kids would never have to wonder where he was.

His boy, or at least the one born with the gift, didn't play with a lurking anger; his competitive instincts were cloaked in softer fabric. He would almost never fight. He was handsome in a different way—not along the square, straight, crew-cut lines of the 1950s, but skinny, feminine in a way. And bright enough, though school was beside the point. Everybody who saw him at the rink, nearly from the earliest days, understood where his destiny lay, that he would be the next one. Even before his voice had changed, the press flocked to Brantford to see the wonder child, to ask him how it felt to be so special. There would be no more eureka moments, no more accidental discoveries of unknown hockey genius, stumbled upon in a chilly old barn of an arena. Wayne Gretzky we knew before we knew what he really was or what he really meant. (By the time the *next* one came along, in Cole Harbour, Nova Scotia, the path was so familiar, the tale had been so processed, that it would seem stage-managed, contrived, reduced almost to cliché.)

The story of the nurturing, demanding dad, the ridiculous scoring feats in minor hockey, the parents end-running the system, the short career in junior, the jump to a rebel professional league—it was all played out under the lights. As before, our hero would change the game, would reimagine it with his genius, would set the National Hockey League on an entirely new course, would be its face shining among the heathens, its image and salvation. For the country, he would come to represent something else—not just the embodiment of national identity wrapped up in a game, but what it felt like to have that bought and sold.

The same story, and different.

A chapter closes.

It was the wrong place, the wrong uniform, but the trappings, the setting, were beside the point. It didn't really matter now whether he was a Bruin or a Blackhawk. The end had come, as he had long known it would, prematurely, painfully, bitterly. In 1978, Bobby Orr was thirty years old, and he wouldn't be playing hockey anymore.

He had stumbled through six games at the beginning of that final season with Chicago before finally surrendering to the knifing pain in his left knee, wrecked and repaired, wrecked and repaired again. All that remained was to make official what was obvious, to share the bad tidings with the world.

Orr had never been comfortable with public intimacy, even the feigned, phony kind that was fast becoming the currency of celebrity. He was imbued with the stoicism of his forebears, their natural reserve, a shyness bordering on the antisocial that had fully kicked in when he left Oshawa for Boston as a teen. The walls he had erected only grew thicker as they wanted more of him. The modern world was redefining sports stardom, with everything, every personal detail, fair game, and he hated that. But now here he was at a press conference, laid bare under the bright lights, with shutters clicking, cameras whirring, and Bobby Orr began to cry. "I'm very, very happy that I attempted to play again," he said, reading carefully, deliberately from his script. "I now know for sure that my leg—" He paused, trying to hold back the emotion. "—cannot handle playing."

He continued, haltingly.

"I am disappointed but I am relieved. I would not want to go through the rest of my life thinking, well, maybe there was that chance. I now know I am no longer able to play."

The saviour of the Boston franchise, the sport's first breakout superstar, the face of the great expansion, the liberated athlete-as-entrepreneur, for awhile the greatest earner in all of professional sports, departed the scene in a very different world than the one he had entered as an eighteen-year-old in 1966. Players were chattel then. Owners were conservative and omnipotent. Hockey was a funny little regional six-team operation, cobwebbed, musty, unchanged for decades.

Nearly all of the players had agents now, and they had a union, and they might wind up showcasing their skills in a whole host of exotic locales, since the NHL had continued adding teams in fits and starts after doubling the original half-dozen, driven by the lure of quick money and a phantom American television audience. The established league couldn't move fast enough to satisfy the imagined demand, so another loop was cobbled together by hockey hustlers, though on the shakiest of foundations. Veteran players, Orr's contemporaries, cashed in enthusiastically, bolting the NHL monopoly for the chance to earn big money playing in strange uniforms for slapdash teams with silly names, that might fold in the face of a strong breeze. The World Hockey Association and Boston's penurious owners had more to do with breaking up the Bruins' dynasty than had any rising foe. Even Bobby Orr had briefly flirted with becoming a Minnesota Fighting Saint, following the path of Gerry Cheevers and Derek Sanderson and the rest of those who had fled Boston Garden, before he finally signed the fateful deal with Chicago.

He and Alan Eagleson had helped build this new world, exploiting the leverage created as the greatest player the game had ever seen, the greatest product it had ever produced, to break the shackles. Now he, though not Alan Eagleson, was about to exit, stage left. For an unhappy retirement. For a cloistered personal life. For near financial ruin. For a period in which he would be so estranged from the game that had defined him, and that he had so helped define, that his two sons would never feel the urge, or the encouragement, to even lace up a pair of skates.

A chapter opens.

It is the age of the hero capitalists, of new-money sex appeal, of the art of the deal celebrated as though it were honest-to-God art. Real estate flippers as movie stars, Michael Milken and Ivan Boesky and Donald Trump, blue-suited pin-up boys. Still to come, the crashes and burns and bankruptcies—and in some cases the jail sentences—but for a brief shining moment they are right there at the heart of the zeitgeist, even in the backwaters.

Six days before Bobby Orr announced his retirement in Chicago, two of those high fliers got together in the most northerly metropolis in North America to play what was, next to high-stakes backgammon, their favourite game. Nelson Skalbania and Peter Pocklington shared a simple set of business principles: buy low, sell high; calculate risk and reward; use other people's money as often as possible; run circles around the stodgy old guard, with their inherited wealth, their safety-first instincts; take chances they never would; search out the cutting edge and ride it, even as you started to bleed a little. Both of them, business-wise, were on the make, always looking for one-night stands and not a partner for life.

There were also differences, though those matching thick, full, dark beards could make them appear, on the surface, almost to be the brothers on the cough drop package. (Skalbania felt compelled to point out that when it came to facial hair, and by implication to other things, he was the *sui generis* and Pocklington the knock-off.) Skalbania hailed from Vancouver, earned a structural engineering degree from prestigious Cal Tech, then ditched his profession to make his first fortune in real estate, where he loved the adrenaline rush of the big score. Pocklington came from square southwestern Ontario, though he was more than happy to morph, as were so many others, into an oil-boom Alberta free-enterpriser. He quit school early and started out selling used cars—including the family's own, without his father's permission. In business he could play the bully, and he was a bit rough around the edges. Some of his schemes were over and done with in an instant, and some investments he hung on to until they had maxed out, until the moment *the asset had begun to depreciate.* Remember that phrase.

Among the things they had in common were that neither knew a damn thing about hockey and neither let the fact that they didn't know a damn thing about hockey prevent them from sinking money into the business of the game. Skalbania was the first to get into the World Hockey Association, and he fit right in with its wild and woolly cast of promoters and dreamers and pretenders. Like the rest, he bet that any sports franchise—anywhere—at the bargain-basement prices they were asking just had to be worth more. And then there was the larger play, the big game of chicken, which required surviving long enough that the NHL owners would have no real choice but to let the interlopers join their club. That strategy had worked—once, for the American Football League, to the massive enrichment of its owners when they forced their way into the National Football League. It would never really work again, though it would be attempted by every fly-by-night league that followed, no matter what the sport.

The Edmonton Oilers were originally run by hockey maverick Wild Bill Hunter and owned in large part by a wealthy local named Dr. Charles Allard, who bought the franchise for only $25,000 but still couldn't make it pay. Allard knew Skalbania from financing some of his real estate forays, and was delighted to sell him the hockey team, adding the sincere verbal assurance that it certainly wouldn't lose more than $300,000 a year. Skalbania lost $300,000 in his first month. With no quick turnaround in sight, he naturally sought an exit strategy. Enter Pocklington, his sort-of pal and sort-of rival, who very much liked the idea of upping his public profile, of becoming a bit of a star himself. Skalbania sold Pocklington half of the Oilers in a steakhouse, in public, with a bunch of sports reporters looking on (a classic grandstand play), taking a Rolls Royce, a selection of fine art, and a diamond ring plucked straight from the finger of Pocklington's loyal wife, Eva, as payment (in addition to which, Pocklington assumed half of the Oilers' not-insubstantial debt, and half of their liabilities, which was worth a whole lot more to Skalbania in the moment than any piece of jewellery). Pocklington got lost driving to the rink the first time he went to see *his* Oilers play.

Skalbania also owned a second-last-legs WHA franchise in Indianapolis, Indiana, a city whose fondness for ice hockey remained a closely guarded secret. If he hadn't bought the Racers they would have folded, and if they *had* folded the WHA would have been down to six shaky teams, which certainly would not bode well for the future. As late as the spring of 1978, Skalbania was still talking brave talk, fending off the doubters, even as the league seemed to be crumbling around him. He told an Indianapolis newspaperman, apparently with a straight face, "There's going to be a WHA next year come hell or high water. Nuts to everyone else. That's N-U-T-S." And he still had one wild, visionary, crazy-bold card to play.

The NHL had rules about who could play in their league and who couldn't, beginning with nineteen-year-olds selected in the annual amateur draft. Understandably, the now-desperate WHA owners weren't much interested in protocol, or worried about being accused of exploiting child labour. In Birmingham, Alabama —another dormant shinny hotbed—owner Johnny F. Bassett signed his underage "Baby Bulls" before they could be drafted, kids tired of playing for sixty bucks a week in the service of junior teams that turned a tidy profit. It was Bassett who encouraged Skalbania to give it a try. He said he couldn't afford to sign any more underage players himself, but if he could, if he did, there was a seventeen-year-old playing junior in the Soo who was really something special. He'd seen him for the first time way, way back, as a ten-year-old kid in Brantford. "I'm pretty much tapped out, Nelson," Bassett said, "so this one is all yours."

The existence of a teen messiah may have been news to Skalbania, but it wasn't to most any other hockey-loving Canadian. Wayne Gretzky's story, a familiar replay of the national shinny ur-myth, had already been well circulated. But even though Skalbania had never seen him play, he was more than happy to buy Gretzky, just like that. He flew him up to Vancouver with his mom and dad and his agent, Gus Badali, invited them all to his mansion, challenged Gretzky to a six-mile race (Skalbania was a fitness buff), lost handily and, based on that experience, decided that that the kid was the real deal. This was a year before the NHL would allow its worst team to have first crack at Gretzky through the draft, and thus a year before Gretzky could otherwise earn a hockey salary—and then, at nothing close to his true market value. Skalbania gave him a $50,000 signing bonus and promised him crazy money because it might save his team and his league. And the moment it became obvious that that wasn't going to happen, that Indianapolis remained immune to hockey and to Gretzky's charms, Skalbania moved to cash out. Just eight games into a season in which the

Indianapolis Racers would be out of business after game twenty-five, Skalbania called Michael Gobuty, the co-owner of the Winnipeg Jets, with a sporting proposition. To make sure he had an option, a bit of leverage if required, he got in touch with fellow-traveller Peter Pocklington as well.

Time, memory and self-mythologizing render the picture a little fuzzy here. As Skalbania recalls it, he flew to Winnipeg, with Gobuty on board. John Ferguson, who ran the Jets, was waiting at the airport. "You're not going to pay that kind of money to a seventeen-year-old," Big John said, and who was Gobuty to argue? So that was that. Skalbania immediately called Pocklington and cut a deal. Others remember it differently, remember Fergie as being plenty enthusiastic, but cash was the issue—Skalbania needed as much as he could get, and Pocklington was willing to pay more, which sounds about right. Gretzky was told to board a private jet in Indianapolis, along with the other players who were thrown in —his future best man, Eddie Mio, and Peter Driscoll—not knowing exactly where the plane was headed. The pilot didn't know, either, and didn't know who was paying for the trip, but he took off on a northerly heading, on a wing and a prayer, *and* in possession of Mio's credit card. Somewhere up there, he was contacted by radio and instructed to hang a left and chart a course for Edmonton.

They called it a trade, but it wasn't a trade. More like a real estate transaction. There were other players involved, for the optics, but at base it was a straight cash-for-flesh exchange. The age of professional athletes as chattel might have already drawn to a close, but Wayne Gretzky was bought and sold like any commodity. In the papers, they said the price was $850,000. In private, Pocklington maintained it was $700,000—though, like a gambler who crows over every win and grows stone quiet over losses, he wanted very badly for everyone to believe that he was the smartest guy in the room. In private, Skalbania said he never got all of his cash in any case.

A decade later, Gretzky would be sold again, though again they tried to call it a trade. His price had gone way up. Pocklington would have a much harder time convincing the outside world that he'd got the better of the deal. And at that press conference, there would also be crying.

But Gretzky's tears were different.

Chapter Two

THE PRODIGY BUSINESS

.

THERE WAS A BOY, neither strange nor enchanted, which was as ordained. To be ordinary in every aspect but one— that was essential. To emerge from humble origins, to demonstrate skills and determination, yet to remain on some level unaware, unspoiled, happy just to have the chance to lace up and play the only game that mattered. That was the link between the heroes of a vague, distant past, the forebears Gordie Howe and Maurice Richard, and the first true modern, Bobby Orr, who followed in their footsteps. Soon enough would come a generation of young supermen: Mario Lemieux and Eric Lindros, evidence of the evolution of the species, bigger and stronger than previous generations. But *that* would be different. That would feel like science. It was a rational conclusion that they'd be better at whatever they attempted than the average mortal. This story still felt like magic. Wayne Gretzky's arrival was more like an incarnation of the Dalai Lama, who after he dies returns as a boy, waiting only to be discovered and acknowledged. He would be born to a decent, hard-working family, a hockey genius sprouted straight from the landscape, from the rocks and trees and ice and snow. That's what Canada did.

Gretzky would be fundamentally unlike any other hockey player who had ever lived, in ways that were far more difficult to articulate than speed or size or strength, but any Canadian could recite the basic elements of his biography like catechism.

The story hadn't changed, but the prodigy business certainly had in the preceding twenty years. Orr was twelve years old, dominating a game against older boys in Napanee, Ontario, when he was spotted for the first time by outsiders, entirely by chance. He had grown up only a few hours from Toronto, but it was as though he'd been hiding away in the northern bush or the Amazon rainforest, in an exotic, hidden world. The Boston Bruins' brain trust, beneficiaries of dumb luck, went to the rink to scout two other local kids and were instead transfixed at the sight of the diminutive blonde wonder child. They had never even heard his name before. Only by that kismet did the worst team of six in the National Hockey League find itself first in line for the greatest player of his generation. When they persuaded the kid and his old man to sign on the dotted line in return for a used car, a cash bonus and a new stucco job on the family home in Parry Sound, they understood that they owned Orr for the rest of his hockey-playing life. There was no rival league, no such thing as free agency, or agents or unions. They bought him, paid for him, and he was theirs alone.

Consider that, and consider the sound of a child speaking to a radio interviewer faced with an age-old challenge of his profession: how to get a kid to talk into a microphone using something other than monosyllables. Wayne Gretzky was ten years old, and already his story was filtering out: a boy hockey phenom, dominating his hometown league, more than holding his own against older, bigger, stronger kids, piling up unprecedented totals of goals and assists, skating around opponents as though they were inanimate. He was slight and delicate, but there was something about him—great stick and puck skills, for sure, but also an instinct for the game, an ability to see the whole ice, to set the pace, no matter how hard the other team tried to neutralize him, box him in or knock him flat. It was genius, for sure, and if anyone harboured doubts, if anyone wondered whether it might wear off, whether in a few years, the playing field would seem a bit more level, whether when adolescence approached, the kid might be dragged away by girls or a guitar or any of the thousand and one distractions that weren't hockey, they certainly wouldn't let them cloud this happy picture.

In Toronto, in 1971, at a newspaper in its death throes called the *Telegram,* a student reporter named John Iaboni was entrusted with the task of producing a weekly minor hockey page, and loved every minute of his job. The owner, who was about to shut the *Tely* down for good, was named John Bassett. He had once been a partner in the ownership of the Toronto Maple Leafs. His son, Johnny F., was a sport enthusiast who for a time worked at the old man's newspaper (and who would re-enter the story at a later date); *his* son, yet another John Bassett, was playing youth hockey then. In his travels to the rink to watch his boy, Johnny F. had seen something remarkable and passed on a story tip to Iaboni. "There's a kid in Brantford you ought to see," he said. "I'm telling you, he's better than Bobby Orr." It took a second prompt before Iaboni got around to making the trip, arriving at the North Park Arena in Brantford to see the novice Nadrofsky Steelers play the visiting Toronto Kings, no soft touches, undefeated in their own league. The boy, all four feet, ten inches and seventy pounds of him, scored five goals and added two assists in a 7–4 win, and played as though he had the puck on a string. When Iaboni sought him out in the dressing room afterwards, he found a shy, polite kid who was more than happy to talk about his hockey-playing idol—an unlikely one, given the year, given the generation, given that he was speaking of someone of nearly the same vintage as his old man. "Now Gordie Howe is my kind of player," Gretzky said. "He had so many tricks round the net, no wonder he scored so many goals. I'd like to be just like him. And if I couldn't play hockey I'd like to play baseball with the Oakland Athletics and Vida Blue." The story ran on October 28, 1971. Two days later, the *Telegram* closed its doors for good.

And so it began, the commodification of Wayne Gretzky, at an age when the golden children of hockey's past were unnoticed beyond the boundaries of their town or its rink. This one wouldn't be discovered by chance. He wouldn't sneak up on anyone. He would be a surprise only for those who had paid absolutely no attention, who didn't read the sports pages, flick on the radio to hear Peter Gzowski in the morning, or watch *Hockey Night in Canada*. He sure wouldn't be bought for a coat of stucco. He would be able to make choices about where he'd play, he would be able to earn close to fair market value. He would employ an agent by the time he turned thirteen. And he would learn to comfortably spin his own tale, to face down any number of cameras, to smile his shy smile, to charm and disarm, both genuinely personable and, from an early age, acutely aware of his own brand. He would be a perfect Canadian product, not just because of how well he played hockey, but because of how well his life story fit, or occasionally was made to fit, the national myth. Once Iaboni's article appeared, they all began beating a path to his door. Had someone set out to create that character from scratch, they couldn't have done better: ten-year-old Wayne Gretzky, having just scored his 200th goal of the season in novice hockey, en route to scoring 378, beginning his first local radio interview in Brantford, with his doting hockey dad, Walter, standing by his side. The interviewer is Arnold Anderson from radio station CKPC, who, over a career that spanned more than a half-century, would become known as the voice of local sports in Brantford.

"Wayne, scoring two hundred goals is quite the thing no matter what league you're in, isn't it?"

"Yes it is. That's for sure."

"Walter, everybody talks about Wayne and these good moves that he's got. Did you plan them or how did they come along?"

"No, he's worked on most of those moves himself and thought of it. It's just natural talent that he's perfected."

"Has he watched any other players that you know of?"

"Gordie Howe. He's always liked watching him."

"Every time you hear people talking about him also they talk about his skating, the way he's able to go to both sides. This is a big asset, I suppose, for any young hockey player, and for older ones too."

"Oh, that's for sure. Skating is the biggest part of the game. Wayne has skated and skated until he's become the skater he is. He just practises at it always."

"Wayne, how old were you when you started to skate?"

"About three."

"Just three years old, eh? Do you like playing hockey?"

"Yes I do."

"You don't want to make too big a thing out of it, but two hundred goals is a lot of goals. Did you know you were aiming for two hundred the other night when you played here?"

"Yeah."

"I think one of your little friends tried to set you up, didn't he?"

"Yeah."

"Do you like passing the puck and setting other guys up too?"

"Yeah, well, when you're in an easy game and you know he's got no goals all season, you like to set somebody up."

"Walter, you've probably been asked this before, why Wayne is playing in novice, which is the ten-year-olds and under, rather than the older group in peewee. Is there any particular reason for that?"

"I left it up to Wayne himself to decide what he wanted to do. At first he was undecided himself whether to go to peewee or stay in novice. I was glad he stayed in novice. Because he still is ten—he'll be eleven shortly—but the game is still for fun for him. He should have all of the enjoyment a ten-year-old boy gets out of the game. And of course in peewee they are bigger, they're two years older, he could get hurt, he's still only eighty pounds."

Three years later, on the morning of March 24, 1974, thirteen-year-old Gretzky arrived at the CBC Radio studios, housed in a decrepit former private girls' school on Jarvis Street in downtown Toronto, accompanied by his peewee hockey coach. There and then, he would meet for the first time the perfect teller of his tale, and become for a time his muse.

Peter Gzowski was a distinctly Canadian figure. As a writer (he was a newspaper and magazine guy to start), and especially a radio broadcaster, he could juggle the country's contradictions better than anyone—its complex, diverse urban reality and rural roots mythology; its cultural strength and insecurity; its love-hate relationship with the overpowering neighbour to the south—with wit, intelligence, on-air warmth and, when it was called for, a prickly edge. He was known for being equally comfortable interviewing prime ministers and extracting homemade pickle recipes from ordinary folks, but his greatest strength was in constructing a national narrative that could wrap all of that together under the red maple leaf. Radio was, for Gzowski, the perfect medium: intimate, expansive, the studio providing a secure cocoon for his own self-consciousness (on television, where he was required to be concise, glib and artificially effervescent, he failed miserably), and it was on radio—first as host of *This Country in the Morning*, and then *Morningside*—that he tapped so deeply and so well into Canada's elusive identity.

Gretzky would become one of his recurring subjects, interviewed again and again, and the central character in what was arguably Gzowski's best work as a writer, *The Game of Our Lives*. He loved hockey, and in the story of the boy genius from Brantford he heard the echoes of a larger national myth. Gretzky's biography wasn't just the great Canadian fable, but a mirror reflecting a changing country and changing times. All of that begins to come across in the very first encounter between the player and the broadcaster, in which Gzowski became one of the first to try and put Gretzky into context.

Just a few weeks before, Gretzky had played in the famous Quebec City peewee tournament, and there he had been treated for the first time like a full-blown celebrity. His Brantford team (with future NHL goaltender Greg Stefan in net) lost to an Oshawa club in the semifinals. Still, Gretzky was the breakout star, interviewed over and over again, signing autographs for the fans, even having his sticks stolen from behind the Brantford bench by souvenir hunters. Now standing a full five foot two and weighing ninety-three pounds, Gretzky isn't much more expansive than in his first radio interview (though he does seem to have a photographic memory when it comes to his own scoring statistics). But that doesn't get in the way of the story Gzowski clearly has in mind. At one point, he ventures that all of this is "too much pressure to put on a kid." At another, he cites his own experience coaching minor hockey and talks about its occasional ugliness, about the aggressive, angry parents, about how some teams will do anything to cut down a star. (Gretzky acknowledges that he has been on the receiving end of "butt ends and stuff like that," then adds: "It doesn't bother me. When I play, I just try to hit 'em back fairly.") Gzowski doesn't seem to fully grasp the draft system that had been established by both junior and professional hockey, since he talks as though predatory scouts could still sway a kid and his parents with promises of quick money, convince them to sign his life away (Gzowski would have had to be a true seer to anticipate what Nelson Skalbania would one day pull off). The strongest theme of the interview is an intimation of lost innocence: someday, this kid will become a star in the NHL, and something of his poetry and beauty and individuality will inevitably be corrupted.

> "I just want to find out something from a thirteen-year-old phenom and the way the whole thing has got so commercialized. Wayne Gretzky, if you continue to score and to produce, and if your reputation continues for another four or five years until you're eighteen, just how much money do you think someone will pay you to play hockey – if you're as good an eighteen-year-old as you are a thirteen-year-old?"
>
> "I have no idea."
>
> "Just name any amount of money you think. And I'm not saying that you would ask for it, but how much you might be worth."
>
> "I don't really know."
>
> "C'mon, take a stab. Just guess."
>
> "I don't really know."
>
> "Would you believe a million dollars?"
>
> "No, not really."

(When he returned to the story a little more than six years later for *The Game of Our Lives,* which chronicled Edmonton's 1980–81 season, Gzowski found the fresh-faced young men who played for the Oilers, including Gretzky, still remarkably unspoiled for all their fame and [relative] fortune. They were still, in essence, small-town hockey boys hiding behind adult trappings, and the core Canadian-ness of their story remained intact. It was both what Gzowski saw and what he needed to see.)

In other art forms—music, stage and film—the identification and exploitation of precocious talents is a long-established practice. Every so often someone comes along, blessed with startling technical proficiency and startlingly mature aesthetic sensibilities, and if not all—or any—of them were really the next Mozart or Shirley Temple, at least their novelty value might draw a crowd, however briefly. They could be trotted out and promoted, their short life stories and the tales of their discovery grist for the publicity mill. A few might mature into fully formed adult artists, but most would fall by the wayside without that ever happening, and would present the slightly uncomfortable spectacle of the child star as grown-up—no longer cute, rendered ordinary by aging, now too much like the rest of us.

Gretzky, though, would sail through all of the obvious barriers. As a hockey player, he would never take even a sideways step, beginning with that season as a novice, when it seemed as though, all at once, the entire hockey world, the entire country, focused on the miracle of Brantford. The newspaper guys, the television and radio reporters who made the pilgrimage were drawn to the same homey biographical details. As a toddler, Wayne had made a game of shooting a tennis ball at his grandmother's legs as she sat in a comfy chair, happy to provide his first goalposts. He was skating by age three; by age five he was ready to play organized hockey, except that they wouldn't take kids that young. His old man had to all but drag him away from the rink. A year later, he was already playing on a travelling team with ten-year-olds, tucking the too-large jersey in on his stick side because it flapped in the breeze and got in the way. And there was Walter, the archetypal hockey dad, who had built the backyard ice sheet, who created all of those homemade skating and stickhandling drills, who had Wayne watch games on television and, without looking down, trace the movements of the puck with a piece of paper and pen. Gretzky's genius would, at least in part, be the result of a series of learned responses.

(He was in many ways what Malcolm Gladwell would identify as an "outlier" whose extraordinary success was the product not just of innate talent, but also of opportunity and hard work: the "10,000-hour rule," as Gladwell puts it, referring to the necessary time that must be put in, and the necessary circumstances that must allow for it. Gretzky even has the early birthdate—January 26— that Gladwell points out is a common feature of successful athletes, who benefit by being months ahead of their peer group in physical development, though in Gretzky's case that was mitigated by the fact that he wound up playing much of his minor hockey career in leagues with older boys.)

His father—his mentor, his coach, his programmer—was there at his boys' sides nearly every minute he wasn't working. Supportive, prodding, demanding, uncompromising, Wally was the one who even suggested that Wayne ought to try taking a few turns on defence. "You'll be able to play every second shift," he said, "and nobody is going to get mad at you."

Mad. That seemed strange. Why would those nice, warm-hearted, decent small-town Canadians ever get mad at the boy who would become their most famous favourite son? They'd eventually name a recreation centre and a stretch of highway after him, brag about how they knew him when, how they were among the first to understand that he was special. But in the moment, all was not so well; the hockey parents of Brantford weren't so nice and they weren't all that supportive. They didn't much like watching the local boy superstar score all of those goals and get all of that attention and make their own hockey-playing kids seem dead average by comparison. They weren't beaming with pride over the tall poppy. Perhaps, on some level, they thought those Gretzkys, ordinary in every other way, were getting a bit too full of themselves. So they heckled him at hockey games—heckled him even in the off-season, when he played baseball or lacrosse or ran track—asked him who he thought he was, hollered all kinds of mean, spiteful things at a *kid,* celebrated his occasional failures, hated it even more when he scored a goal and gave that little fist pump, as though he was showing up every other boy on the ice. It became uncomfortable enough, untenable enough, that at age fourteen, less than a year after that conversation with Gzowski, Gretzky was driven from his hometown—for hockey reasons, for the more challenging competition he could enjoy playing Junior B in Toronto, but mostly, as he would describe it in his autobiography (written with Rick Reilly), because of "the pressure, the back-biting and the name-calling." He didn't want to leave. He *had* to leave. "That year and the next were the two worst of my life," Gretzky wrote.

There was an implicit sadness there that tended to be glossed over in the telling of the story, because it made for such an uncomfortable fit. (Gretzky would make the sentiment more explicit in an interview with Gordon Edes of the *Los Angeles Times* in 1988: "My brother was three when I left home, my littlest brother. I didn't see my brother grow up, and all of a sudden he's sixteen and he's driving. . . . A lot of people thought I moved away from home to be a hockey player, but that's not why. I moved away to just try to escape all the pressures parents [not his own] place on kids. It's not kids against each other, it's the parents." Edes asked Gretzky if he'd let his own son leave home at age fourteen. "Never. The older I get, the more bitter I am about it. I hate it more now than I did three years ago. The fact that I moved away at fourteen—I wish, if I could go all the way back again, I wouldn't have to do that. I'd be happy to go back and grow up with my family.")

Equally uncomfortable were the more edgy aspects of the Walter figure, sentimentalized and sanitized as the nation's number one hockey dad, a dominant presence in the lives of all four of his boys (sister Kim, the second oldest after Wayne, tends to get short shrift in the family histories—she was a talented track and field athlete who worked for the Canadian National Institute for the Blind and later moved to the Gretzky family farm. Gretzky's mother, Phyllis, also remained out of the limelight, which was as she preferred it. When she died from lung cancer in 2005, she was eulogized as the perfect hockey mom, who didn't really care that much about the game but was there to drive her boys to the rink when Wally couldn't, to watch their games, and to keep the home fires burning. "I looked after the kids and house and Walter went to work and looked after the finances," she once said. The day she gave birth to Brent, Walter was away at a hockey tournament with Wayne. She joked that when he finally got to the hospital, all he wanted to talk about was what happened in the games—she had to remind him that he had another son). There was something unusually intense about Walter's methodology, about the way he turned the sport into an activity that no longer resembled play, into a serious, single-minded, goal-oriented quest. No doubt Wayne loved him for it, the way Tiger Woods loved his old man for sticking a golf club in his hands long before he understood what it was for, for pushing him through the whole prodigy process and turning him into one of the most blinkered athletes in history. "My hero as a kid was a man with constant headaches, ulcers and ringing in his ears," Gretzky wrote. "He's a funny little guy who stays up drinking coffee every night until 3:00 in the morning even though he's got to be at work at 8:00 the next day. He doesn't have to work if he doesn't want to, yet he never misses a day. . . . He's still my coach, but he's also my agent, manager, amateur lawyer, business partner and best friend. He doesn't have a college degree, but he's probably the smartest guy I know."

But what if it hadn't all worked out? What if Wayne hadn't so loved the game, and been so naturally gifted? What if all those hours spent skating around pylons (at the expense of . . . well, hobbies, music, school work) hadn't paid off in the form of the greatest, most lucrative career in professional hockey history?

What if . . . well, what if Wayne Gretzky had been his brother Keith, or his brother Brent, whose hockey careers flattened out in the minor leagues, and who might not have gone that far but for the curiosity and commercial potential that went with their last name? In 1998, Dave Feschuk, writing in the *National Post,* interviewed Brent Gretzky, then toiling away in the hockey boondocks, and came away with one of the most remarkable, counterintuitive quotes in the annals of Canadian sports journalism. Brent spoke wistfully about those happy days in his childhood when the old man was out of town somewhere, "so we could do something with our friends. My dad would come home and we'd be playing with a tennis ball or something and he'd yell at us, 'What do you think I make the rink for, to fool around?' Then he'd go in and get the pylons and pucks out and sure enough, we'd go to work for about three hours. He'd stand there and he'd have the video camera and tape us. Then after dinner we'd watch the video and he'd tell us what we're doing wrong. He was definitely strict about it.

"You didn't even second-guess it. Right after school, get on the ice, go inside, eat dinner, get back on the ice. Even on Saturdays, go on the ice all day long. It was definitely pressed on us, but we loved the game. Without the direction of a father, I don't know where I'd be."

Judy Garland's stage mother would be adjudged a monster by future biographers because of how hard she pushed little Frances Ethel Gumm to succeed, preparing the ground for evil directors and husbands and drug pushers who followed. She became the perpetual tragic victim, and it all traced back to Mom. Because it was hockey, because it was Canada, because things worked out, because his most famous boy turned out so polite, so well-mannered, married happily, raised a family, never said a thing out of turn, no one ever thought twice about Walter Gretzky's uncompromising ways, about all of those hours spent in endless, head-down repetition, the antithesis of pond hockey's unstructured freedom, its spontaneous joys. Surely that wasn't part of the great myth. And when Wayne wound up attached to some unfortunate characters later in life, a naif attracted by power and wealth, no one would connect the dots the way they would with any child star gone bad.

That's because Gretzky came through it all fine, and eventually his brothers came through it all fine, and because the happy Gretzky story was one Canadians needed, more than ever, to be true. Self-consciousness and doubt had crept into the tale of hockey and identity. What had been a tenet of faith a generation earlier—

that it was Canada's game, Canada's invention, Canadians' birthright and theirs alone—was no longer a given. The Soviets had nearly won in '72, the great national wake-up call after which no Canadian could claim clear hockey supremacy as an absolute fact of life. Players from all sorts of different places and different backgrounds were beginning to turn up, and excel, in the National Hockey League, and even though many years later the likes of Don Cherry would still be arguing that essential qualities were conferred by a player's birth certificate, the evidence all around suggested otherwise. At the same time, the country was becoming ever more diverse, especially in the larger urban centres. The notion that everyone had grown up gathered 'round the television set watching *Hockey Night in Canada,* the idea of a shared history involving the Leafs, the Habs, Foster Hewitt and Danny Gallivan, was less and less true, as was the belief that everyone—or at least every boy—had at some stage played the sport.

The NHL had always done its best to blur the lines between hockey the game and cultural given, and hockey the bottom-line business, run by Americans for the benefit of Americans as much as by Canadians for the benefit of Canadians. With further expansion into exotic U.S. locales it became harder and harder to pretend. It was slipping away. It was all slipping away. And in the face of that, the story of homegrown genius, of square, Canadian small-town values, the reassurance that the next greatest player could only come from one place, from one country on earth, that he couldn't have been born in Leningrad or Los Angeles, that he had to come from a Brantford, or at least from a Brantford of the sentimental imagination, was all the more important. Important enough that it was sought out and processed and packaged and refined and exploited as it had never been before.

You couldn't have *that,* and think too hard about a boy made a hometown pariah because he played the national game so well. You couldn't have that while pondering the difficult question of whether the kid really had a say in the matter, whether his calling was really born of the place, the geography, the Canadian character, or was imposed upon him.

And this was also a very different story in another respect. While generation after generation of dutiful hockey heroes played out their careers as unquestioningly as soldiers, bought into the fable that what was good for the NHL (and its owners) was good for hockey and did what they were told to do, how to process the fact that Gretzky would be an iconoclast, that he and his family would do things *their* way, to benefit *their* interests, that they'd turn their backs entirely on the NHL—its history, its tradition, its glories—and subvert its system purely for cash reward? Best to keep the story simple, keep it familiar, make it resonate of the past—and gloss over the fact that what came next was like a small revolution.

As a star rose over southwestern Ontario and many a wise man beat a path to Wayne Gretzky's door, the business of big-league hockey was in the process of being transformed—changes that would allow for his unconventional arrival. The first modern expansion, from six to twelve franchises in 1967, while a great leap forward for the NHL, was hardly an unqualified success. Of the Second Six, only the Philadelphia Flyers would thrive right from the start. All of the others would at some point experience tribulations—the Pittsburgh Penguins with shaky ownership, the Minnesota North Stars eventually moving to Dallas, St. Louis at one point appearing headed to Saskatoon, the Los Angeles Kings struggling to attract consistent audiences in southern California, and the California Golden Seals a wacky, unqualified, white-skated disaster, doomed eventually to relocation and finally extinction. None of that, though, entirely discouraged the owners from pushing forward, from further expanding the boundaries of the game. They understood that the business of selling franchises could be a lucrative one in and of itself, and they still dreamed of the day when a big-money television contract from one of the major American networks might make the NHL less dependent on putting bums in seats while dramatically increasing the value of their teams.

The continuing struggles of expansion teams at least tamped down the temptation, causing the owners to become more cautious and proceed by baby steps. In 1970, the NHL voted to add two teams—in Buffalo, a border town with a long history in minor-league hockey, and Vancouver, which had been on the shortlist for the 1967 expansion, and which, as another west coach beachhead, made the California franchises seem a little less isolated. There were no further plans beyond that, the league's president, Clarence Campbell, announced. Professional hockey had for the time being reached its natural limits. The NHL was standing pat.

But there were other people, with other ideas, who saw an opening in the business of the game. Their model was the American Football League, which successfully challenged the hegemony of the National Football League, eventually forcing its way into the Super Bowl, and then into a full merger. Some had been involved with the American Basketball Association, which used, among other things, a red, white and blue striped ball to differentiate it from the established National Basketball Association. It would crumble eventually, with a few of its teams absorbed by the NBA. Also found on some resumés were a host of less successful, more eccentric sports ventures, from World Team Tennis to a professional roller hockey league to a pro basketball loop limited to players under six feet, four inches—all of them doomed, and all, in their failure, far more indicative of what tended to happen to those bold sports entrepreneurs who attempted to reinvent the wheel. There was one other thing that the founding brain trust of what would become the World Hockey Association had in common: they were ignoramuses when it came to hockey.

For expertise, they hired Wild Bill Hunter, a junior hockey huckster who would be the founding father of the Edmonton (né Alberta) Oilers, and Ben Hatskin, a hockey money man from Winnipeg with experience on the management and ownership side of the sport. The core concept was relatively simple: set up in smaller places where the NHL was disinclined to establish franchises, including western Canada, as well as try to establish a beachhead in larger NHL markets and compete head to head. By the time all was said and done, the WHA would put teams just about anywhere and everywhere it could in an effort to stave off collapse.

It certainly got the NHL's attention. In 1972, in a late attempt to head the WHA off at the pass, the league added two more franchises: the New York Islanders, to sate pent-up hockey demand in a huge market served only by the Rangers and block the WHA from moving into the brand new arena in Uniondale, and the Atlanta Flames, a first incursion in the traditional American South, where they would have to sell the game in a place without scads of displaced Canadians to fill out the crowds. That same season, the WHA opened for business with teams in Cleveland, Boston, New York, Ottawa, Philadelphia, Quebec City, Edmonton, Chicago, Houston, Los Angeles, St. Paul, Minnesota and Winnipeg. The rosters featured a mixed bag of minor leaguers and NHL veterans seeking a payday—and, on that last team, one of the greatest stars in the game. Bobby Hull's signing with the Jets for then-other-worldly sum of $250,000 a year was the WHA's defining moment: they needed to make a splash, and thanks to the cheapskate practices of Chicago Blackhawks owner Bill Wirtz, they found the perfect guy, willing to walk away, turn his back on history and brave the Manitoba winter purely for the chance to be paid what he was worth.

Signing Hull was the coup, the clear demonstration of intent, the shot fired across the NHL's bow. Signing Gordie Howe and his hockey-playing sons Mark and Marty in the league's second season showed creativity and cleverness. Signing other big-name NHL players anxious to finally cash in provided a level of recognition (though it was obviously a short-term solution, and didn't always provide value for money). Signing underage kids right out from under the NHL's nose before they could be drafted, that was something else again—a provocation, a threat, a subversion of the old system, a way to force matters to a head. If the WHA's endgame was independent survival, it could scoop the best talent in its formative stages, build a foundation, create its own stars, while at the same time undermining the competition. And if it was really about elbowing their way in—blackmailing the old league into inviting them to join the club—locking up the teenagers could provide a strategic advantage for the WHA owners. They wouldn't only be brokering markets and arenas and fan bases now; they'd be brokering talent. If you want the kids, they seemed to be telling the NHL, you're going to have to take the rest of us as part of the bargain. If you want access to the stars of tomorrow, you're going to have to open the door.

The Gretzkys were the kind of bedrock, conservative Canadians who ought to have regarded the NHL as a holy of holies. But somewhere along the line, when they stopped playing dutifully within the system, when they started to steer Wayne's hockey career along an independent path, both the kid and the old man took on the look of radicals. After playing for two years in Toronto, Wayne was selected third in the midget draft by the Sault Ste. Marie Greyhounds of the Ontario Hockey League, the prime feeder system for the NHL. At first, the Gretzkys objected, saying that he wouldn't play in the Soo because it was too far from home, only to relent. In December 1977, as a sixteen-year-old, he made the Canadian team that went to the World Junior Championships, a side that wound up winning a bronze medal. Thereafter, he would be expected to play out his time in the Soo and fill arenas around the OHL, to wait patiently for his nineteenth birthday and the chance to enter the NHL draft. Then he would be the surefire first-overall pick, awarded to the league's worst team from the previous season (unless they'd been foolish enough to trade that pick away), which would hold his exclusive rights. In the days before the WHA came along, Gretzky's choices would have been to sign for whatever that team was willing to pay him, to withhold his services in the hopes of getting more, or to forget about playing professional hockey altogether.

As a rookie entering the league, even the greatest junior player had precious little leverage. He'd have an agent at his side during negotiations (Al Eagleson and Bobby Orr had paved the way for a legion of others in that regard), but if he wanted to play in the best hockey league in the world, there wasn't really a choice to be made. In the end, what Canadian boy could resist the chance to fulfill the dream, to put on one of those uniforms, to skate onto the ice at the Montreal Forum or Maple Leaf Gardens or the Chicago Stadium or Boston Garden, to play where his heroes played? That's exactly what the NHL owners counted on.

But Wayne Gretzky said no to all that. He wouldn't wait for the draft. He wouldn't play by the old rules. He wouldn't let history and hero worship and romance and propaganda get in the way of making as much money as he could, as soon as possible. He listened when Nelson Skalbania called. He flew out to Vancouver and signed a contract, then headed for the great unknown in Indianapolis. He'd get to play against Gordie Howe and Bobby Hull. The competition was a big step up from junior, but it was still a B league, a fringe league, just barely hanging on. And if it survived, as far as Gretzky knew, that would be it, his final destination. "When I signed, I thought I was never going to play in the NHL," he said. "I never thought that was possible." The day of the dutiful, dumb hockey star who mistook a business for a game was done; in his place stood the athlete/entrepreneur who understood that it was really about looking after number one.

Though the trip was circuitous, that's how Gretzky wound up in Edmonton, which represented the perfect backdrop, the final piece of the mythic puzzle. The Oilers, with a brand new arena and a loyal fan base, had better odds of survival than most of the WHA teams—and a better chance of being absorbed into the NHL if the league could hold on long enough to force a merger. More than that, it was the place itself, the surroundings, and the teammates, that fit so well. Gretzky's story would have had plenty of dramatic juice had he suited up for his childhood heroes, the Detroit Red Wings, or for the Montreal Canadiens, or for the team very much in need of deliverance in Toronto. But this would be even better. This would be a chance to leave a mark in the most northerly outpost of North American professional sport, in a city small enough to fully, completely appreciate him, in a community undivided in its passion for the national game. There he would be coached by a gruff up-and-comer getting his first shot behind the bench, happy to encourage a freewheeling offensive style once he had the right players. And there he would eventually play with a group of other young, bright talents (interspersed with the odd role-playing veteran), who would grow up together like a high school class, who would complement his own skills, who would learn to understand the nuance and rhythm of Gretzky's play. The Oilers would evolve into something much more than just a supporting cast (after he was gone, they'd prove that definitively by winning a Stanley Cup on their own), while skating on the best, fastest, hardest, smoothest ice in the hockey world.

It was poetry. It was sweet and sentimental and perfect. Forget old rooting interests. Anyone who had grown up in Canada, hearing the tribal tales, knew this was where Wayne Gretzky belonged.

Chapter Three

A GOLDEN AGE OF HUSTLERS

THE MOMENT HAD ARRIVED when the label "used-car sales-man" ceased being a pejorative, and for Peter Pocklington the timing couldn't have been better. Not literally, perhaps, since old punchlines die hard, but figuratively for sure. What expired was the idea of vulgar money, the belief that there was a difference between institutional, generational wealth and that newly minted. A good thing, in many ways, since class distinctions also fell by the wayside, since parentage and heritage and old school ties also lost some of their import. With the tumbling barriers came a generation of loud, pushy, wealthy folks who refused to play by the established rules, who were not to everyone's taste.

Certainly by the early 1980s, the beginnings of a decade marked by high living and large hair, the pendulum had swung far the other way. Money, the topic any decent Canadian had once refrained from discussing in polite company (along with sex and religion), came out of the closet with spandex, headbands and lines of cocaine at suburban dinner parties. The origin of the filthy lucre wasn't important, except that audacious was better than cautious, flashy was better than discreet, and new was certainly better than old. Profit for the sake of profit, the thrill of the hustle, the joy of a well-wrought scheme, the orgasmic payoff from closing a deal. It no longer mattered so much who your daddy was; simply being rich, and especially the process of getting rich, could make you a star. Business and show business had crossed. Middle-aged white guys in good suits with fat wallets developed a pop-star aura, fuelled by magazine covers and fawning profiles. Vanity press discourses on how to get the better of the other guy shared space on bookstore shelves with Tom Wolfe's definitive fictional take on the era, *The Bonfire of the Vanities.* By the time Ivan Boesky delivered his famous call to arms—a kind of "Ask not what your country can do for you, ask what you can do for yourself" address—the era of the hero capitalists was both in full swing and steaming inevitably towards the rocks. "I think greed is all right, by the way," Boesky told a rapt audience at the University of California, Berkeley on May 18, 1986. "I think greed is healthy. You can be greedy and still feel good about yourself."

Soon enough, Oliver Stone would distill those sentiments down to "Greed is good." His film *Wall Street,* released in 1988—an eventful year—was a cautionary tale of the evils of value-free avarice, personified by one of the great, odious characters of the screen, Gordon Gecko. His doppelganger but for the coif, Donald Trump —*Spy* magazine, exploiting the overriding cynicism of the age for humour, would saddle him with the capsule description "short-fingered vulgarian"—had already given the world *The Art of the Deal,* his up-from-the-upper-middle-class (his father was a small-scale developer in Queens) Horatio Alger story, and would soon enough lapse into full-blown self-parody, culminating two decades later in reality television. Boesky graced the cover of *TIME* magazine in 1986, but by then he was on his way to jail—rolling over on buddy Michael Milken in an attempt to mollify the prosecutors—and the bloom was off the rose. But even as Boesky and Milken and the rest were trading in their Hugo Boss suits for prison stripes, their spiritual children remained, loads of fast-buck artists treading a fine line between the creative creation of profit, and outright illegality.

In Canada, our own Boswell to the moneyed classes was several steps ahead of the Yanks. Peter C. Newman published *The Canadian Establishment* in 1975 to great acclaim, a book about the country's true power brokers and their stuffy old-money empires, including just enough of their heretofore hidden, quirky, humanizing habits to lift the characters off the page, to top the WASPy world of good schools and private clubs with a dollop of gossipy sex appeal. It was a national best-seller, and it naturally spawned a sequel. Newman later explained that he had mulled over several possibilities before it became obvious that he should chronicle a shift of wealth and influence that was even then ongoing. "Power is passing into new hands," he wrote in the rather breathless introduction to *The Acquisitors,* published in 1981. "An exotic new strain of bravura entrepreneurs has bullied its way into contention, shaking Canada's Establishment to the very filaments of its elegant roots. The Establishment quivers at its furthest reaches, like a forest at climax yielding to a regeneration that starts not from its own seed but springs out of altogether different species."

They weren't just new and different and unsettling to the old order. They were of lower caste, in many ways like the guy working the car lot in a loud sports jacket, pushing lemons on the unsuspecting. For their chronicler, they were obviously loads of fun, less concerned with bloodlines, tradition or decorum. "They're the fresh and very different breed of business leaders who are strangers, by birth and behaviour, to the Canadian Establishment, yet cannot be denied its membership. They welcome risk, have succeeded by their own efforts, and combine a *macho* approach to business with extravagant lifestyle. They have dared to prise the riches of new resource frontiers, gambled on real estate, chanced the miraculous possibilities of space-age technology, divined the whims and desires of a consumer society on a spending spree, and railroaded the Canadian tradition of government subsidy into everything from offshore oil to horror films."

By the time Wayne Gretzky caused the fates of Bruce McNall and Peter Pocklington to become intertwined—one on the rise, apparently invincible, a California Midas comfortable in the company of the most glamorous crowd on earth, the other scrambling for cash and resorting to desperate measures during a temporary downturn—the hero capitalist era had already pushed well into its decadent phase. Those on the sidelines who had celebrated all of that money-making moxie were equally happy to indulge in *schadenfreude* as the nouveau riche hustlers tumbled one by one. But in that moment, both McNall and Pocklington could still convincingly play the role of Masters of the Universe. Both, as far as the outside world understood, were concerned only with that next scheme and that next fortune.

Newman obviously loved—or at least loved as a subject—Nelson Skalbania, the flamboyant real estate hustler who had brought Gretzky into the World Hockey Association, brought Pocklington into his orbit, into prominence, into the spotlight provided by professional sport, and might have brought Gretzky to Vancouver years later if his audacious, half-crazy plan hadn't crumbled at the last moment when others got cold feet. He was—still is—a character out of fiction, one who has straddled the line between the big score and ruin, never content to take his winnings and walk away from the table. There is, for Skalbania, always one more hand to play, one more roll of the dice.

Pocklington wasn't quite so unique or intriguing to Newman, though he certainly had his quirks and eccentricities. In method, in style, in backgammon proclivities, in facial hair, he seemed to casual observers a bit like Skalbania-lite. (Skalbania bristles at the comparison. Were they different cats? he's asked. "I hope so," he says. "He's got a grade eight education. Came up through the car business. He's a little more abrasive. Very quick, though. Rightly or wrongly, he's quick. Makes his mind up very quick. And maybe is more of a bull in a china shop.") Without the Oilers, Pocklington would have remained just another of the nouveau riche who had made his fortune in real estate, in the meat business, who bought buildings and bought jewellery and bought name-brand art for the cachet, who dropped famous names (Paul Newman and President Gerald Ford were particular favourites), who raced jet boats, who liked to play games of chance over everything and anything, including who would pick up big restaurant tabs—none of which made him unique then and there. Other than his delusions of someday running the country, he was a car salesman writ large—not that there was any longer anything wrong with that—though Newman struggled mightily to make him sound like more. "He is a compulsive achiever with eccentric political views whose intimates firmly believe he will one day be Prime Minister of Canada," Newman wrote. "His daredevil exploits and noncomformist lifestyle have taken him over the edge of normal existence. Participant in a sport that courts death, he lives in a Scheherazade world of luxury and self-indulgence."

It doesn't really matter whether every detail of his biography was true. What mattered was how Pocklington told it, how he framed himself, how he spun his own creation myth, who he wanted to be and how he wanted to be seen. Born in relative comfort in London, Ontario, where his father, Basil, worked in the insurance industry (the defining business in what was a quiet, conservative town), baby Peter seems to have emerged from the womb ready to sell an Oldsmobile to the obstetrician. At the tender age of five, he plucked chestnuts off a neighbour's lawn, packaged them up and sold them back to her. At the age of six, he picked cherries from the tree, packed them in jars with tap water, then attempted to peddle the mixture as "preserves." At nine, with his parents away from home, he and a group of pals tore down an old barn on the property and sold the wood as lumber. At fourteen, he traded a bicycle and a hundred bucks for a Model A roadster that he was too young to drive, then turned around and sold the car for five hundred dollars. No sentimentalist, he sold his own Christmas presents. As a teenager, with his parents again absent (you'd think they'd have learned by then), he sold the family Cadillac for $2,800 in cash plus a '56 Plymouth, which he in turn turned around for eight hundred bucks. The old man was a bit taken aback when he returned, but since the kid got more than the trade-in value, he smiled the smile of an indulgent parent and patted young Peter on the head.

In a different parable, written at a different point in history, the moral of those episodes might have been interpreted rather negatively. Let's see . . . he was duplicitous, he misled trusting neighbours, he pulled the wool over his parents' eyes, he cared more for money than for the feelings of others, he was indifferent to education. George Washington couldn't tell a lie: Peter Pocklington could, at least little white ones, when they might help him close a sale. You could make the case that the picture painted was of a young man on the road to ruin, perhaps to incarceration. But in the age of the hero capitalists, the story told by Pocklington while sitting in his mansion high above the Saskatchewan River, drinking fine wine and surrounded by modern masterpieces, proclaiming his intellectual debt to Ayn Rand and talking about how the country must establish a flat-rate income tax, was the mythic beginning of a master salesman, one whose skills were drawn from real-world experience, who was self-made, who was a natural champion of free will and free enterprise and a natural leader of men.

Pocklington liked to explain that he was "fired from school"— that one day, at age seventeen, the principal called him into his office and suggested that he had to choose between his outside, entrepreneurial interests and achieving the basic requirements of his diploma. Young Peter didn't find that a tough decision at all. Briefly, at age nineteen, he made his one pass at the square life, signing on as a management trainee with the Robert Simpson Company, then the national rival to the department store giant Eaton's. In his own telling he walked away, boldly declaring that he was worth ten times what they were paying him. (Simpsons' side of that story, like Simpsons itself, is lost in the mists of history.) His calling, he understood, was in the car business. Even before taking the Simpsons job, while on a summer trip to visit relatives in Manitoba, he had figured out that used cars on the prairie were both undervalued and in better shape than their equivalents in Ontario, which were rotted by road salt. He'd ship cars east and sell them for a tidy profit. By age twenty-three, he was leasing his own dealership, Freeway Ford in Tilbury, Ontario, and already dabbling in real estate. Two years later, he bought a dealership outright in nearby Chatham: Maple City Ford. His mentor in the world of cars and the world at large, Pocklington liked to recount, was a legendary salesman named King Ringer—the guy who he said invented the "sales manager" pitch. ("I'd love to be able to sell it to you for that price. But I have to take it to the sales manager first. . . ." Even if the sales manager wasn't really there.) The great secrets Ringer taught him, Pocklington said, applied to any business venture. "It's all just selling cars, only with more zeroes," he told Peter Gzowski in 1982. "Like the difference between your bank loans and mine. Same game, more zeroes. I learned very early that you should sell when everyone else is buying, and vice versa. When you're buying, always give people more than they're asking, and get it back on the terms. If you offer what sounds like enough, you can give them zero interest. Greed overcomes good judgment. That what the King taught me, and that's what I still know."

By 1971, the great minds at Ford Canada, recognizing a young up-and-comer in their midst, put Pocklington in touch with a dealer in Edmonton who was selling out. He jumped at the opportunity to move west, to the land of less-fettered free enterprise, invested heavily in television advertising, employed his considerable force of personality to great advantage, and prospered. Pocklington sunk his profits into real estate, which was where he first came into contact with Skalbania, who became a bit of a mentor. By the time Skalbania strolled over to his table at The Steak Loft in 1976, offering a chance to buy into the World Hockey Association, they had already done plenty of business together, and Pocklington had already gambled on much bigger deals, and won.

"The world was simple," Pocklington said. "All I had to do was conquer it."

One Friday night in 1978, the phone rang at the home of Jim Matheson, the fine hockey writer of the *Edmonton Journal*. He was well into a dinner with Rod Phillips, the Oilers' play-by-play man, and their wives, and by the time the phone rang he was feeling rather . . . relaxed.

Nelson Skalbania was calling, completely out of the blue. Matheson had come to know him well as the owner—then the half-owner—of the hometown Oilers.

"What do you know about this kid Gretzky?" Skalbania asked.

"I've seen him on TV," Matheson said, "and I've read some stories."

"Is he any good? I'm thinking of signing him for Indianapolis."

Gretzky's reputation was already widespread in the hockey world. By now he had been named rookie of the year with the Sault Ste. Marie Greyhounds, hadn't looked out of place as a sixteen-year-old playing for Canada's team at the World Junior Championships, and had received extensive coverage in the sporting press. But none of that made any impression on Skalbania, at least not until Johnny Bassett gave him the heads-up.

"I've got his dad out here with him in Vancouver," Skalbania continued. "Why don't you fly out?"

Matheson didn't think that was such a great idea, not in the middle of dinner, not in his current state of mind. "I don't think I can do that, Nelson. Why don't you stop here on your way back?" he suggested, half-seriously.

So Skalbania, being Skalbania, did. The next day, Matheson and Phillips hunkered down in a hotel room across the street from Edmonton's old downtown airport, waiting for his private jet to land, hoping that none of their media competition had been tipped about what was going to happen. When Skalbania arrived and they ventured over to the tarmac, out of the plane stepped a skinny, long-haired teenager who looked like he couldn't have weighed much more than 160 pounds, clutching a yellow legal pad in his hands. Even then Gretzky hated flying, and writing out his own contract in longhand must have at least provided a diversion during the flight over the Rockies.

Skalbania announced that he was going to pay Gretzky $850,000 a season—in a city that really had nothing to do with the story. From there, he and his guests flew on to Indianapolis, to a town too indifferent even to be curious, to a place that would hardly get to know Gretzky before he was gone.

"Heck, if it doesn't work out," Skalbania told Matheson, "I've got a boat and he can swab the decks."

It didn't work out—not for Skalbania, not in Indianapolis. With the Racers, Gretzky entered a dressing room filled with grizzled minor-league lifers. The coach, Pat Stapleton, resented everything about him; the fans (such as they were) were ambivalent to his presence; and the team was dying, in any case, of entirely natural causes. But when the time came for Skalbania to cut his losses, Gretzky had at least shown himself to be far more than a deck-hand. Even in the dodgy economy of the WHA, he had value—not just because he might improve a team and move a few tickets, but because, in the ongoing game of chicken with the NHL, whoever had Gretzky on their roster had a significant card to play when it came to forcing their way into the established league. Pocklington had the cash in hand and was ready to move when the Winnipeg Jets got cold feet.

Never mind selling cars to rubes, or cherries and water as jam: this was easily was the best deal he'd ever make. Soon enough he would be staging a ceremony at centre ice in the Northlands Coliseum, where Gretzky, on January 26, 1979—his eighteenth birthday—signed a twenty-one-year personal-services contract (that is, not with the team per se, but with its owner). The implication was that he had committed his entire professional hockey career, wherever it might take him, to Peter Pocklington in return for a sum between $4 million and $5 million. (Gretzky says that he didn't actually sign his own name in front of the crowd—that on the advice of his friend and teammate Garnet "Ace" Bailey, he signed it "Ace," for a lark, and only got around to putting his own name on the deal afterwards, behind closed doors.) The relationship between Pocklington and Gretzky was permanent, even if the Oilers or the World Hockey Association were not. "The contract is for personal services," Pocklington said. "There's no way anyone's going to touch him when we join the NHL."

And that's how it would be. When the merger finally happened, two WHA players were exempted from the draft by which the

NHL teams would reclaim the "property" lured away from them by the breakaway league: the ancient Gordie Howe, who would remain with the Hartford (né New England) Whalers, and Gretzky, who would never be selected in the NHL entry draft and who would remain an Edmonton Oiler when the franchise was absorbed into the NHL. Pocklington, with the "lifetime" deal, had both helped push the merger forward and secured his own future, joining a club that otherwise might not have welcomed someone like him as a member. (As time went on, the NHL would get considerably less picky about who owned its teams, and would in fact lead all professional sports in the number of league governors who were eventually led away in handcuffs.)

What Wayne Gretzky did for Peter Pocklington's fortunes, for his public profile, for his ego, for his larger aspirations, was undeniable. With Gretzky on the payroll, with the young Oilers maturing together, growing into a magnificent hockey powerhouse, rolling to four Stanley Cups in five years, Pocklington became, nearly as much as the players, a local hero. He had delivered for the people of Edmonton, he had put the town on the map, he had made it not just a City of Champions, but almost a hockey mecca, the place where the game's greatest aesthetic expression (at least since the last Canadiens dynasty) had been allowed to flourish.

Even in his darkest hours, Edmontonians stood by him. In the recession years of 1982 and 1983, Pocklington hit a personal rocky patch. He was forced to fold the Edmonton Drillers soccer team, sell Westown Ford, was left helpless to prevent his drilling company and another car dealership from falling into receivership. He lost control of Fidelity Trust, and sold parts of the Gainers meat processing company and a real estate holding company. In order to stay afloat, Pocklington was left with no choice but to borrow heavily, putting up the Oilers and the team's player contracts (not including Gretzky's personal-services contract, but including coach Glen Sather's very similar deal) as collateral. Pocklington's financial travails became a front-page news story, but it didn't matter that the curtain had been pulled back, temporarily, revealing the inner workings of the sports fantasy as a bottom-line proposition. As long as the Oilers were winning, he was them and they were him, and whatever he'd done to secure his interests, whatever behind-the-scenes relationships might have be strained or broken, the hockey-loving public remained four-square behind their team, and therefore four-square behind good old Peter Puck.

That would be his launching pad to greater challenges, or so Pocklington imagined. In 1983, despite having little or no grassroots support, he launched a quixotic campaign for the leadership of the Progressive Conservative Party of Canada, a quest that happened to coincide with the temporary downturn in his financial fortunes. Pocklington was undaunted, and his ego was such that he was convinced Canadians were longing for his brand of small-government conservatism (which had hardened for Pocklington, as it had for many Albertans, in reaction to Pierre Trudeau and the National Energy Program in the 1970s). His central policy platform was the same kind of flat-rate income tax system espoused by right-wing American thinkers like William F. Buckley Jr.

During the campaign, some of his more colourful personality traits and biographical details naturally came to the fore. Old stories were revisited, including Pocklington's claim to have been briefly held hostage by Mexican bandits when his jet boat broke down during a race, and the entirely real hostage-taking at his house in Edmonton a year earlier, from which he had emerged shaken but unscathed. There was also juicy gossip about his relationship with psychic advisor Rita Burns, who was in the process of suing him, and who claimed in court—among other salacious and unproven suggestions—that Pocklington was in the habit of looking at himself in the mirror and proclaiming himself a god. "We all have a few skeletons in our closet," Pocklington acknowledged.

At his side during the party convention in Edmonton was Wayne Gretzky, not for the last time lending the weight of presence to an owner in a time of need, a signal not just of Pocklington's success in life, like a fancy wristwatch, but also a symbolic affirmation of his core Canadian-ness, of his connection to home, to values, to the needs of the honest working man. He might prefer champagne to beer, he might dress in expensive suits and ride around in a Rolls Royce, but if Gretz liked him, if he had been blessed by the humble hockey god from Brantford, then at some essential level he must be all right. It was a nice touch (as was using the Oiler colours, orange and blue, in all of his campaign materials), but it wasn't nearly enough to make Pocklington's vanity run credible. On the first ballot, he finished with 102 votes, sixth among eight candidates, beating out only two from the party's fringe. He did make the right call in the immediate aftermath of that humiliation, passing on Joe Clark and John Crosbie and moving immediately into the camp of the eventual winner, Brian Mulroney, before the second ballot. Pocklington thought that Mulroney might want to make him finance minister in a new Tory government. He was wrong about that (though when he became prime minister, Mulroney did at least put him on a committee to look into the tax system, which went nowhere.)

Still, what a thing for the kid who dropped out of high school, what a thing for a car salesman, to be communing with statesmen, to be sharing his big ideas, to be a mover and shaker on the national stage. Peter Pocklington might have fallen short as a politician, his business empire might have sprung a few leaks, he might have been embarrassed a bit by his psychic friend. But he was a player, far bigger than the Skalbanias of the world, bigger than some of those guys who inherited their dough and status by birthright. All, when you boiled it down, because of Wayne Gretzky.

What Pocklington had done for Gretzky was less well understood. It wasn't just the salary he paid him, or the faith he had shown in Sather, elevating him from player to player-coach to running his hockey team, or the magnificent supporting cast he empowered his coach and general manager to assemble, but also how he filled, for the young star, a different kind of need.

Both Pocklington and Sather would regularly be described as "father figures" to Gretzky—though of course he had never lacked in the father department, with Walter forever remaining the dominant influence in his life. His old man provided counsel in hockey matters and in business matters, was there with praise and criticism as required, was very much a part of the Oiler culture. What Pocklington and Sather *could* offer, though, was a window to a wider world that was entirely alien to both the senior and junior Gretzkys. Walter would never get rich working for Bell, and Wayne had arrived in Edmonton still a teenager—an unsophisticated, undereducated teenager whose entire life had played out, whose entire being had been defined, in a series of hockey rinks. Now, for the first time, he had real money in his pocket, he had a peer group among his teammates (in kid hockey, he had become an outcast in his own town because of his prodigy status, and he wasn't in junior hockey or in Indianapolis long enough to forge a lot of strong bonds), he had all of the wine, women and song he could handle in a fishbowl environment, but he knew next to nothing about life outside of the game. Sather was a hockey guy, albeit significantly smarter than the average bear, and Pocklington was hardly worldly when he arrived in Alberta. But both had parlayed their positions, their wealth (Sather would make his own fortune in real estate, in part by investing in and around Banff), their opportunities, into a level of sophistication. They were there to ease Gretzky into the world of investment, they could introduce him to fine restaurants, they could offer wise counsel and teach him things he might never have learned on his own.

As the boys got a little older and a little wilder, as the Oilers started to sow their wild oats around Edmonton and around the NHL, Pocklington and Sather could also provide some protection. It would be said over and over again that Edmonton, especially in those days, was a small town grown large, that the population boom that so radically changed the numbers on the sign when you crossed the city limits hadn't really changed its essential, intimate character. The Oilers, unlike hockey players in large American cities, would never be anonymous at home. Despite that, despite the fact that their every move in public could be charted, there remained a reverent, deferential quality among the fans.

Though there were surely pockets of resentment, because these young men had become so rich, so privileged, by playing the same game that any self-respecting Canadian would certainly play for free, the bottom line was that wagons would be circled in times of trouble. Just how wild those days were has long been a subject of conjecture. Certainly there was plenty of the usual stuff: Mark Messier's colourful traffic record, Dave Hunter's impaired driving and Grant Fuhr's disastrous finances were all on the public record. There was lots of booze and there were plenty of women. Occasionally, there'd be a fist fight, when someone said the wrong thing to the wrong person. But in all of those matters, the Edmonton constabulary seems to have understood its role in protecting the local treasures, and seems to have been open to a call from the coach or the owner when a particularly sticky situation emerged.

Drugs were the wild card, though, because unlike drinking and fighting and chasing women, their use wasn't considered a healthy recreation for hockey heroes. Cocaine was very much in vogue; it was everywhere there was money and opportunity, which certainly included the NHL (the New York Rangers' Don Murdoch had already been suspended for being caught using the drug, though the league did its best to portray that as an isolated incident). As the Oilers became stars, and as the stories began to filter out about the life the grown-men/adolescents were living, reporters (invariably out-of-towners) occasionally tried to paint a picture of a northern Alberta bacchanal. Only one real exposé reached print, though, and because one of its co-authors, Don Ramsay, was a troubled individual in his own right (as a news reporter at the *Toronto Sun*, he had partly manufactured a story that led to one of the largest libel settlements in Canadian history), it was widely dismissed, especially among the ever-protective hockey press. But looking back at the *Sports Illustrated* story from May 12, 1986, looking at the other byline (the respected reporter Arman Keteyian) and especially looking at some of the on-the-record quotes, it clearly wasn't just a fantasy exercise. A named RCMP officer says flat out that there "are [cocaine] users on the club." Max Offenberger, well known as a psychologist employed by sports franchises and by leagues (he was hired by Sather for the 1983–84 season), says of the Oilers: "The club came too far, too young, too fast. They had too much money and too much freedom. They did what they wanted to do. It was 'we want it and we want it now.'" And Sather himself at the very least opens the door to speculation. "I'm not so naive to think that no one on this hockey club has been exposed to something they shouldn't have," he said. "Any kind of drugs you want to find I'm sure has been exposed to this team at one time or another. If a guy goes to a party, gets drunk, or sniffs a line of cocaine, or smokes a joint, that doesn't make him a compulsive user or dealer or anything. That makes him a guy who went to a party and had a good time. If it becomes a habit, if he gets caught, then you've got a problem. But until it's a problem I can't do anything with it."

What Gretzky learned in those days, with Sather's help and insulated by Pocklington's influence, was how to stay out of trouble, to avoid making the dumb mistake. He didn't steer clear of, or stay aloof from, his teammates (by all accounts, he was very much one of the boys), but he was also never the poor sap who gets caught. Gretzky had been a public figure for most of his young life, had learned early to play that role comfortably, to give just enough, and to hold just enough back (a quality and a balance that would always elude the shy/angry Bobby Orr). But it was in Edmonton that Gretzky learned to coat himself in Teflon. All hell might be breaking loose around him, but nothing stuck—not a single smudge. That was the case during the crazy 1980s in Edmonton, and that was still the case during the Rick Tocchet gambling scandal in 2006. He seemed able to effortlessly remain above it all.

That applied, also, to the way Gretzky would remain largely untouched by the flashy company he kept, the series of fast-buck operators to whom he pledged his allegiance. Gretzky liked money—not just having it and spending it, but the smell of it, the shine of it, the sparkle, the veneer of dead-obvious wealth. The hero capitalists, who walked around with wallets bulging, who drove the fanciest cars, who flew in private jets, who ordered the most expensive bottle on the list, were oh so seductive. Skalbania was the first, and Nelson knew enough to play that card to the hilt, flying Wayne and his family out to the palatial digs in Vancouver.

Then Skalbania sold him to Pocklington, and Peter was more than happy to lay it on thick, to show him the paintings and let him ride in the Rolls Royce. "Those guys—they were flashy," says a long-time friend of Gretzky. "They showed their worth. They had private jets. They had bling. There are other people who are much more well heeled who don't need to do that. He fell for it. The *stuff.* The cement pond." (That last reference, for those too young to remember, is to a 1960s situation comedy called *The Beverly Hillbillies,* in which country hicks strike it rich and move in among the wealthy—marvelling even at the sight of a swimming pool.)

It would become a recurring theme in Gretzky's adult life. On the rink, he was nearly infallible; his instincts never let him down. It was as though he could see around corners, could anticipate events before they happened, could read the strengths and weaknesses of both his opponents and his teammates, and exploit every advantage.

Away from the rink, he wouldn't have nearly the same foresight, he would be bought and paid for and used like a hood ornament, he would be let down and embarrassed when those he had mistaken for titans turned out to be just like old King Ringer, playing an advantage, sucking in the rubes.

Chapter Four

HOCKEY HOLLYWOOD

I N A PLACE WHERE IT IS ALL about looks, all about perfect
faces attached to perfect bodies, Bruce McNall was an anomaly, though of course money changes everything. He was
charismatic, magnetic, but certainly no leading man; round and
soft, with a big head, an ever-ready grin and giggle—an infant's look,
really, wrapped up in a well-tailored suit. He could be obsequious,
but was mostly endearing. He didn't set off alarms. You smiled with
him—and at him—automatically, the way you would a cute baby in
a stroller. You were drawn to his generosity, to his enthusiasm, to his
grand sense of fun. And that's where it all began.

McNall grew up a brainy, overweight kid in what he has
described as a chilly, middle-class academic family in Arcadia, a
Los Angeles suburb, a domestic environment in which success
would be measured not in dollars and cents, but in the letters that
might be appended to the end of a name. No athlete, no jock, not
even a hanger-on, really, McNall found a calling in collecting
coins, a lonely boy's pursuit if ever there was one. But what is for
most a solitary hobby became, for McNall, an entrée to the wider
world. Coins connected him with others, made him friends, gave

him a purpose, created a social life, eventually made him wealthy.

It wasn't just his growing expertise that opened the doors, though his real knowledge of the ancient world had him headed to graduate school before his true calling became clear. What McNall could do best, they didn't teach from textbooks. He could take those coins and tell a story. He could place one in your hand and make you dream of great emperors, of battles won and lost, of the events that shaped the world. In a catalogue somewhere, each piece of precious metal had an assigned value, based on its rarity and condition, but that dry, lifeless calculation wasn't what McNall was selling. It was the *idea* of the coin, of where it had been and who might have held it before you. It was the thrill of possessing it, like Gollum and his precious. It was McNall's own barely containable joy, rubbing off, filling the room. You weren't being hustled. You weren't being sold a bill of goods. You were instead being led by the hand into a more exciting place, made a partner in a great adventure. In a place where everyone has a pitch, everyone has a sitcom or a screenplay they've written, needs financing for a block-buster, is backing a starlet whose career is ready to take off, knows of a real estate play that can't fail or a famous chef who needs a few bucks to create the next place to be, the sense of excitement that came with Bruce McNall was somehow different, somehow seemed more genuine. He made enemies—plenty of them. He hurt people. But years later, even some of those he bilked can't help but remember him fondly, remember the fun they had while he was lifting their wallets.

On this sunny southern California afternoon in 2008, McNall is telling his story again in much-diminished circumstances. The office in downtown Santa Monica he inhabits is a casual rental, a phone number, an address and an answering service. The people out front, working the phones, are selling God knows what. McNall's own glass box looks freshly occupied and largely empty. There is a single beat-up piece of leather furniture; a framed poster from *WarGames*, one of the movies he produced back in the good old days, is propped up on the floor; and one—but only one—of the great big horse-racing trophies his stable won sits on a credenza.

Not surprisingly, after almost six hard years in prison, he seems physically diminished. His hair is thinning, his features have coarsened, his wardrobe—today a golf shirt and slacks—certainly isn't reminiscent of days gone by. But he is back making deals—though those who visited him behind bars, who stuck by him, including Wayne Gretzky, might argue that he never really stopped. Even in the joint, at least when he wasn't stuck in solitary confinement for real or trumped-up misbehaviour, McNall was working the room. Alan Thicke, the actor, comedian, writer, composer, a pal from back when, went to see McNall on the inside several times. During one of those trips, they were standing outside in the prison yard, and Bruce beckoned for a guard, the way he might have once summoned a maître d' at the most exclusive place in town. "Are you hungry?" he asked Thicke. "What do you want? What do you feel like? KFC? McDonald's? Popeye's? In-N-Out Burger? We've got 'em all here." The guard dutifully took the take-out order, and soon enough the food arrived. It was the kind of thing that prison administrators tended to frown upon, even from a nice, gentle, endearing white-collar crook.

McNall currently serves as a matchmaker for those with money who want to sink part of their fortune into the movies and be sprinkled with a bit of magic dust, a time-honoured tradition in Hollywood. It is a job McNall can still do well, earning a producer's credit when things work out. (On IMDB, the Internet Movie Database, his production credits end abruptly in 1990 after several familiar titles, including *Weekend at Bernie's* and *Mr. Mom*. They resume in 2005, with the likes of *Camille, Autopsy* and *Pool Boys*.) Not that it's likely to make him rich again. Until he makes whole those who were left holding the bag, a portion of everything he earns goes straight to the people he ripped off. And what a bag it was—a huge, phony web of investments, underwritten by bank loans secured under false pretences, a massive fraudulent house of cards, the foundation of which was that Bruce McNall charm. So confident was he in his greatest asset that he believed, right up until the very end, that he would save himself, that there would be one more big deal to fix everything. There had been close calls before; he'd been right there on the brink, and no one had suspected a thing. Bruce kept right on smiling.

Those were the days—the game seven semifinal win over Toronto at Maple Leaf Gardens, the what-ifs of the Stanley Cup final against the Montreal Canadiens, Marty McSorley's illegal stick and the ensuing penalty that turned the momentum of the series in the Habs' favour. If McNall had been honest with himself, if he was seeing straight, he would have understood that he was on his way to jail even as his greatest triumph—putting hockey on the front page in Los Angeles—was playing out according to the grand, wildly ambitious plan. The coins, the antiquities, the horses, the Honus Wagner baseball card, the Toronto Argonauts, the movie deals, and still the conversation always comes back to hockey. The Kings were only part of Bruce McNall's empire, but you believe him when he says that they were where his heart was all along.

Since his fall from grace, there have been a whole lot of *mea culpa*s, not just from McNall and his associates, but from the legions who were seduced, who were sucked in, who in hindsight figure they should have seen it coming. McNall now acknowledges that real people lost real money because of his machinations, that it wasn't just faceless banks and their complicit executives who suffered. "I didn't feel at that moment that what we were doing was that wrong," he says. "It was sort of like going to a hooker—it's a crime, but a victimless crime. That's how I felt. It wasn't until later on I realized that there are a lot of victims who come out of these things, family and friends who get very badly hurt."

Besides that pain, and those emptied bank accounts, McNall's most lasting impact was on the National Hockey League. More than any commissioner or owner, he set the sport on a new course. McNall had a vision for hockey. He revolutionized past practices, he played the pied piper and convinced just about everyone to follow. So much about the business of the game today, including the man at the top, the man he hired, commissioner Gary Bettman (though McNall now believes that he got the wrong guy), can be traced directly to him. For a moment, McNall made real the long-standing fantasy that big-league hockey could be sold anywhere, to anyone. He set the stage for a wildly lucrative expansion. He showed the way for a host of hockey entrepreneurs who followed.

And now, McNall acknowledges that he just might have led the NHL down a blind alley. "We were right about the game," McNall says, "but in some ways I think we were wrong. I think Wayne and I were so passionate about the game that we thought if we exposed it to anybody, that they'd get it. And I'm not sure that was really the case. You look at some of these expansion areas and you wonder if in fact what we did. . . . I'm not so sure we were right."

It is not exactly an unbroken line, but still, it is possible to trace the history of ice hockey in Los Angeles all the way back to the 1920s—coinciding, naturally, with the arrival of artificial rinks. The California Amateur Hockey Association was formed in 1925, and the first organized game took place in February of that year, when the Hollywood Athletic Club beat the Los Angeles Monarchs at the Palais de Glace. Hockey was booming back east as well—the NHL, formed in 1917, would expand from its Canadian base into the United States and grow to ten franchises, becoming the second most important professional team sport in North America behind baseball before the 1929 stock market crash wiped out four teams and any true big-league pretensions. But there was no chance of the NHL (or any other league, for that matter) reaching California then, even at the peak of optimism. It was a multiple-day train trip both from the NHL's most westerly outposts and from any true, indigenous hockey culture. So hockey in California remained, by necessity, a small, isolated, local proposition. A first modest professional league, with teams playing in a rink called the Polar Palace, fell victim to the Depression. Only after the Second World War did the sport establish itself for good, with a string of minor-league franchises that continued right up until the Los Angeles Kings' arrival in 1967 (Bill Barilko played for the Hollywood Wolves before being called up by the Maple Leafs to score his fateful goal). Hockey in California was a cult sport, with a dedicated but miniscule following, and a cult sport it would remain, arguably, until the day Wayne Gretzky arrived in town.

That said, from the moment in the early 1960s when it became clear that the NHL was considering expansion (as with baseball, jet air travel had opened up the possibility of west coast teams), there was no shortage of interest in owning the Los Angeles franchise. It is always thus with professional sports, whatever the game, whatever the league, whatever the true bottom-line prospects. There are a finite number of teams available, and there is a unique appeal to ownership. It is one thing to have become rich in real estate or through family, to have brilliantly accumulated a fortune or to have fallen into one by dumb luck. But by owning a team, wealth can instantly be translated into a public profile, into being part of the daily water-cooler conversation. That's why there's nearly always a lineup of buyers, and that's why those who build business empires by being cool, rational and calculating are prone to losing their minds, spending romantically and frittering away the kids' inheritance in the pursuit of a piece of silverware. It's a big part of what keeps the sports world turning—not quite the old P.T. Barnum axiom that there's a sucker born every minute, but that there is a sports-crazy boy in a grown man's body with a rich man's bank account ever ready to live out his fantasy.

Though there were other suitors, the obvious and best candidate to bring the NHL to Los Angeles was a brash expatriate Canadian businessman named Jack Kent Cooke, who had a passion for sports, whose point of origin suggested he ought to understand the game. Cooke had only recently left Toronto and his Canadian citizenship behind in frustration after having had his original sports dream thwarted—unfairly, in his mind. He began his business life as a Depression-era travelling salesman, pushing soap and encyclopedias before falling into the hurly-burly world of commercial radio, where he would make his first fortune. As proprietor of the Toronto radio station CKEY, Cooke was known for big, loud, garish promotions, which certainly made him stand out in what was then a staid, square, blue-law-abiding, buttoned-down town. He would bring the same philosophy to his sports businesses, the first of which was the Toronto Maple Leafs baseball club of the International League, which Cooke purchased in 1951. Like Bill

Veeck, he served up minor-league baseball with a healthy dose of promotional sizzle, running wild contests, bringing in comely B-movie actresses, tarting up the grand old game to lure in paying customers. All the while, he told everyone who would listen of his plan to bring major-league baseball to Toronto, asserting that the city was ready to join the ranks of New York and Boston and Chicago (a riff which, ironically, would eventually help undermine his own minor-league enterprise). Cooke failed in bids to buy the Philadelphia Athletics, St. Louis Browns and Detroit Tigers, and was rebuffed in his every effort to secure an expansion franchise from either the American or National League. During the brief moments when it looked like the independent Continental League might get off the ground, he was an enthusiastic proponent. But when that dream died as well, when the city failed to build a new ballpark, and especially when he lost a bid for Toronto's first commercial television licence, Cooke packed his bags and headed for Los Angeles in frustration. His application for U.S. citizenship was fast-tracked through Congress—then as now, it helped to have powerful friends—and he set about building an American cable television empire. In 1961, Cooke bought a 25 per cent interest in the Washington Redskins, which turned out to be a brilliant investment in a league just beginning its phenomenal rise to become the continent's dominant sports enterprise, thanks in large part to its unique compatibility with television. (Cooke would eventually become majority, and then sole, owner of the franchise.) Four years later, he bought the Los Angeles Lakers of the National Basketball Association, a franchise that had moved west from Minneapolis in 1960, and began planning to construct the greatest, most lavish sports arena the continent had yet seen, a true west coast rival to the storied Madison Square Garden.

Hockey would seem, in some ways, a natural fit—a second occupant for the arena, a fresh attraction for the area. And in a city of that size, with that kind of wealth, surely there were enough potential customers (including all those other Canadian expats who, like Cooke, had headed west to seek fame and fortune) to justify the cost of setting up shop. Now that it was a coast-to-coast enterprise, the National Hockey League would naturally begin to attract serious interest from one of the three networks, and through television would be introduced to a mass audience that had no first-hand experience of natural ice, shinny or Gordie Howe. The game was fast and violent and apparently of the moment. Once they saw it, folks would naturally be turned on.

Not for the first time, and not for the last, that tenet of belief among hockey fans—the notion that the virtues of their favourite game were self-evident and irresistible—would be put to the test. Cooke built his palace on Manchester Boulevard in otherwise dreary Inglewood, where it was immediately dubbed The Fabulous Forum—a circular structure with magnificent white columns, meant to be suggestive of the real thing in Rome, or at least of the set for some sandal-and-toga epic on a Hollywood back lot. There, his basketball team, led by Jerry West and Wilt Chamberlain, soon became the toast of the town, a perennial contender that finally claimed a championship in 1972, while attracting Hollywood's A-list to its games.

Basketball, people in California knew. It was an American game (though invented by a Canadian) played in every high school, recreation centre and church basement. Hockey, they knew not so much. There is a story, perhaps apocryphal, about the Kings' first official practice at the Long Beach Arena (they played there, and at the L.A. Sports Arena, until construction of the Forum was completed in December of their inaugural season), and how the team's supply of pucks had somehow been misplaced. Replacements certainly weren't readily available in that neighbourhood, or in any other in southern California. Years later, Cooke would famously wonder aloud whether all of those former Canadians living in Los Angeles had moved there because they hated hockey, since they clearly weren't filling his rink. The truth is, he owed a debt to at least one of them, Larry Mann, a working Canadian actor with a long list of television credits who had set up shop in L.A., and who deserves recognition as the Kings' first, and most loyal, fan. He was there to watch that inaugural practice, and when the pucks didn't turn up, he found one stashed in the glove compartment of his car (as any good Canadian boy would). The players were careful not to lose it.

Other than a few devoted souls like Mann who understood the game and recognized some of the players who had been acquired in the expansion draft—the most famous of them the great, and greatly troubled, goaltender Terry Sawchuk—the sport was slow to catch on with the larger public. Cooke's promotional instincts failed him, and those he hired to run the hockey club didn't make things any easier by embarking on what turned out to be a disastrous development strategy, sacrificing long-range planning, in the form of draft choices, for short-term gain, in the form of fading talent with vaguely familiar names. Over and over again, they traded away picks for veteran players they were convinced would spur an instant turnaround, or at least sell a few tickets for a team that didn't average more than ten thousand fans a game until its sixth season in the league. The strategy didn't work. The Kings remained mired in mediocrity, an afterthought in the big city, a perpetual money loser, the Lakers' ugly stepsister.

Cooke's eventual decision to sell all of his Los Angeles sports properties had little to do with his frustrations involving the Kings, and a whole lot to do with his always complicated personal life (he would be married five times before his death in 1997). He never stopped loving being the boss. "I'd like to attend an athletic contest every night—365 days a year—and see a team I own," he once said. "It's a personal indulgence. Money ceases to be an object after a while." But he did stop loving his first wife, the former Barbara Jean Carnegie of Toronto. Their divorce settlement, the largest in California history, paid her $41 million, on top of which Cooke incurred enormous legal costs. (The presiding judge was one Joseph Wapner, who would later become famous on television's *The People's Court.*)

Just as soon as his assets were unfrozen following the divorce decree, Cooke began looking for a way to come up with the cash for his now ex-wife. By then, he owned 85 per cent of the Redskins, and the football team had become both his primary passion and a valuable asset. At the same time, there was a buyer in California ready and willing to purchase not just the other jewels of his sports empire there (the Forum, the Lakers), but also the money-losing Kings, like a piece of parsley tucked beside a restaurant sandwich. For Dr. Jerry Buss, who would come up with the cash to complete what was then the largest sports transaction ever (there was also a non-sports component involved in the deal, a thirteen-thousand-acre ranch in the California mountains), it wasn't just the opportunity to play out the familiar boyhood dream, but also a chance to parlay the money he had earned as an exceptionally savvy real estate speculator and buy his way in among the stars. He certainly liked sports—or at least one of them. "Well, I was a mild hockey fan," Buss says today, "and a major basketball fan." But what he liked even more was hitting the nightclubs, being ushered in past the lineups, behind the velvet ropes, being offered the best table at the best places in town, getting his picture in the papers, his name in the gossip columns, and especially dating the most beautiful women in a city overflowing with them (he kept their pictures filed away neatly in an album, just for the memories). You could do some of that simply because you were a kid who had grown up dirt-poor, then struck it very rich in the land of opportunity. But you could do it a whole lot more easily if you were also the owner of the city's most glamorous sports franchise, if you were the keeper of courtside seats, if you were part of the story every time they won or they lost. Buss paid $67.5 million for the Lakers, the Kings, the Forum and the ranch, and got his name in lights.

A *Sports Illustrated* story written just after the deal was completed provides a clear picture of his feelings in that moment of triumph. Buss was positively bubbly about the possibilities, about the potential for growth and winning championships—at least until he started to talk about hockey. "With the Kings, you have the all-important question: Can hockey ever be a West Coast sport?" Buss wondered. "I don't think anyone knows the answer to that. The Kings definitely lose money every year. In their very best year they lost $200,000. In the worst year they lost $1.5 million. They average about $700,000 a year in losses. However, in the first few operating years, the tax treatment would be such as to allow a break-even situation as regards cash flow. To make money steadily, the Kings have to sell another 3,000 season tickets. If they can, great. If not, I've made a bad deal."

Buss was born and grew up in a place as far from the bright lights of Hollywood as could be imagined, a tiny coal mining town in Wyoming (not far, as it turned out, from where Bruce McNall's father was born). He left home early and lived above a pool hall for a spell, did time as a gandy dancer on the Union Pacific Railroad (no dancing involved, but plenty of dirty, dangerous work), before finally understanding that he was academically inclined. He put himself through the University of Wyoming while working as a chemist for the Bureau of Mines, then moved to Los Angeles to study chemistry at the University of Southern California, completing both a master's degree and a doctorate by the time he was twenty-four years old. Buss worked for a short time in the aerospace industry, developing weapons technology while holding his nose, but his real dream was to teach. In the interests of subsidizing that career, of making enough money on the side so that working as a university instructor wouldn't be a financial hardship, he decided to try his hand at real estate, in partnership with a friend named Frank Mariani. Buss's first investment, a thousand dollars in a West Los Angeles apartment building, was the beginning of a career that would take him away from science and the academic life, and make him both rich and famous.

As his fortune grew, Buss came to enjoy some of the side benefits life on the fringes of Hollywood could provide. But sports ownership would provide his real entrée to the world of celebrity. His first purchase was a franchise in World Team Tennis, a bright idea designed to capitalize on the 1970s craze that had made stars of Billie Jean King, Chris Evert, Jimmy Connors and Björn Borg, and had spurred a huge participation boom. The league was a flop, but Buss was undeterred, and when Cooke came calling he was more than willing to write the cheque.

This is how William Oscar Johnson described Buss in *Sports Illustrated* in 1979, just after he bought the Lakers and Kings:

His persona is an amalgam of Horatio Alger and Hugh Hefner; of sugar daddy, devoted father, accountant, real estate wheeler-dealer and aerospace scientist. Buss comes on in a manner that mixes cowboy swagger with movie star glamour, college professor smarts with pool hustler chic. He habitually wears a pair of almost disgustingly shabby Levi's, a Western shirt open to reveal the gray hairs of his chest, and shiny black cowboy boots. His hair is silvery, long and curly at the nape of the neck, with a thick-woven thatch on top, which proves baldness is indeed not necessary. He is tall and handsome in a way that is vaguely mindful of a ravaged Robert Redford crossed with a slightly rejuvenated Ronald Reagan. His smile displays perfect teeth, which are every bit as white and well made as the $127,500 Rolls-Royce Camargue he drives. He is, in a sense, the archetype of a certain breed of Bel Air millionaire—acquisitive, aggressive, restless, obsessed with good looks and rich in an assortment of playthings, playmates and possessions that ordinary men can only covet.

Yet Buss says he is a devotee of Camus and Sartre, and in his real estate office associates habitually call him Doctor Buss. This refers to a Ph.D. in physical chemistry that he earned at USC in 1957 at the age of 24. One of his doctoral dissertations was entitled "The Bond Dissociation Energy of Toluene," another, he says, dealt with "thermochemical prediction." For a brief time he taught chemistry at USC. But, he says, "Actually, I'm probably more of a mathematician than a chemist. To some people, numbers are as comfortable as words. They fascinate me, they're my passion. I'll notice the number of miles on the odometer of a friend's car, and I'll figure how much he drives. Then, maybe weeks later, I'll call him up and ask if I can go for a ride with him and watch while his odometer turns past 100,000 miles."

The same month that Buss bought the Lakers, the team selected point guard Earvin "Magic" Johnson from Michigan State University with the first pick in the 1979 National Basketball Association draft, and in that moment the die was cast. Johnson would help lead the franchise to a championship in his rookie season—the first of five the "Showtime" Lakers would win during his tenure. They became the most famous basketball team in the world, and the great team rivalry with the Boston Celtics—and the personal one between Johnson and Larry Bird—pushed the NBA to the forefront of American professional sports for the first time. To be lucky enough to land a courtside seat at a Lakers game required being very rich or very famous or very beautiful. The celebrity fans, like Jack Nicholson, became almost as much a part of the event as the players themselves.

On the hockey side, Buss straightened out the Kings' operation, banned the practice of trading away draft choices, and did his best to set the franchise on a path towards respectability. During his watch, the team kept its picks, employed Marcel Dionne, who would go on to become one of the greatest scorers in NHL history, and yet still sputtered along, some seasons quite good, most mediocre-to-bad. But more significantly, they were still the Kings, it was still hockey, and nothing about the team or the sport really turned Buss's crank. Unlike the Lakers, they didn't help his bottom line, and they didn't particularly enhance his social life.

On April 10, 1982, the Kings would enjoy the most glorious victory to that point in franchise history. It was game three of a best-of-five first-round playoff series against Wayne Gretzky and the Edmonton Oilers, then a very young, very talented, very cocky, but not yet battle-hardened squad. The Kings had split the first two games, and were trailing 5–0 entering the third period at the Forum, with any hope of winning the series surely slipping away against the high-flying team from the north. They were still down by three with ten minutes left. Then they roared back in stunning fashion to claim a wildly unlikely victory (and won again in Edmonton to eliminate the Oilers from the playoffs, before falling themselves in the next round). The game was dubbed "The Miracle on Manchester," and for the long-suffering loyalists who had stuck by the least-glamorous team in town, it was the closest thing they had experienced to winning a Stanley Cup.

But when they looked up at the owner's private box during the ecstatic celebration afterwards, they couldn't help but notice that

Buss had already left the building. He had ducked out early. No doubt, he had something better to do.

Before finally throwing in the towel and selling the Kings, Buss did have one very bright idea. The league's biggest star, its one real marquee attraction, was toiling away in Edmonton, a relative back-water. That surely couldn't be good for the long-term interests of the sport. Putting Gretzky in Los Angeles might be enough to revive his moribund team. Buss knew the Oilers' owner, Peter Pocklington, from meetings of the board of governors and they were friendly, to a point. He knew a little bit about Pocklington's mercurial business life outside of hockey, his cyclical ups and downs. Maybe there was an opportunity there. Maybe there was a deal that made sense for him, sense for Pocklington and sense for the NHL. "I approached Peter Pocklington and said, 'Why don't you sell me Gretzky?'" Buss remembers. "My reasoning was—you have a fabulously valuable asset which is depreciating. It has to be going down by three million dollars a year. There has to come a time when you can't afford this depreciating asset anymore, while you can still get some value for it. I was deadly serious."

Buss had made his pitch. "[Pocklington] laughed and dismissed it and that was kind of that."

Jerry Buss also liked to collect coins. Not the ancient stuff, not the Greeks and Romans, but American coins, and it was through that hobby he first heard the name Bruce McNall. "I had kind of been aware of [McNall] as a coin dealer," Buss says. "I was a very big coin collector in those days. I didn't know him very well. I knew him as a coin dealer and I started becoming acquainted with him as a hockey fan. . . . He seemed to be incredibly successful and incredibly intelligent. He had a lot of things going at the same time. He was into racehorses. He was into motion pictures. And he wanted to get into sports. He had all of the trappings of very suc-cessful and wealthy individual."

According to McNall, another of Buss's hobbies was high-stakes gambling, which he says caused Buss to regularly suffer a case of the shorts. McNall says that Buss frequently asked to borrow money from him—a thousand here, a couple of thousand there—and Bruce was happy to oblige. So they were pals, sort of, and had a business relationship, sort of, and McNall had certainly come to love hockey, deciding that it was *his* game. He became a fixture around the Forum when the Kings played, known to fans and players alike.

As Buss remembers it, the impetus to sell the Kings came when he was presented with another sports business opportunity. "I had really been interested in buying a [National Football League] team," he says. (In the end, that bid would not come to fruition.) "There wasn't an official rule that you couldn't own too many franchises, but it was kind of an unwritten rule that if you owned in basketball and hockey, you probably wouldn't get a football franchise. So I started negotiating for the Dallas Cowboys. I kind of reached an agreement on it—one that didn't last very long. At that point I realized I had a better chance to get a team if I would sell the hockey team. I was losing a lot of money with it. Bruce was there. He wanted it. It just kind of started to fall into place."

Not hard to imagine what Buss was thinking. Hockey in L.A. was a non-starter, but it would be nice to keep the Kings as a paying tenant in his arena. And here was this wide-eyed guy who clearly loved the game, who loved the attention, who by all accounts was worth a whole lot of money, who never seemed to have trouble coming up with cash. First sell him a piece, with the option to buy more. Cut a generous deal that allowed him to get into sports ownership without having to pay for the whole thing up front. Let him be seduced before the cruel realities of selling the game in southern California set in. Make your problem somebody else's problem. Get while the getting was good. The machinations couldn't have been clearer if a cartoon thought balloon had popped out of Jerry Buss's head.

What McNall was thinking behind that ever-present smile was not yet so obvious. He just seemed so darned happy to be there.

Chapter Five

BRUCE'S BIG IDEA

S PAGO. THAT WOULD BE THE STAGE. A restaurant so filled with famous people that its chef, Wolfgang Puck, had become a bit of a star himself. Never mind the food, it was all about the buzz. In ancient times there was the Brown Derby, and then there was Chasen's and now Spago—hip because it was; and because it was, the hip came out. Someday that would pass, someday they'd move down the street or around the block, but in Los Angeles in 1987, *this* was the place to be seen. So rent the joint, for a king's ransom. Call in every marker from every celebrity you'd ever met. Work the publicists, convince them that this was a primo photo op. This was going to be big, this was going to be lavish, with great food, great booze, packed with other stars, and all of it free to those who could attract the spotlight. The occasion? Well, something to do with hockey, but who watched hockey—and in any event, that was really beside the point, wasn't it? Roll out the red carpet and they'd come out of habit, celebrities in descending alphabetical order—the A-list, the B-list, the C-list—there to fete something or other, have their pictures taken, soak up the goodies and then move on.

On the night, the place sure looked the part. Though paparazzi culture wasn't yet what it would become, the shooters staked out their spots on the sidewalk, jostling for the best positions, since Spago was a good bet on most nights, and on a night like this, with the spotlights shining, pretty much a sure thing. Passers-by, gawkers, autograph seekers filled the last of the available space, pushing forward for a glimpse. Then the limos began pulling up to the curb, one after another, the invited guests piled out, and at least a few of them were instantly recognizable: Goldie Hawn and her longtime companion, Kurt Russell; and Tom Hanks, one of the biggest movie stars in the world—and one of the few who might have actually spent a night or two watching the Los Angeles Kings. Finally, another car rolled up, this one carrying the guests of honour. The photographers raised their cameras in anticipation, the autograph hounds stood with paper and pens at the ready. Out climbed three young men—good-looking guys, buff, and a bit awkward as if blinded by the bright lights, as if bewildered by the whole situation. The flashes started firing—then stopped. The fans started hollering, until it dawned on them that they couldn't put a name to any one of those faces. Their attention soon enough was drawn elsewhere, to the next car, and the next, in the hopes that they contained a someone, leaving Luc Robitaille, Jimmy Carson and Steve Duchesne to stroll into their own coming-out party, pretty much unmolested.

Bruce McNall had his hockey team now—a money-losing hockey team in a great big city oblivious to its charms and largely illiterate in the sport, but he was a man not easily discouraged. He was also a man with great faith in his own ability to work magic. The coin business that he began as a hobby had been transformed into an investment vehicle for the über-wealthy: movie moguls, tycoons, even the famously eccentric, politically extreme Hunt brothers William Herbert and Nelson Bunker (who had once tried to corner the silver market), all of them convinced to sink millions into the collections McNall would build for them. Coins led naturally to other antiquities, and from there to sports memorabilia, and then to sports ownership, with the Kings and with a stable of racehorses. And movies were part of the equation, of course, because a few million invested in that business could also give you access to the currency of celebrity, which went a long way in this town. To run that side of the operation, McNall hired David Begelman, a man with a checkered past and an expensive lifestyle. But that didn't matter, because they had the ready cash and they were bold as brass. There were flops, but there were also hits—*WarGames, The Fabulous Baker Boys*—which meant that Bruce McNall, the coin nerd, was now a bona fide Hollywood producer.

No one looked too closely at where the money was coming from. If they had, they would have discovered a series of banks, all convinced to approve loans on the basis of past schemes built in turn on past loans—a house of cards constructed on the foundation of McNall's personal charm and not much else. He figured out early how easy it was to talk others into buying into his dreams by appealing to their own fantasies. Stoke their imaginations and they'd make decisions to free up huge sums of money without fretting over the financial fine points. Put a banker next to a movie star, entrance a billionaire with tales of the Greek and Roman ancients—or of a famous ballplayer from the early 1900s depicted on a cigarette card. Press an artifact, a piece of metal, a bit of cardboard, into their hands and they became like wide-eyed kids who had to have the latest toy. (And with the bankers, he also realized that the farther out on a limb they went, the more exposed they were, the more money they gave him based on the flimsiest of pretences, the less likely they were to call his bluff or call his loans. They were all in this together, and so it was in their interest as much as his to keep the cash flowing. Others, he just flat-out bribed.)

The same mix of schmooze and audacity and charm, McNall reasoned, could be brought to bear on hockey. Surely the game, with all the virtues that he had come to love—its speed and toughness and skill—could be sexed up in Los Angeles, made glamorous, made the hottest ticket in town with just the right amount of stardust applied. Once ticket buyers were sold on the notion that the rink was where the hip and the beautiful went, they would decide for themselves that they needed to be seen at The Forum. That's how Hollywood worked.

But where to begin? The National Hockey League wasn't a novelty act anymore, and the Kings were little more than an afterthought in the overcrowded southern California sports landscape. The Forum was still Fabulous, but only because that's where the Lakers played. In the local hierarchy, hockey sat somewhere behind professional basketball, baseball and football *and* the glamorous college teams of USC and UCLA, in the same murky professional sports netherworld where games like soccer struggled for recognition. The Kings were a small-time attraction with a committed following of zealots, who numbered just enough to fill about half of the seats on most nights (and who had long ago mastered the art of buying a five-dollar ticket in the upper sections, then working their way down to the vast empty spaces closer to the ice as the game progressed and the ushers lost interest). Presumably, the hockey hard core would stick around, no matter what, but there weren't enough of them, they didn't spend enough, they were a bit down-market, and they certainly weren't famous. Only occasionally could the odd recognizable face be found among the Kings' faithful—one of the Canadian expat actors and comedians, perhaps, homesick for the national game, or someone like the great Canadian jockey Sandy Hawley, whose career had taken him to the California tracks and who liked to moonlight as an off-ice official, working as a timekeeper in the penalty box. But the really big stars, the kind who might make the world sit up and notice the Kings, still wanted to be courtside at Lakers games.

McNall considered his assets. The Kings didn't have a player on their roster with anything near the name recognition of a Magic Johnson or Kareem Abdul-Jabbar. But they did have Bernie Nicholls, a first-rate NHL scorer, and through the draft they had begun to assemble a cast of young talent. There was Carson, an American chosen second overall in the 1986 draft, who scored 79 points as a rookie in 1986–87, and Robitaille, a handsome devil with an exotic French-Canadian accent who scored 84 points that same season and was named the NHL's rookie of the year. McNall decided that beyond representing the on-ice future of the hockey team, the two young guns would become the foundation of his marketing strategy, that one way or another he would put their names in lights. "As long as I'm here," he told the two of them, "I'll never trade you guys." He tried to encourage fans and the press to think of Robitaille and Carson as Butch Cassidy and the Sundance Kid, as hunky hockey-playing glamour boys. They would be treated like stars in the land of stars, even if the public hadn't yet caught on. He would create the right presentation, the right environment, drop them into the kind of surroundings associated with the rich and famous and let the market draw its own conclusions. And so the Hollywood party at Spago, which for the players would become one of those great shared memories, though it wasn't quite so much fun in the moment. "Nobody knew who in the heck we were," Robitaille remembers, laughing. "We got out of the car and the paparazzi were taking pictures of everybody but us."

It wasn't cheap, it bombed, and it began to dawn on McNall that he had bought into a chicken-and-egg predicament. If hockey didn't matter in Los Angeles, you couldn't make a hockey player a star; but without hockey-playing stars, you couldn't make hockey matter. The players, though—especially those who had suffered through the relative indifference of the Jerry Buss years—at least appreciated what McNall was trying to do, and were thrilled to work for a happy, engaged, fun-loving, free-spending owner. "We didn't like it—we loved it," Robitaille says. "We had never seen that. He joked—he'd go, 'I don't know anything about hockey.' He asked us questions. He was a participant owner. He loved to be with the guys. He loved to go on the road and take guys out for dinner and tell us stories about his business.

"He always came into the dressing room and brought someone and introduced them—the celebrities. As a player, you suddenly started to feel the team is important. He made us feel great about us. And you felt you had to perform. That's the way this town is. The purists of hockey might say, 'Oh man, this is wrong.' But when you're a person and you see someone you see on TV, you might just pick it up a bit that night. In Bruce, we saw somebody that cared. We cared to the point that when we lost, we felt bad for him —we genuinely felt bad for him."

The Kings' diehard fans soon came to love McNall, too. They saw in him, in his obvious passion for the game, one of their own. They adored the fact that, unlike Buss, his sports priorities were undivided. The team seemed to be coming together on the ice, finally; the owner was a nice, smiley guy who didn't hide in a private box, who was more than happy to show his face and press the flesh. For those who could remember all the way back to the first expansion years, to the peripatetic ownership of Jack Kent Cooke, to the few brief moments of encouragement when it seemed the Kings were rounding into something decent, to the hopes inevitably dashed, simply having an owner who was visible, pleasant, engaged and gave a damn was a large, comforting step forward.

And being liked was a big part of it for Bruce McNall. He pined to be part of a crowd, to be one of the boys, to be on a team, and the Kings and the little community surrounding them gave him all of that. But the precarious nature of his personal finances required moving forward relentlessly, keeping the cash flowing and growing; otherwise, like a shark stilled in the water, he'd die. Hockey in Los Angeles couldn't remain a money-losing minority passion. There wasn't time for slow, steady, incremental growth. McNall couldn't be the guy who made the Kings respectable, solid, decent, a break-even proposition. It had to be a whole lot more than that, and it had to happen fast, or it would be all over.

What he needed was something beyond hockey. What he needed was a big idea.

Several thousand miles to the north, the owner of another hockey team, in a much more hockey-loving town, in a much more hockey-loving country, had already ridden a string of championships and the subsequent surge in local pride to become a small-city celebrity in his own right, and for some folks, at least, a bit of a hero. Peter Pocklington had paid the bills and enjoyed the benefits of what had become an iconic franchise—not just for Edmonton, but for anyone who loved the game. Heady stuff, indeed, the very reason he had moved beyond cars and real estate and meat products in the first place. And yet here he was, contemplating a transaction that he knew, even in his ego-driven haze, could bring it all tumbling down. But, like McNall, Pocklington was not a man short on self-regard.

It was almost certainly on a golf course in a sunny southern clime that he first mentioned the unmentionable: a thought, a solution to his own business challenges, the boldest of bold strokes that had been kicking around in his head for some time. "What do you think would happen," Pocklington said with a smile to one of his playing partners, shooting the shit between shots, "if I ever got rid of Wayne Gretzky? What do you think they'd do to me? Do you think there'd be riots in the streets?" Just a crazy hypothetical, a wild what-if scenario that surely would never happen. Gretzky out of Edmonton? Not in a million years. Peter Puck, the sono-fabitch, was messing with them, being intentionally outrageous—probably trying to put them off their game to win the money riding on the next putt. But if they didn't immediately break into helpless fits of laughter or stiffen up in righteous indignation, Pocklington, a few holes later, might have eased into the topic that had come to dominate his private thoughts. Gretzky, the saint and icon and small-town Canadian boy, wasn't all he was cracked up to be, he'd tell them. Nothing wildly scandalous, though maybe there were a few boys-will-be-boys tales thrown in to titillate his pals. But then he'd go on. About how Wayne was getting a little too big for his britches. About how that self-effacing public image concealed what had become a monstrous ego. About how the new girlfriend, the actress, the blonde, the Yankee Jezebel, had him wrapped around her finger, how she didn't want to be in Edmonton at all. Wayne actually preferred hanging out with her flashy Hollywood friends. And the old man, Walter, everybody's favourite hockey dad? Let me tell you, he's a royal pain in the ass.

It was a dry run, a rehearsal, practice for saying what Pocklington increasingly believed he was going to have to say soon enough in front of the microphones, under the television lights, to a no doubt hostile audience. He believed the stuff about Gretzky's growing self-love, and the same for the pernicious thoughts about the missus, though casting her in the role of female seducer/ betrayer was a cliché that dated all the way back to the (not Boston) Garden. What was really driving Pocklington towards the previously unthinkable, though, was a series of unpleasant realities of an entirely bottom-line nature, and it certainly wasn't the first time he'd felt such a pinch. His varied business interests, always a boom-bust-boom proposition, were experiencing one of their periodic downturns, while at the same time his most valuable asset might be planning his exit in any case.

Back in 1983, right about the time he was being celebrated for his financial acumen by Peter Gzowski in *Saturday Night* magazine (". . . the thrill of dancing on thin ice was behind him as he entered his forties . . . his companies in real estate, automotive sales, finance, professional sport, and food processing were grossing more than a billion dollars a year. They were solid."), while he was trying desperately to be taken seriously as a would-be prime minister, Pocklington had in fact been teetering on the brink of insolvency (that would be around the same time that Jerry Buss had smelled blood, and came asking about a Gretzky trade, only to be rebuffed). He had come back from the brink, but now there was the ongoing debacle of the Gainers meat-packing plant, where a long, angry strike, during which Pocklington enthusiastically employed scab labour in an attempt to break the union, essentially killed the business. (In Edmonton, more progressive politically than the rest of Alberta, and a solid labour town, the Gainers strike certainly didn't win Pocklington any friends, a situation that was exacerbated when the news broke that the great free enterpriser had been bailed out by his pals in the provincial government.) Real estate had taken a dip. Other of his businesses were hemorrhaging. There was at least one looming lawsuit.

Pocklington was becoming increasingly uncomfortable, feeling increasingly boxed in, and a big infusion of cash certainly couldn't hurt. The hockey end of his ledger was pretty much maxed out. The Oilers were selling all of the seats at Northlands Coliseum at the price the market would bear and the team invariably went deep into the playoffs (all of those home dates represented found money since, in the curious NHL system, the players weren't paid for the post-season, aside from bonus money delivered by the league). Beyond that there was nothing left to tap. At the same time, NHL salaries, unimpeded by any kind of cap system, were escalating at a rate that Pocklington knew he couldn't match in new revenue. Would ticket buyers and sponsors remain onside, even if Pocklington invested a few million dollars less in the payroll, even if the team shed its most famous, and most expensive, star? Just as long as the Oilers kept on winning, wouldn't the fans stick around in any case? Wouldn't it at least be worth rolling the dice?

And about that asset—for in Pocklington's calculations, that's what Wayne Gretzky had become, not a person, not a hockey player, not a shinny genius, not a star, but flesh and blood and brain with a defined value in the economic calculus of professional hockey. Gretzky was twenty-six years old, certainly not ancient for a player, but statistically, historically, closing in on the point where he might be expected to peak. Any professional athlete has a shelf life, and most reach their top earning years after the most productive parts of their career are actually past. Young stars tend to be underpaid relative to their real value, and grizzled veterans who are rewarded for their name and past glories are overpaid. The trick for a general manager, for an owner, is to have more of the former than the latter, to cut ties when it makes practical—and not emotional—sense.

During the 1987–88 season, Gretzky suffered injuries that limited him to sixty-four games—not necessarily a sign of Father Time's work itself, but certainly the older a player gets, the more fragile he becomes. In part because of the weeks spent on the shelf, he had been supplanted by Mario Lemieux both as the NHL's leading scorer and as its most valuable player. The torch, it seemed, had been passed, and the betting was it wouldn't be passed back. Pocklington was paying the highest salary in the league to an athlete who may well have no longer been its best—a disparity between production and reward that could only become worse over time. Plus, most significant of all, Gretzky's contract was itself a ticking time bomb.

He was still working under the twenty-one-year personal-services deal that he had signed as an eighteen-year-old, which provided enormous security, but also eliminated any negotiating leverage. Under financial duress, Pocklington needed to attach Gretzky directly to the Oilers, since he was the key to the team's value, and therefore the owner's equity. Gretzky and his advisors were more than happy to oblige—to a point. Sure, they'd tear up the old contract and sign a conventional five-year deal with the Oilers, with one addition: Gretzky could walk away after three years, without consequence, if he chose to retire. Plus, at the contract's conclusion, under the terms of the collective agreement between the players and the owners, Gretzky would be eligible for free agency at age thirty-one, opening the door to greener pastures. It would represent a chance for the most valuable commodity in the game to find out what he was really worth on the open market, a move that would be applauded by every other player in the league and by the union that represented them. "I wanted to get paid my fair value," Gretzky said years later. "I owed it to myself to do it and I felt that I really owed it to my teammates. At that time there were guys making a million dollars plus and we were making $250,000 or $300,000."

The day he signed the new contract, Gretzky was absolutely aware of its implications. He wasn't oblivious to the business of hockey. He understood the economic realities of Edmonton. He knew that Pocklington, if he was thinking like a businessman, wouldn't let the deal play out to its conclusion and risk being left with nothing. "I said, I've just traded my life away," Gretzky acknowledged in a 1992 interview. "I'll be traded before the five years are up."

The Gretzky camp still maintains that any threat was implicit—that it was always his desire to continue playing in Edmonton. He would have been happy to go back and sign a new contract with the Oilers, they claim, just as long as it ensured that he remained the highest-paid player in the game. Still, given the size of the market, given Pocklington's travails, just how likely was that?

—

It had been a symbiotic relationship. Pocklington compensated Gretzky fairly, and had supported Glen Sather by giving him the autonomy and resources to assemble a first-rate supporting cast, while largely refraining from meddling in hockey matters—though the nasty parting with Paul Coffey over money suggested that the good times might be drawing to a close. On the personal front, he had acted as a bit of a mentor, especially in the early days, even if they weren't so close anymore. (The relationship between Gretzky and Pocklington had, in fact, cooled so much that they were hardly speaking during his final season with the Oilers.)

There were certainly worse places where Gretzky might have played out the prime years of his career, and worse owners who might have signed his cheques. It must have been a rare day, as the Oilers were winning Stanley Cups, as the players enjoyed the lifestyle of extremely big fish in a smallish pond, when Gretzky wished that hockey fate had landed him somewhere else. Wayne Gretzky *and* Peter Pocklington put Edmonton on the map. Wayne Gretzky *and* Peter Pocklington brought the city the Stanley Cup, made it the number one hockey town in a hockey nation, made the folks down the road in Calgary jealous for a change.

And Pocklington had to know that the day Skalbania phoned out of the blue, offering him a seventeen-year-old hockey player for ready cash, had been just about the luckiest day of his life. He had to know that getting rid of Gretzky, however rational the impulse, would traumatize the city, and maybe the entire country. It was going to get emotional. People were going to be upset. They would immediately start looking for someone to blame. He'd be right there in the bull's eye.

But ego, hubris, clouded his thoughts, made him a bit delusional, made him believe this was a battle of equals, the hero owner trading the hero player—who wasn't really the great guy they all thought he was, who was under the thumb of his American girlfriend, who didn't really want to be in Edmonton anymore. Pocklington convinced himself that he could stand up and sell that story, that he could solve his financial problems in one fell swoop while telling Edmontonians that their adopted favourite son, their most famous fellow citizen, their city's one iconic presence, was leaving of his own volition, that he was quitting town and quitting his loyal fans for his own selfish motives. Heck, it wasn't like the *team* was leaving. It wasn't like they'd finish last without him. Sather was still there. They would get loads of talent back in a trade, and once they started winning again, once they won a Stanley Cup without Wayne Gretzky, the fans would have fallen out of love with old what's-his-name and would be celebrating the owner for his shrewd, bold move, for cutting the cord at just the right time.

Nelson Skalbania says that he made the first move. Like a hoary plot device, he had reappeared in the story, there to set things in motion at the beginning, and now back in a supporting role at the end. It wasn't a secret in the circles in which both travelled that Pocklington was in a wee bit of distress, and having been in distress a few times himself, Skalbania knew the drill, knew that what were weak moments for some were moments of opportunity for others. The law of the jungle, the law of the business hustler, and no hard feelings. When others had inquired before, making far-fetched pitches about Gretzky, Pocklington had been able to confidently rebuff them—or at least had never received an offer he couldn't refuse. This time, Pocklington was all ears. "He needed money," Skalbania remembers. "There's nothing the matter with that. He had problems in some of his other business ventures. And you know Gretzky's not going to play forever. Let me tell you when not to sell a player—when he can't play anymore. From Peter's standpoint, if he was sitting on an oil well pumping out a lot of revenue, he never would have sold. The trouble is he was in a bunch of businesses that were struggling. It was strictly a business deal. . . . What do you do when you're broke or having trouble? You sell your best asset, because that's the only thing you can sell. Which is the reverse of what you usually do—usually, you should sell your shit and keep your good asset. I never did that, either, by the way—even though that's a good rule. I used to sell my better stuff to pay for the shit that I should have sold. In his case, [Pocklington's] most readily saleable immediate cash asset was Wayne. Remember, at that time Wayne wasn't young. And to get $15 million was a lot of money."

It had been a long time since Skalbania had been in the hockey business. But in this case, not being part of the NHL's inner circle might actually work to his advantage. He could move discreetly, without setting off alarms, even while the season was still underway, putting together a deal with all kinds of moving parts. The Vancouver Canucks were owned by a publicly traded company. Jim Pattison, an aggressive British Columbia–based entrepreneur, was interested in putting some of his money into gaining marketing rights for the team—or at least he was interested if Wayne Gretzky could somehow be part of the package. Enter the great facilitator: Skalbania cooked up a scheme in which he and Pattison would buy 51 per cent of the Canucks at a market price of a bit more than $5 million; they would then pay Pocklington $15 million for Gretzky, betting that the value of the team would increase enormously with him on the roster. As an inducement to make the move, Gretzky would be given 25 per cent of the franchise himself. And as the cherry on top, Pocklington would slip Gretzky $2 million of the cash he received.

Hard to imagine that even the NHL, which was forever playing fast and loose with the rules of business, would approve such a transaction: a player sold for cash, a player holding equity in a team, and a player, in effect, pocketing a portion of his own sale price. Surely it would have been shot down by president John Ziegler or the board of governors if it had ever seen the light of day. Which it didn't. "I went to Pocklington. I said, Would you do a deal? He said 'Yes,'" Skalbania remembers. "I was only going to get a few shares in the Canucks. Maybe they never took me seriously. I think they used me. McNall jumped at it because he figured it was going to go to Vancouver. I think they used me to really trigger McNall. It never had a chance on this end. I don't think the [Canucks' owners] thought it was a serious offer from Peter."

That's how the conversation started, just before the beginning of the Stanley Cup playoffs in the spring of 1988. Skalbania (in fact, first it was his daughter Rosanda, testing the waters, and then

Nelson following) calling Gretzky's representative, Michael Barnett, with his pitch: "I've got a deal in place. Peter is sure about it. Wayne can come to the team and own a piece of the hockey club. Do you think he'd be interested? He's already won three Cups. Now he can come to a great city and have a piece of the club." Skalbania started working on Walter Gretzky as well. He knew him from the WHA, from the day in Vancouver when Wayne beat him in a foot race and signed his first professional contract, and he understood how much influence the father still had with his son. Barnett and Wally talked about it, talked about the fact that Pocklington was apparently shopping Gretzky without having the courtesy to speak to him about it, and decided to keep that knowledge to themselves until the last game was played—ideally until the Cup was raised—lest it distract from the holy quest.

Chapter Six

THE LAST PERFECT MOMENT (I)
MAY 26, 1988

S OMEONE MUST HAVE INTERVENED—a higher power, a guiding intelligence, or perhaps it was just one of the rats. They lurked in the dark, dank spaces of Boston Garden, a pile that had long since crossed the line from charming heritage building to irredeemable dump. Anyone privileged with backstage access first took an elevator in the office next door (the arena was above street level—above a railway station, in fact), then walked through a grubby passageway that emerged beneath the stands. The place smelled of elephants, an odour hard to forget, the legacy of circuses past that had leached right into the brick. And every once in awhile, out of the corner of your eye, a dark shadow might be seen disappearing into a nook or cranny. Their ancestors must have been there to see Eddie Shore.

In the fourth game of the 1988 Stanley Cup final, on May 24, the Edmonton Oilers had just scored to tie the Boston Bruins, 3–3, seventeen minutes into the second period. Winners of three of the past four Stanley Cups, the Oilers had taken the first three games of the series, making a Boston comeback a virtual impossibility (only one team in that position, the 1942 Toronto Maple Leafs, had ever battled back to win the Cup). But at the very least the B's might save face in front of the home fans, and in their fantasies they could steal the next game in Edmonton and return here down 3–2, and then . . . well, somebody would opine that you have to take it one game at a time. This night, at least, they were playing well enough to win.

Conditions had been far from perfect. Hot late-spring weather, unreliable air conditioning, antique ice-making technology, all had combined to create a slow track, over which hung a low blanket of indoor fog. The Oilers, who thrived on speed and skill, weren't a team built to play on slush, and though they had won game three in those same circumstances, they were struggling a bit to complete the sweep against a foe desperate to avoid that humiliation on home ice.

Then the lights went out and wouldn't come back on, and more than one person who had experienced the Garden's peculiar charms figured that a rat had bitten into the wrong wire at the wrong time and had gone up in a puff of electrical smoke. According to the statutes of the National Hockey League—section 27-12, to be precise, as President John Ziegler would later explain—the power outage constituted an act of God, and when God intervened to end a hockey playoff game before its conclusion, the law of the league was crystal clear: it would be completed not now, not the next day, but at the conclusion of the series, and then only if necessary.

So game four, which was really game five, though not really, would be played in a rink where, even in late May, when by rights no one should have even been contemplating winter sport, the ice would be as hard and fast as on a prairie pond in January. Edmonton had taken to calling itself the City of Champions, and not without reason, given what the Oilers and football Eskimos had accomplished over the past decade and a half. It would now be granted the unexpected opportunity to watch another champion anointed at home. In those days, it seemed part of the natural order that Canadian teams would regularly win the Stanley Cup, but there was still something pure and right and special about bringing these particular boys back to Alberta to hoist the mug once more.

In the minds of most of the people in the stands, of those watching on television, there was no separation, no demarcation between hockey, the cultural given, and the business of the National Hockey League, though there always should have been. The former was a game that grew out of climate and geography, an organic connection to long, cold winters and vast, open space, to the point that hockey was the single simplest short-form explanation of what made a Canadian a Canadian. The local rink was part town hall, part church, and gathering there was an expression of community, of belonging. The game and its players were mythologized, invested with idealized qualities which, by extension, were also our own: toughness, honesty, the triumph of effort and heart. Understanding hockey implicitly, as birthright, was like the Canadian secret handshake; for the new arrival, learning its nuances was a necessary rite of passage. Americans didn't get it—*couldn't* get it, except in a few border outposts and in Minnesota, which was, by virtue of its climate, liberal politics and the fact that they broadcast all ninety minutes of *As It Happens* on the local public radio station, sort of a Canada-lite, in any case. The game was ours, by definition, or at least it was until the penny dropped and we realized that we were not alone in this galaxy, that there were Russians and Swedes and Finns who felt much the same way. Then the national founding myth required a minor adjustment: that really, we *cared about it* more than they did, the flimsy evidence resting on the finale of the '72 series, regular victories in the World Junior Championships, the 2002 Olympic gold medal (never mind what happened in '98 or '06) and the entirely meaningless fact that, until 2008, no NHL team captained by a European had won the Stanley Cup.

The National Hockey League, by contrast, was a largely American-based entertainment business, with an American president and mostly American team owners who called the shots according to their needs. Forget about playing the nostalgia card: it had always been thus. Two-thirds of the Original Six were based in the United States, and when the league embarked on its first great expansion, adding six franchises all at once, not a single one was located north of the great unguarded border. The NHL would take the pure products of Canadian hockey culture, compensate them for their talents, make them stars, but the minute they cashed that first cheque—really, the minute they signed over their allegiance to an NHL team as a teenager—they straddled the line between culture and commerce, becoming a product.

When the line between hockey and the hockey business was blurred, most often intentionally by money guys trying to sucker some poor Canadian into following his heart instead of his head, it was time to start feeling for your wallet. Gordie Howe, God love him, didn't give up a raise in favour of a new hockey jacket because he was stupid; he did it because, in that moment, in his naïveté, he honestly believed that those extra dollars might be the difference between the success or failure of the Detroit Red Wings. If the Wings started losing money, hockey would be in trouble, and if hockey was in trouble he might well wind up back on the farm in Floral, Saskatchewan, working all day in the summer and freezing his behind off in the winter. Surely the game that had given him this life was worth protecting, even if it meant forgoing the extra dollars that the best player in hockey had to know he deserved.

Later, when the players weren't quite as certain to be innocent farm boys, when the spectator base became more sophisticated in the ways of the sports–entertainment complex, when the notion of mercenary professional athletes with feet of clay eventually replaced the hockey-card saints, Canadians understood that, in indulging their fantasies of heroes and home teams and pure motives, it was more often than not a case of suspending disbelief. They could still do that, to a point. They could hold the hockey/Canada/NHL trinity together, one holy of holies in three indivisible parts. They could hang on, like Gordie and his jacket, to the notion that what was good for the NHL was good for the game, and by extension, good for Canada. But not even the true, blinded zealots would be able to convince themselves that selling the perfect Canadian player from the perfect Canadian team in the perfect Canadian hockey town to foreigners of suspect motives in a place with palm trees was really in our own best interest.

—

Here, in Edmonton, on this night, there is absolutely nothing to disrupt the fantasy. Here, in front of people who know and understand and care, a remarkable group of players has enjoyed an extended adolescence together, professional hockey as extra years of high school—complete with plenty of wild times off the ice—and then matured as a single, flawless shinny organism with all of its component parts: skill guys and tough guys, playmakers and scorers, grinders and role players, journeymen and the greatest celebrity the game would ever produce. Not in New York or Los Angeles, but in Edmonton, which wasn't even the richest or most glamorous city in Alberta, never mind the country or the continent. It is as though, when some hockey higher power was apportioning talent, the decision was based not on where it could generate the most money or the most attention but on where it would matter most, where it could transform an entire city's self-image. If you want to see the best hockey team on earth, if you want to experience the fullest expression of the sport's aesthetics, if you want to witness the triumph of speed and skill, a repudiation of the goonish crimes the Philadelphia Flyers of the 1970s perpetrated against the game, this was it, here it was, in Edmonton. And after they win the Cup tonight? Well, they're still young, they're still getting better. They lost Paul Coffey over money, and look what happened: didn't miss a beat. Same place, same time, next year. It's not just the players. It's Glen Sather as well. He is not entirely beloved by his team. He's rubbed some of them the wrong way by pushing hard, by criticizing them in the press, and yes, by playing hardball with Coffey over his contract and forcing a friend and a great player out of town. Gretzky, and others, have certainly started to tire of Sather's act. But there's no doubting the skill and savvy of the architect. He is widely regarded as the smartest hockey man on the planet right now, his signature on this, his masterpiece.

Live, in the Northlands Coliseum, the boards are still pristine white, uncluttered by advertising, the only logos on the ice those of the club and the publicly owned building. It's not a crowd of high rollers in the stands, not even the familiar men in dark suits who, on all of those *Hockey Night in Canada* broadcasts past, could be seen standing and applauding dutifully in the best seats at Maple Leaf Gardens or the Montreal Forum. There's a bit of money floating around, but not so much of the old, dry establishment sort. You can still smell the ink drying on some of those bills, and social status is conferred for reasons other than birthright, last name, the proper schools. Alberta, land of opportunity, bastion of free enterprise, rich in resources, free fertile ground for strivers and dreamers from anywhere, from any background, bent on becoming rich and on personal reinvention—just like the guy who owns the local hockey team. But at base, Edmonton is a working-class town filled with working-class people who are here on their own hook, not on the cushion of expense-account write-offs. That's the Oilers' crowd.

Across the country, the fans tune in to hear the familiar voices of Bob Cole, the warm, folksy signature of *Hockey Night in Canada,* always betraying a hint of his native Newfoundland, and Harry Neale, his sharp, funny, occasionally acerbic sidekick, who long ago gave up the uncertain life of coaching and running hockey teams, having found his real home in the broadcast booth. They will give full points to the Bruins for trying hard, for achieving to a degree, but it's clear from the opening moments of the broadcast that everyone understands they are here to tell a story of dynastic greatness, not of the triumph of some plucky underdog. The Oilers have lost only two games in the entire playoffs, and it is hard to imagine them losing here. Don Cherry, though he wears his Bruins heart on his sleeve, has already opined that the only way Boston can win is if goaltender Andy Moog, the ex-Oiler, steals the game for them. And Cole, over a shot of Gretzky—who, for the playoffs, has traded his short-on-top, long-in-the-back hockey mullet for an old-fashioned crew cut (he will explain, with a smile, that someone told him it could get hot in Boston; and just maybe, he had the wit to shoot for the 1966-vintage Bobby Orr look)—delivers the opening line of a familiar script:

"A win tonight for the Oilers and that will be it for another season, and another Stanley Cup . . ."

The Bruins, though, decline to play the role of ritual sacrifice, at least through the first twenty minutes. They open the scoring forty-three seconds in, with Steve Kasper putting one past Grant Fuhr from a tough angle, and though the Oilers get that goal back— not from one of the glamour boys, but from the unlikely sniper Normand Lacombe—Boston restores its lead soon after, when Ken Linseman, another ex-Oiler, scores while his team holds a two-man advantage.

And then Gretzky takes over. These are the last moments of a frustrating season in which he was limited to sixty-four games because of knee and eye injuries, in which he surrendered the league scoring title for the first time in eight seasons, the most valuable player award for the first time in nine—in both cases, eclipsed by Mario Lemieux, a remarkable physical specimen with magnificent talents who, at season's end, has been widely acknowledged as the new greatest player in the game. At least until Gretzky, with one of the finest playoff performances in the history of the sport, reminds everyone that the king wasn't quite dead yet.

Throughout his career, just as it was with Orr, even hockey's eggheads would struggle to explain just what made Gretzky exceptional. The new wave of super athletes were coming to the fore as they had already in other sports: giants possessed with fine, sophisticated skills, the likes of Lemieux and Eric Lindros. What made them dominant was self-evident. But Gretzky was built along modest, ordinary, mortal lines. Though in other athletic endeavours he had natural gifts and coordination that might make him stand out back home in the relatively shallow pond of Brantford, Ontario— he was a decent distance runner, a very good ballplayer—his supreme hockey skills, which evolved from boyhood to manhood without missing a beat, were inexplicable through anything visible to the naked eye.

In researching his definitive account of the Oilers' glory days, *The Game of Our Lives,* Peter Gzowski persuaded Gretzky to watch a videotape of himself playing and describe what he was thinking as the game progressed. (Gzowski rightly suspected that what made Gretzky different must be found inside his head.) Hockey is tricky that way: Ted Williams could offer up a treatise on the science of hitting a baseball, reducing it almost to pure mathematics (though what Williams knew, he found almost impossible to impart on lesser beings). You can do that in a game with stops and starts, break it down into its component parts, analyze acts of athletic brilliance in terms of their biomechanics. Even in soccer, where, most of the time, the play flows freely (and for those who know both sports, the best points of comparison for Wayne Gretzky are the greatest soccer players, who move through space, anticipate openings and angles, view all of the moving pieces as though looking down from above), there are set plays when it's possible to diagram the act of putting the ball where you want it and getting someone else on the end.

Hockey's speed and fluidity work against that kind of deconstruction. Which is why, when Gretzky watched himself at Gzowski's behest, he could explain, but not really, and the sports scientists called upon to speak to reaction time and pattern memorization and all the rest can suggest but not define. No doubt, somewhere in the great code there is a mathematical and biological and cognitive formula for one-off greatness, the firing of synapses and chemical processes and connection between brain and muscle, intuition, action and the creative impulse. No doubt, some of Gretzky's responses were also programmed on the backyard rink, where over and over again, under his father's guidance, he worked at the game's basic skills. But there were two other genetically-similar hockey-playing brothers who, on the same tiny patch of ice, did the same things at the same time, and they came out as merely above average. So until someone distills the genetic formula that separates the genius from the master technician (and perhaps even after that happens), there is nothing to do but sit back and watch in wonder.

Yes, genius is a word thrown around way too casually by sportswriters and broadcasters, but it does apply to those few athletes who bring something original to the table, as much as it does to singular artists of any kind. Gretzky as a hockey player was part of a very short list of those who both reimagined the way the sport might be played, and possessed the skills to fully express that vision (there's a much longer list of great players who operated within the boundaries as traditionally defined, all of them celebrated, but not the same). On the roll call of dominant individual athletes in all team sports, he is probably closer to Diego Maradona than to Howe or Rocket Richard. He was an above-average skater, but below average in pure physical strength; a hard, accurate shooter, though it wouldn't become his signature in the style of Bobby Hull. Unlike almost any of the great hockey icons before him, who at some point would be called upon to demonstrate their toughness as a rite of passage, no one looked at Gretzky and expected him to defend himself with his fists in the sport's time-honoured fashion. That was someone else's job, riding shotgun for the superstar, but, arguably for the first time in hockey history, that was deemed to be just fine.

The easiest test of genius comes from looking at who came before and who came after. There was no direct model for Gretzky's game among players of the near or distant past. Since his retirement, the NHL has gone through several distinct phases, from the negative, defensive-oriented trap (which evolved, in an era of greed-driven over-expansion, as coaches and general managers sought a way to make disciplined but talent-poor teams competitive in a hurry) to the relatively free-flowing game that has marked the period since the 2004–05 NHL lockout. Through all of that, there has not been a single player to emerge who looks like him, who plays like him, who controls the game on the ice like him. Wayne Gretzky was a one-off, which is a different thing than simply being very, very good. And it was through those unique Gretzkyesque qualities that he decided his final game as an Edmonton Oiler.

He begins late in the first period, inside his own blue line. The Bruins are killing a penalty, and Rick Middleton, a veteran playing what will turn out to be his final NHL game, skates tentatively into the offensive zone. He makes a careless, lazy error, dropping a back pass to no one in particular that is scooped up by Esa Tikkanen, leaving two Bruins hopelessly out of the play. The Finnish winger, both a skill guy and an agitator, who will enjoy a long and productive

NHL career with several different teams, is one of the essential cogs of the Oiler machine who is rarely spoken of as part of the Edmonton pantheon. He immediately flips the puck to Gretzky, who, anticipating the turnover, is already fully committed to the counter-attack, skating down the right wing towards the Bruins' goal. He accepts the pass in the neutral zone, cruises past centre and the Boston blue line, then stops hard along the boards. It's a trademark move, one of the many ways Gretzky has invented to create space for himself within the fixed confines of a hockey rink. The defenders know exactly what he's up to, but are left with an unenviable choice: close him down, and be burned by a pass to an open man, or stay with the other Oilers, and leave Gretzky free to skate in and shoot or create a chance for someone else around the net.

Gretzky plays a quick game of pass-and-return with Jari Kurri, who has automatically moved in behind him at the point. After giving the puck back to Gretzky, Kurri slides to the centre of the ice and towards the goal, finding a comfortable place in the slot, understanding from all of those games they have played together what will happen next. Glenn Anderson, also party to the unspoken communication, moves directly in front of the Boston net, screening Moog's view. Gretzky's return pass to Kurri is delivered with a flip of the wrist, not flat along the ice where it might be deflected. It lands soft and deadened, as if on a tee, and Kurri meets it without pausing, driving a slap shot on goal, hoping to catch Moog still moving or blinded.

The shot, which looks like it is headed in, strikes something—or rather, some*one*—in front of the net and ricochets into the corner. There the choreography breaks down and dumb luck takes over, as happens so often in any sport: Tikkanen tracks down the rebound and dumps the puck immediately back towards the front of the net, where Anderson is still causing havoc. It hits the leg of Bruins defenceman Gord Kluzak and deflects behind Moog to tie the score at two.

Gone are the last vestiges of Boston's confidence. Early in the second period, Mike Krushelnyski is left alone in front of Moog, where he takes a pass from the hard-working grinder Kevin

McClelland and puts Edmonton ahead, 3–2. The crowd at Northlands begins to feel it now, cheering almost constantly. The game is free-flowing, fast, with few whistles, and at that pace, in that style, no one can skate with the home team.

"The Oilers are coming," Neale quips, "and I'm afraid the Bruins are going."

Now Gretzky hardly seems to step off the ice. His shifts get longer and longer, and why would Glen Sather want it otherwise? They're on a power play near the second period's halfway point, and Tikkanen has the puck at the left point. He holds it and holds it and holds it while Lacombe parks himself in front of Moog, drawing the attention of two Boston defencemen, screening the goaltender. Another Boston checker stands in front of Tikkanen, hoping to block his shot. Gretzky was, for a moment, along the boards, but now he has somehow disappeared from Boston's radar. Impossible, you'd think, to lose Number 99, but he has made himself invisible so many times before. Everyone in the building is waiting for the slap shot. Gretzky slips behind the Bruins' goal, emerging beside the far post, all alone. Tikkanen has, of course, been following his teammate's progress, and instead of letting it rip, cuts down on his swing and fires a half–slap pass to Gretzky, standing on the goal line, two feet to the left of the Boston net. In one motion, Gretzky stops the puck with his left skate, directs it to his stick, and tucks it into the empty corner before Moog has a chance to react.

"He gives you an imitation of Pele, the soccer star, before he shows you Gretzky the hockey star," Neale says.

It is over, really, with half a game still to play, and everyone understands that: the Bruins, who have bravely done their best; the Oilers, who are now in the process of putting a cherry on top; the fans in Edmonton, who have seen all of this before, but certainly don't sound the least bit jaded. You can't take your eyes off Gretzky. He plays his own shifts with his own line as well as, it seems, with at least two others. He plays on the power play, and kills penalties in an aggressive, attacking style. He is actually speeding up as the game moves along. And except for the moment when

Michael Thelvén, a Swedish defenceman who would spend parts of five seasons with the Bruins, manages to time that skate-over-the-blue-line-and-stop-hard manoeuvre perfectly and levels Gretzky with a bodycheck, he is able to command the ice all but unmolested. It has always been one of his most remarkable qualities—in a game in which it is considered perfectly fair to physically beat down a talented foe in order to neutralize him, no one has intimidated him, almost no one has touched him. Though every coach going back to minor hockey must have instructed his guys to pound that will-o'-the-wisp SOB and get him off the ice, they just couldn't do it. That wasn't because a Dave Semenko or Marty McSorley was waiting to dole out vengeance, but because of Gretzky's elusiveness—and especially because those who overcommitted to the task of doing him harm found immediately that their aggression was turned against them, that he'd exploit it and make them pay, which is the best self-defence technique of all.

There are just ten seconds remaining in the second period when Boston is forced to turn over the puck behind the Edmonton net, thanks to some fine work by Steve Smith and Kevin Lowe—this incarnation of the Oilers is a bit more responsible defensively, by necessity, than some of its high-flying predecessors. Gretzky picks it up inside his own blue line, glances up at the clock high above centre ice, then tears down the left wing. Cole will later opine that perhaps someone on the Oiler bench hollered at him, telling him how little time remained. Harry thinks that maybe he just has a clock built right into his brain—he's Gretzky, so wouldn't it figure?

Whatever the case, as he crosses the Boston blue line with only a few moments remaining in the period, Gretzky seems absolutely unhurried, unflustered, as though this scenario has played out in his head already, and he knows how it ends. The Boston defenders back off, he makes a quick turn inside the line, and then, with not a heartbeat to waste, flutters another soft pass to the corner of the net, where Craig Simpson has arrived to tap it behind Moog.

"Wow. Two seconds left, and don't think he didn't call it," Cole says.

"Craig Simpson is on the end of a masterpiece by the master himself, Number 99, Wayne Gretzky," Neale chips in.

The assist is Gretzky's thirty-first of the playoffs, breaking his own record—in just nineteen games. The point is his thirteenth of the final, breaking his idol Gordie Howe's record, set against the Montreal Canadiens way back in 1955. Even the faintest hope of a Boston comeback is extinguished now as the teams head to the dressing room for the second intermission.

With the outcome all but decided, the final twenty minutes—the final twenty minutes of so many things—will now well and truly be *played*. In the sport-as-entertainment business, the joy that draws us to games in the first place is all too often sucked out by worldly concerns. For the players, it's a job; for the owners, an investment; for the television network, programming; for the advertisers, it's a vehicle. But now, for one period at least, the greatest team in hockey can act like kids throwing their sticks into the middle of the ice to pick teams for a game of shinny.

Still, the opening shot of the period after *Hockey Night in Canada* returns from a commercial break isn't of a player. It is of a comely blonde sitting in the stands between Gretzky's youngest brother, Glen, and his mother, Phyllis. Glen has been living in Edmonton for the past year with Wayne and Janet Jones, finishing up his final year of high school. (This was Glen's graduation night, and with Walter and Phyllis and sister Kim he had to scramble from the ceremonies at the Jubilee Auditorium, grabbing his diploma, walking off stage, jumping into a car and arriving just in time for the second period, moments before he was seen on camera.) Jones, though, is the story, with the wedding coming up in July. "There's the future Mrs. Wayne Gretzky," Cole tells the audience. She is Marilyn Monroe to our Joe DiMaggio, though presumably without the baggage, without the desperately unhappy ending. Gretzky used to have a hometown Edmonton girlfriend, Vikki Moss, an aspiring singer who by osmosis became a modest celebrity. When they split and he became engaged to Jones, an American starlet typecast as a golden-haired goddess in *The Flamingo Kid*, there was hardly a hint of small-town Canadian resentment, a flicker of concern that our native son might have gone all Hollywood. Such was the faith in Gretzky's feet-on-the-ground clear-headedness that, if Wayne had chosen Janet, she must be all right, whatever the trappings, and such was the allure of the national icon that it was only natural that a world-class beauty would fall for him.

The third period flies by with hardly a whistle, with hardly a pause. Tikkanen scores a goal early, pouncing on a puck that should have been touched by a Bruin for icing, but instead takes a weird bounce right out in front of Moog. Kasper answers back for the Bruins. In the no-defence portion of the game, both goaltenders have a chance to shine—it's the first time in the game that Edmonton's Grant Fuhr really rates a mention—and Gretzky doesn't want to come to the bench. "He's famous for his four-minute shifts," Neale says. "He must have learned that from Phil Esposito . . ."

He sure doesn't float through those long stretches on the ice. Gretzky is working like mad, forechecking doggedly. At one point, pinned behind the Boston net, he kicks the puck out to Tikkanen, who is so surprised by the move that he doesn't know quite how to handle his gift. Late in the period, there's a scramble in front of the Bruins' goal as Moog grabs a loose puck out of the air. Kurri takes a little swipe at the goalie's glove with his stick, to which Moog understandably takes exception, responding with a shove. Into the centre of the minor melee skates not an enforcer, but Wayne Gretzky, getting right in the face of his old teammate. It doesn't take a skilled lip-reader in the television audience to make out what the All-Canadian Boy is saying: "Fuck you! Fuck you!" The real language of hockey rarely makes its way over the airwaves (though there was at least one memorable Bobby Clarke moment with an open mike, when the same word escaped his near-toothless mouth), but a few scandalized grannies aside, at this stage in history, it can only enhance Gretzky's image—the superstar once again revealed to be an ordinary guy.

The only hint of Gretzky backing off, of him taking this game and this Stanley Cup for granted, comes when he finds himself with the puck, skating towards the Boston blue line, and only Reed

Larson, a journeyman defenceman, stands in his path to the Boston goal. The crowd noise rises in anticipation of some great one-on-one move, but Gretzky opts instead to quietly dump the puck into the Bruins' end, then skates to the Oilers bench, a huge smile breaking out across his mug.

"He's saving himself for his honeymoon," Neale says, cracking wise.

Now, the final seconds tick down. The Edmonton fans are on their feet.

"Was there ever any doubt?" Cole wonders aloud.

Well, Bob, yes, there was—when eight Oilers held out in training camp over pay disputes with the owner; when Gretzky was hurt, twice; when there were questions about whether Fuhr could handle the load of a full season between the pipes; when the Oilers finished second behind the hated Calgary Flames in the Smythe Division. Only when they swept Calgary aside—and how sweet that was for an Edmontonian, the second city putting it to the first city one more time—did the Oilers' destiny become absolutely clear, was the dynasty's progress assured. And now, at the siren, it is official.

Before Ziegler presents the Cup, he awards the Conn Smythe Trophy, cast as a replica of Smythe's great hockey temple, Maple Leaf Gardens, to the most valuable player in the post-season. There is no debate: Gretzky, with his helmet off, his retro crew cut showing, gets hugged and head-rubbed by his teammates, and in that moment, the armour shed, the boy in all of them is allowed to shine through.

"He's a great guy, a fabulous hockey player. He's just something else for this game of hockey," Cole says. In the course of less than a year—361 days, to be exact—Gretzky has captained two NHL champions, plus the Canada Cup–winning team that temporarily restored his countrymen's chauvinism regarding the national game.

Even before the Oilers lift the Stanley Cup high, before they take turns skating it around the Northlands ice, speculation on the television broadcast and around the hockey world has turned to what comes next. There are seven players on the Oilers' roster (albeit most of them in minor roles) who weren't there the year before. Glen Sather has tinkered with the team, understanding that in professional sport there is no standing still. In the coming off-season, there is surely more to come.

"I'll bet you that Glen Sather makes one or two changes before next season," Neale says, and if you could have whispered in his ear at that moment what one of those changes would be, no doubt he'd have fallen over dead. "And you might see this scene again. It's going to be tough to dethrone the Edmonton Oilers."

It seems the only real question hanging over the franchise is the fate of John Muckler, Sather's long-time assistant, who pines for the chance to run a team on his own. But nearly everyone assumes that they'll work that out somehow, that Sather will move full time to the front office, that Muckler will get his shot, that, a few minor adjustments aside, most of this same cast will be right back here a year from now, because why would it be any different? Why would you mess with this perfect creation?

Peter Pocklington has made his way to the team bench during the celebration, standing between Sather and Muckler, wearing a conservative suit and tie. Eventually, Gretzky beckons him to come out on the ice, and because unlike other years the fans have been held back, because security is tight, because the team is essentially alone, in that instant a tradition is born: the players gather round the Cup for a photo opportunity at the captain's behest, and are joined by the coaches and their assistants, the trainers, the club-house boy Joey Moss (brother of Wayne's old girlfriend), whose friendship with Gretzky and life triumphs despite Down's syndrome had long been one of the sport's great heart-warming tales. Finally, the owner slides into the happy mob scene, front and centre, right behind the silverware. It looks like an old-time team photo, the players more sprawled than posed, and the joy of the moment is self-evident.

The team finally retreats to the dressing room. Pocklington, now wearing a snazzy blue Oilers windbreaker (the better to deal with all of that flying champagne), is asked to step in front of the camera by the CBC's Chris Cuthbert. The celebration plays out behind him as he says a few words. "Well, you know, all year long, we wondered if they still had that in them." He smiles in a great big cat-with-the-canary way that a neutral might read as insincere, and punctuates his thoughts with a smug little laugh—"Huh, huh, huh!"—that adds to the air of self-love.

Does he remember the speech he gave his team before the play-offs, the one that might have inspired them at the end of a troubled season to again reach such heights?

"Huh, huh, huh! . . . Well, that's really between the club and I. But one of the things we talked about—and all believe—is that we as a club become what we think about. If we believe we're great and we're going to do whatever we have to do to conquer whatever, they always make it. That team philosophy has built them for nine years and I think it will do another nine or ten."

In the heat of the moment, it's not entirely articulate, but you can catch his drift. And who's to argue with success? Edmonton acquired its big-league professional hockey franchise only by virtue of the birth of a rebel league, and got into the NHL only because the old-guard hockey establishment, which never would have expanded there by choice, was anxious to kill off that pesky competitor. Pocklington, who wasn't a fan, fell into sports ownership by chance. He inherited Sather, who would seamlessly make the transition from player to coach to executive, and lucked into Gretzky. All of that a happy fluke, but the rest was by design, and if believing in their greatness was part of what made the Oilers great (a typical bit of Pocklingtonian New Age business malarkey), there was also magnificent hockey logic in the team's construction. But no one was pretending that all of the self-hypnosis and savvy talent assessment in the world could have created this without the contribution of the best player in the world.

Now he moves into the television spotlight. Gretzky is wearing a sky blue T-shirt that hangs off his chest, like adult's clothing on a kid, and his torso seems ridiculously small, disappearing inside hockey pants that appear enormous as they come up over his narrow hips.

"The ending is great," Gretzky says. "It gets better every year we win. It's more exciting. I'm really thrilled."

Asked about his own performance during the playoffs, he acknowledges feeling fresher than usual at this time of year, because of those games missed with injuries. Then he figuratively steps aside, talking about Fuhr and Mark Messier—"Either one of them could have won the Conn Smythe"—and especially about Lowe, who has finished the playoffs wearing a cast to protect a broken wrist and full body armour to shield two broken ribs. "That's pretty amazing for a guy to do that."

"How do you top this?" Cuthbert asks, shifting the conversation to the night's other great theme. "I know how Wayne Gretzky does. You've got something planned for July?"

"I'm excited about my wedding . . ."

Glenn Anderson jumps in and pours half a bottle of champagne over Gretzky's head. "That's cold!" Wayne giggles. It was Anderson who started the champagne dousing the minute he got in the room, and he's not about to stop. The life of the party, but there's just a hint of malevolence there as well, a bit of an uncomfortable edge, as though he's getting a little bit too much pleasure out of causing discomfort—everyone knows the type.

"I'm excited about the wedding," Gretzky continues. "The wedding would have been a great day no matter what, because it's something I'll treasure for the rest of my life. But winning this will make it even more exciting. It's a great team, it's a great city. We should all be proud of everything that's gone on this year—our team, our fans. It's just been tremendous."

Then, as Cuthbert is signing off:

"I just want to say hello to my two grandmothers, who I know are watching. Hello!"

And that's it. The last real comforting glimpse of Wayne Gretzky, Edmonton Oiler, calling out to the old folks back home—exactly what you'd expect from the decent Canadian kid the country understood him to be.

—

The party had shifted to a local restaurant by the time his father pulled him aside and delivered the news that he'd been keeping to himself for most of the playoffs, lest it distract his boy, lest it derail what mattered most—to win one with the team, to again reach the goal for which he'd trained his entire life, to play the game with focused, blinkered, unparalleled excellence.

He's going to get rid of you, Wally said. It's probably already done. Pocklington is going to trade you or he's going to sell you, he's already shopping you around, there's not a thing you can do about it, and for that I'll never forgive him. This isn't the beginning, or the middle. There isn't going to be a next year—at least not in Edmonton, not in Canada. This is the end.

Wayne said it wasn't true—it couldn't be true. He would talk to Peter and straighten the whole thing out in the morning. But in his head and in his gut, he must have known, not for the first time in his life, that the old man was right.

Chapter Seven

A STAR IN STAR-VILLE

WAYNE GRETZKY LIKED Los Angeles. He liked the weather, liked the culture, liked having access to the hidden, privileged, alluring world of celebrity. It was his own place, one he had discovered, separate from the game and separate from his family, the forces that had driven nearly every day of his existence. It was a city where he could live, and live very well.

Since leaving Brantford behind, since leaving high school behind, too immersed in his art form to graduate, he had moved on to Toronto and Sault Ste. Marie, Indianapolis and Edmonton, but all of those were hockey destinations, where the cycle of practices and games had long since become the rhythm of his life. Gretzky was on his own before reaching the age of legal majority, but the lot of a hockey player, junior or professional, is to be encased in a protective cocoon, to relax into relative infantilism. They are told where to be and when to show up. They pick their seat on the bus or the plane and go along for the ride. They don't have to book anything or check into a hotel on their own; they feed themselves only when team meals aren't available. Their basic needs are accounted for, and free time is most often spent in the company of teammates—like the insular communities of soldiers or of cops, the only ones who can really understand.

When they do branch out, when they hit the town for a meal or a few beers, when they chase girls or wait to be chased, it is done under a spotlight. Canadians, by nature, tend to keep an appropriate distance from their heroes. They're deferential when asking for autographs, aren't inclined to interrupt anyone's meal. They respect personal space, arguably more so in a relatively small city like Edmonton, where the people were like Brantford people, and for the young Gretzky, there was comfort in that (though the truth was, the Brantford people themselves hadn't treated him so well as a kid). Still, even junior hockey players have a difficult time completely disappearing into the background, and even in an Edmonton, anyone identified as an Oiler, let alone the most famous hockey player in the world, the most famous human being in the country, would find it difficult to enjoy even a moment when it felt like no one was looking. (Though it could become a bit of a lark at times. A buddy of Gretzky's remembers an elaborate game of bait and switch they employed to get a girl into his apartment without anyone catching on.) As Gretzky grew older, as the security of the familiar became less important, as he looked to enjoy his wealth and spread his wings a bit and experience the wider world, Edmonton for all of its virtues started to become for him more than a little claustrophobic.

He would get away in the off-season, travelling to celebrity golf or tennis tournaments, visiting back home to Ontario, a couple of times embarking on trips to Europe. (These included one memorable junket to the Soviet Union in 1983, where he and his family visited the home of the great Russian goaltender Vladislav Tretiak, a trip captured for posterity by documentary filmmakers. The highlight is a scene in which a clearly tipsy Gretzky, after a long night of vodka toasts, encourages his girlfriend Vikki Moss to try caviar for the first time: "It doesn't taste like anything," Gretzky claims, though Moss, understandably, seems skeptical.) And long before he first met Bruce McNall, Los Angeles had become Gretzky's de facto second home. His first real Hollywood encounter was back in

1981, when the National Hockey League staged its annual All-Star festivities in Los Angeles, kicked off by a glittery gala attended by as many stars as the league could muster. Though hockey still wasn't front of mind in L.A., this one-off event, featuring the best players in the game and some of the bigger names in the entertainment world, would at least suggest that the two could be combined in a natural mix. Professional athletes, like anyone else, tend to be dumbstruck in the presence of those they see on the big and small screen, and movie stars, TV stars and famous musicians are drawn to athletes because, for all of their wealth and privilege and fame, they can't be like the jocks with their magical, unattainable skills. Who knows how many of them are having flashbacks to high school, to the years spent hanging out in the band room or with the drama club, envious of the football captain and the cheerleader?

Called upon by the league to bring it all together, to produce this show of shows, was a Canadian expatriate who may well have qualified as L.A.'s greatest hockey wannabe—his claim to fame was that he'd once had his nose broken by Gordie Howe during the course of a "celebrity" game, and his support for the Kings extended all the way back to the Jack Kent Cooke era. Alan Thicke, the former high school homecoming king of Kirkland Lake, Ontario, was a remarkably successful showbiz jack of all trades. He sang and acted. He invented and hosted game shows. He wrote, performed and recorded the theme music for television shows. He developed and starred in a long-running, highly rated situation comedy, *Growing Pains*. And perhaps most significantly, at least when it came to the hockey crowd, he had been the host of a daytime talk show (and, very briefly, of a would-be late-night rival to Johnny Carson's *Tonight Show, Thicke of the Night*). Hockey players are among the world's great consumers of afternoon television, since virtually all of their games are played at night, leaving them with many empty hours between the morning skate and trip to the rink. Sitting in yet another hotel room in another town, there's not much else to do. So they knew and appreciated Thicke's art, and Thicke very much liked meeting hockey players. That especially applied when the greatest team of the era, the Edmonton Oilers, rolled through Los Angeles. Thicke appreciated their remarkable talent, and also came to understand that in person, they were a particularly appealing group—unaffected, in many ways just kids. "These were really babes in the woods," Thicke remembers. "Wayne was the only guy with experience in a city even the size of Indianapolis. They were small-town Canadian boys and they were fish out of water in L.A. I felt somewhat responsible for acclimatizing Wayne, and to a lesser degree the other guys, with L.A. They were starstruck, but we broke them in. They would come to town, they would play a game, I'd bring some celebrities to the game. We'd have a drink afterwards. A couple of times they would come to a recording studio where I would be with [record producer and fellow Canadian] David Foster—we'd be doing music for my show." Thicke knew enough to add a few beautiful women to the mix. "Morgan Fairchild or Kirstie Alley, Mimi Rogers. They were babes at the time. The guys were impressed just to see or hang out with them. . . .

"But then, they always had another agenda. They'd be there for half an hour or an hour and then be ready to go to a club or a bar. Wayne would invariably let them go, because by that time he was into the project that was going on. It showed me a guy who, whatever he was touching at the moment, wanted to absorb it and understand it and be excellent at it and excel. The other guys were ready to go. Wayne, by the end of the night, would be directing the sax player when to do the fills. He got into it and would eschew the party opportunity in favour of staying there in the studio."

It was in Los Angeles that Gretzky began to fully comprehend the growing magnitude of his own celebrity. In Canada, in a hockey culture, he understood that he was pretty much the ne plus ultra. But here he was, in the company of those who were famous on an entirely different level, and as much as he was thrilled to meet them, they were at least equally enthralled at the prospect of meeting him. "He was mature," Thicke remembers. "Mature beyond his years, and responsible, respectful. He had that Elvis kind of respect for adults and authority. Wayne always called people 'mister.' And he would always introduce himself as Wayne

Gretzky, which was beyond the pale, because everybody knew who he was. It was a touch of humility. Even leaving phone messages. It was 'Wayne Gretzky.' When he met everybody, even with people sitting there in awe waiting to shake his hand, it was 'Wayne Gretzky.' . . . He wasn't worldly, except to the extent that he knew he was either a celebrity or a celebrity in training, and he'd better keep his nose clean. He was worldly enough to know not to be too worldly. He was aware of the impression he made and aware of his privacy. Those days helped break him in and tell him that L.A. was okay. He started to see that the celebrities were more in awe of him than vice versa."

There was also something else that had begun to draw Gretzky's attention southward: his first real girlfriend, Vikki Moss. They had met in Edmonton, her hometown, in 1980 after he saw her singing in a nightclub and asked her out. That might sound a bit late for a first love, but consider the transient life Gretzky had lived. Leaving home at fourteen, a junior in the Soo at sixteen, a pro in Indianapolis at seventeen, then on to the Oilers; there were girls, no doubt, "puck bunnies" and others, but precious little chance to really get to know them. It was only in Edmonton that he really settled in. When Moss and Gretzky became a couple and the relationship became public knowledge, it made her, by association, just about the most famous woman in town, a position she very much enjoyed, especially because of what it meant for her burgeoning singing career. The two of them were an item for the local gossip columns (such as they were) and shared the burden and privilege of local celebrity. "It's something that's going to be there and you can't run from it," Gretzky said during a fabulously awkward joint appearance with Moss on the *Tommy Banks Live* television show in January 1981. He looked like a blushing schoolboy sitting beside Moss, who was the embodiment of 1980s glamour in a slinky black dress, with big, blonde disco hair. "We know that there's nothing that you can do about it. We're on our best behaviour when we're out in public."

"*You* are," Moss quipped back.

She was, by any measure, a bit more street-smart than Wayne, and a bit more rough around the edges. Along with her, Gretzky embraced her family, to the point where he put some of them on his payroll. Moss's mother took over the administration of Gretzky's booming fan club, and her brother Joey, born with Down's syndrome, wound up with a job as the Oilers' clubhouse boy (Gretzky had grown up with an aunt who had the same condition, and so was from the start an understanding friend). Moss suffered from no shortage of ambition, and in her own element was as much of a careerist as Gretzky was, though not blessed with an equivalent talent. Through him, she would be introduced to the super-producer Foster, who was part of Thicke's circle in Los Angeles, and who advised her that if she really wanted to break into the music business, she should move there full time. For several years, at least in part as a favour to Gretzky, Foster became her mentor and producer, and placed one of the tracks he recorded with her on the soundtrack of the very-'8os Brat Pack film *St. Elmo's Fire.* (That was the peak. Moss would eventually fade from view, marry a music producer and settle in Los Angeles, leaving show business behind.) Moss spent more and more time in California, while Gretzky was home and away with the Oilers. He would follow her to California as often as he could, which increased his familiarity with, and fondness for, the place. But the long separations put pressure on the relationship. It would be written often after the fact that he split with Moss because she refused to sacrifice her singing ambitions to be with him. That wasn't quite right. It was less about the fact that she had an independent career and more because Moss was elsewhere, that she felt she needed to be in the city where stars were made, and though Gretzky tried to hang on, though he was distraught at the thought of breaking up, he couldn't be in two places at once. (Tellingly, in Gretzky's autobiography, written in collaboration with Rick Reilly, Moss's role in his life is reduced to a single passing reference. He was only a bit more expansive in a 1988 interview with the *Los Angeles Times.* "Vikki and I had a great relationship," Gretzky said. "We spent seven years together. She was great for my career; her family was great to me.

It was just a situation that didn't work out. Things happen for a reason. . . . It's ironic that we're both in L.A. It's frustrating to see people disappointed in their lives. You only live once. I've been real lucky. She was nice to me, and my wife is just great.")

In June of 1986, after the Oilers had been eliminated from the play-offs, temporarily interrupting their Stanley Cup dynasty, Gretzky was killing time in California. Things were rocky with Moss, but he was still trying to remain available. One night, Thicke received a phone call from his hockey-playing friend, who was holed up in nearby Palm Springs. Gretzky said he needed to get away for a bit, that he had a pair of tickets for a Los Angeles Lakers–Boston Celtics playoff game at the Forum and wondered if Thicke was interested. (The tickets came courtesy of another new Los Angeles chum, Bruce McNall.) They went to the game, sat courtside among the stars, and then afterwards repaired to the exclusive Forum Club, which was where the glamorous in-crowd guests who could always be found at Lakers games socialized among themselves. Thicke knew a lot of the people in the room, including an old acquaintance, a strikingly attractive blonde dancer and actress not too far removed from her breakthrough role as Matt Dillon's object of desire in the 1984 hit *The Flamingo Kid.* Janet Jones hailed originally from St. Louis before moving to California to pursue her show-business career. After struggling through the early days, tak-ing whatever work came her way (including a stint as a featured dancer on the television series *Dance Fever,* a strange remnant of the disco era hosted by the incomparable Denny Terrio that, given the current craze for the genre, seems to have actually been ahead of its time. Though it apparently didn't make much of an impression on either of them, one of the celebrity judges during her time on the show was Gretzky.), her career was then in rapid ascendance. She had just appeared in the film adaptation of the long-running Broadway hit *A Chorus Line,* and seemed bound for at least mod-est stardom. Thicke knew Jones from the celebrity tennis circuit, to which she was attracted both because she was a decent athlete and because she had been the girlfriend of tennis professionals Vitas

Gerulaitis and Nels Van Patten (she had also been paired for a time with the actor Bruce Willis—as one Gretzky friend observes today, without undue cruelty, "She didn't date any plumbers.").

"This is my friend Janet Jones," Thicke said. "Janet—I'd like you to meet Wayne Gretzky."

It happened fast—as he would confess to radio DJ Howard Stern a few years later, *everything* happened very fast. ("That's why they call you The Great One," Stern said.) There was a post-game dinner at a restaurant in the San Fernando Valley with Thicke and a few of his friends. (Two years later, when Jones and Gretzky were married in Edmonton, Thicke bought the chairs from the restaurant where they had sat that first night, and gave them as a wedding present.) The next morning, Gretzky phoned one of his buddies. "You're not going to believe this," he said. "You know that chick from *The Flamingo Kid?*" Soon enough, Moss was history, and at the training camp for the Canada Cup tournament the following September, Gretzky went public with the fact that there was a new woman in his life (which, in Edmonton at least, was treated as very big news). He was deeply involved with someone who was a minor celebrity in her own right, whose career and whose inclinations tied her very much to Southern California. Now he was, all but officially, a man with two homes.

By then, Gretzky, was also in the early, blissful stages of another burgeoning relationship—with McNall, the jolly, generous hockey superfan, the Hollywood social maven, the life of the party. As McNall recalls it, their first encounter came soon after he bought a piece of the Los Angeles Kings from Jerry Buss in 1986. Standing near the players' bench doing a television interview, he felt a sharp smack across his backside and turned to see Gretzky skating by, having just given him a playful whack with his stick.

"Congratulations on buying the team," Gretzky said.

"Thanks," said McNall. "You know I'd love to get you here."

"Yeah, right," Gretzky hollered back. "Good luck."

Joking, playful chat, but the idea, and the possibilities, were already percolating in McNall's fertile imagination. Buss had mentioned in passing his conversation with Peter Pocklington way back when, and how he thought that trading for Gretzky and bringing him to Los Angeles was the one sure way to put hockey on the map in Southern California. From his own business experience, McNall had independently come to understand how you could generate enthusiasm and close a sale based not on what your product was in the cold, hard light of day, but on the way it might be romantically imagined. Hockey would always be hockey, a sport alien to most of the population of Southern California, and the NHL would never be a marketing goliath like the National Football League, or even the National Basketball Association. As much as McNall believed it himself, he was never going to be able to sell people on the pure virtues of the sport alone. Even Gretzky himself, for all of his name recognition and star power, wouldn't attract non-believers to the game because of what he did on the ice. They didn't really understand that. They didn't know why he was special, why he mattered, why he was different than anyone else wearing a helmet and skates.

But the *idea* of Wayne Gretzky was something else again. It was like the idea of all those ancient coins he'd sold to so many rich guys for more than their objective value, like the idea of making movies that he'd sold to investors in his film company, the idea of becoming part of Hollywood by writing a great big cheque. What McNall realized, what he would distill and package and sell once he claimed his prize, was the marketing power of a simple notion: Wayne Gretzky is the greatest hockey player in the world, perhaps the greatest who has ever lived. A chance to see him is like a chance to hear Artur Rubinstein or the Beatles in concert, to gaze upon the *Mona Lisa* or *Guernica*, to see Nureyev in full flight. You might not understand the fine points. You might not have the vocabulary to describe it, or the expertise to know what makes him unique. But consider yourself lucky, consider yourself blessed, to have this rarest of opportunities, to be in the presence of true one-off genius, to be able to tell your grandchildren that you were there, that you saw Wayne Gretzky do—well, whatever it was he did.

That sales pitch, as McNall had already learned, wouldn't work with just a very good hockey player, like Luc Robitaille or Jimmy Carson. It wouldn't work with a very good hockey team—probably not even with a Stanley Cup contender, because those were hockey conversations. The idea of the greatest player of all time transcended hockey. The idea of Wayne Gretzky transcended the real value of any real athlete on the ice. The idea of the brightest star shining here in a land of stars would unlock every door.

Now to make it happen. The conversation with Buss had started the wheels turning, followed by the first fleeting contact with Gretzky himself, who McNall learned was spending more and more time in Los Angeles of his own volition. "He was transitioning down here," McNall says. "He liked it here. He had friends here, like Thicke and others, that were Canadians who moved here. His allegiances were starting to come down here." McNall made sure that he became part of that. He cozied up to Gretzky at every opportunity. He charmed and flattered him; introduced him to famous people; indulged him and indulged Janet when they met socially. Nothing was too good or too extravagant for his new pals. It was a seduction, plain and simple, and McNall, as he had already proven while separating so many of the rich and powerful from their money, could be a real Don Juan when the occasion demanded. He continued to probe, gently, on whether Gretzky might accept a move from Edmonton—usually framing it as a joke, trying never to seem too anxious or too serious. To do more would be to risk a tampering charge (under NHL rules, he couldn't even flirt with a player under contract to another team). According to McNall, Gretzky didn't reveal more than a flicker of interest at the beginning. He acknowledged that he liked Los Angeles, liked the people there, liked McNall, that it was where his wife was most comfortable. But he didn't particularly want to leave Edmonton, certainly didn't want to leave his teammates, didn't want to leave the best hockey team in the world. Bruce seemed like a lovely guy, and all that sunshine sure was nice, but an Oiler he was, and an Oiler he would remain, at least until his contract expired. Not that he didn't understand the implications of that contract. Not that he didn't realize that it might at some point be in Pocklington's interest to get rid of him. But for the time being, Gretzky wasn't inclined to force the issue.

Were it not for some unpleasantries in the Alberta meat-packing business, for some sly negotiating, for Peter Pocklington's delusional belief that he could get away with it, the McNall–Gretzky relationship might have remained forever unconsummated. When the door was opened, though, when the opportunity presented itself, McNall knew just what to do.

In the spring of 1988, he began hearing the same rumbles others had heard in NHL circles. Something was up with Pocklington. Something was up with Gretzky. Crazy talk on the face of it, but it didn't go away, and as the pieces came together it made more and more sense. Time to become a bit bolder, he figured. At the NHL awards banquet in June, McNall found himself sitting a row behind Pocklington. With that big, broad, signature smile on his face, McNall leaned forward and wondered if they might be able to do a little business, wondered if Pocklington might be willing to talk about trading Gretzky, and Pocklington didn't say no. Or at least that's the way Pocklington remembered it happening–that it was McNall who initiated the discussion, and that he himself was a passive player until approached with a sporting proposition.

McNall tells a rather different story. He says that from the very beginning, every time he crossed paths with Pocklington at a board of governors meeting, he'd ask in a half-joking way whether he was willing to trade Gretzky yet, and every time Peter would tell him he was crazy, it was out of the question, it would never happen. Then, one day in June 1988, in advance of the upcoming NHL draft, Pocklington called McNall at his office, completely out of the blue. "Are you serious about Gretzky?" he asked. They met secretly at the draft, and there Pocklington laid out his terms: he needed fifteen million dollars, period. "When I met with him, he opened right up," McNall says. "He knew what he wanted immediately. It wasn't even like a negotiation. It was automatic. He said, 'I want fifteen million U.S. cash. And I need some players to make it look like a trade.' That fifteen million dollars never changed. Once he said that and I knew I could do it, I said, 'Let's make this happen.' Once I agreed to the basic economic terms, that's when I thought this could happen."

Pocklington still says, and perhaps on some level still believes, that it really wasn't all about him and all about the money. He was really only acceding to Gretzky's wishes, doing what was best for all concerned—including the sport of hockey itself. He stepped aside, unwilling to stand in the way of Gretzky's, or the NHL's, larger destiny. "Everyone has a moment when times change, and times did change and times had changed in Wayne's life," he told filmmaker Don Metz in a 2008 interview commemorating the twentieth anniversary of the Gretzky trade. "He had got married. I'm sure there was a little bit of pressure from his new wife to feel more comfortable in Los Angeles. But maybe those were excuses I made, too. Realize that number one, it was a good business deal for Edmonton, it was a great business deal for hockey, it was a great business deal for L.A." Since the bottom line seems to have been the extraordinary selling price, which was never up for negotiation, perhaps he ought to at least have added one more clause: "it was a great business deal for me."

McNall broke the news to his hockey people that he was working on a Gretzky trade even before his face-to-face meeting with Pocklington, just so they'd be prepared. The Kings' general manger, Rogatien Vachon, and everyone else on the scouting staff were shocked, not to mention skeptical that it could ever really happen. (That would be the sum total of Vachon's involvement in the process, which suggests just how important he was considered to the Kings' operation, even if his title might have suggested otherwise.)

In Edmonton, Pocklington decided to play things a little closer to the vest. Glen Sather had built and coached the team to four Stanley Cups. He was Pocklington's friend, his confidant, and at times his business partner outside of hockey. But in this, the most crucial moment in the franchise's history, Pocklington chose to leave Sather in the dark, at least at the beginning. He'd find out soon enough, after it was a fait accompli, after there was nothing he could do to stop it. (Pocklington and Sather would eventually celebrate one more championship, drink together once more from the Stanley Cup, and find a way to work together for several more seasons after that, and years later, when Pocklington got in trouble, Sather would come up with his bail money, but their relationship was fundamentally altered. "I never really trusted him after that," Sather says.)

Whatever Pocklington's intentions, whatever McNall's desires, there wouldn't be a deal unless Gretzky gave it his blessing. In theory, the Oilers could have traded him against his wishes. In practice, both sides understood that they could never survive the backlash that would be created by forcing an icon to change uniforms—and with only four seasons remaining on his contract, only two of those guaranteed, any team willing to pay fifteen million dollars for his services would need Gretzky to commit to an extension.

So some persuasion was in order, but McNall still lacked formal permission even to speak to Gretzky—Pocklington wasn't going to surrender that privilege until he knew the money was on the table. But those were other people's rules, for which McNall was no stickler. Just as soon as he returned from the draft, McNall discreetly contacted Gretzky—it would have been tampering, in the NHL's eyes, if the league had ever found out about it—and found someone hurt, confused, angry and ambivalent about what to do next. After the Stanley Cup victory, his dad, Walter, and his agent, Mike Barnett, had let him in on the scheme cooked up by Nelson Skalbania that would have made him a Vancouver Canuck, and about Pocklington's part in it. When Gretzky and Pocklington had their annual end-of season meeting, Pocklington denied that anything was up. But now Gretzky no longer believed what Pocklington had been telling him. The story was coming at him from too many directions.

Not long after his meeting with Pocklington, Gretzky sat down in New York with Barnett. When he signed what turned out to be his last Oilers contract, Gretzky had predicted that he would probably be traded before it was finished, that Pocklington wouldn't have much choice. Now that prediction was coming true. "I know he's going to do it," Gretzky said. "There are only two teams that I'll go to if I'm going to be part of this. It's L.A. or Detroit." Detroit because it was close to Brantford, because it had been Gordie Howe's team; Los Angeles because he already felt at home there, because his wife wanted to be there, because he understood that he could make a whole lot more off-ice money there, and because he already very much liked Bruce McNall. Call him, Gretzky said. See if he's interested.

So Barnett did. "We've got some real issues here," he said. "Wayne thinks he's being shopped, and if you're interested, we'd like you to get in the game."

"He is," McNall said, "and I am."

It was then that Gretzky and Barnett learned that discussions between Pocklington and McNall had already been ongoing on for some weeks, without their knowledge. And though McNall claims that he still wasn't yet sure that Gretzky's heart was really in it, it's extremely telling that Gretzky almost immediately took an interest in the hockey side of the "trade," discussing which players he wanted to come with him from Edmonton to Los Angeles (Marty McSorley, Mike Krushelnyski), telling McNall that if the Kings were going to surrender multiple draft choices, they ought to be staggered over several seasons to avoid crippling the club in the short term. That certainly sounded like someone in the process of discarding any sentimental attachment to the old uniform, to his old teammates, to his old hometown. And from the very beginning, Gretzky embraced the idea that by coming to California and playing in a huge media market, he could help transform the business of hockey in the United States. Through his years as a pro, in both the WHA and NHL, he had seen the by-products of overly ambitious expansion, seen how hockey failed to permanently take root in the so-called non-traditional markets, seen all of the empty seats in places like L.A. Now he believed that he had a chance to single-handedly alter the hockey landscape. "Wayne was very much behind that," McNall says. "He knew his importance. He wasn't oblivious to his importance." He knew, also, that in Los Angeles he could become an entirely different level of commodity than he had been in Edmonton. Gretzky had signed plenty of endorsement deals in Canada, earning more than his hockey salary. But imagine how the Gretzky business might expand if even a small slice of America bought in.

Despite all of that, McNall still felt the need to bring Gretzky fully onside. He didn't want to spend fifteen million dollars on a reluctant superstar. What followed was one of those moments that came to define the man. He summoned Gretzky to his office in Century City, invited him in and closed the door. It was just the two of them in the room. A secretary buzzed over the intercom to let him know that Pocklington was on the line. That part was pre-arranged. McNall punched the button to activate his speaker phone, and Pocklington answered, unaware that Gretzky was listening. McNall certainly wasn't about to enlighten him.

Cordially, the owners began chatting. They exchanged pleasantries, talked a little hockey. Then Pocklington started to become more expansive, opening up to his new pal, talking—and just perhaps, with McNall gently steering the conversation in a particular direction—about how he really felt. Working himself into a lather, Pocklington expounded on all the things that bugged him about Gretzky and his family. The old man, Walter, was an unpleasant meddler. The new wife, Janet, was a manipulator who was pulling Wayne's strings. (As McNall remembers it, Pocklington may well have uttered a phrase beginning with the words, "Well, whatever that bitch wants . . .") Pocklington called Gretzky a crybaby and a whiner (foreshadowing some particularly ill-chosen words to come). He laid out his grievances, confided his frustrations and resentments, all for McNall's apparently sympathetic ear, all with Gretzky silently listening, silently seething.

That did it. As far as McNall is concerned, that was the moment that Wayne Gretzky departed Edmonton for Los Angeles. That's when McNall had him, heart, mind and soul.

Afterwards, they went out for dinner at Matteo's in Westwood, and entered into a long, deep conversation. They talked about Gretzky's situation, about hockey, about what it might mean for the NHL to have him playing in Los Angeles. McNall laid out an early version of his plan for continental expansion, which would become the league's guiding business principle for the next twenty years: with Gretzky on board, they could sell hockey anywhere, they could create new markets in places even where the game was alien. They could dot the American Sun Belt with franchises, all of them generating millions of dollars in revenues for the owners. They could attract real financial players to the league, not the two-bit operators of the past. They could lock up an American network television deal, something that had long eluded the league's grasp.

They also talked about Gretzky's own contract. Obviously, McNall would want—and need—him to make a longer commitment, and for that he would compensate him handsomely. He offered three million dollars a year—the same amount Magic Johnson was making with the Lakers, and an unheard of sum for a hockey player in that era. Gretzky indicated that he'd be happy with two million, more than double what he was making in Edmonton, and that he'd rather McNall spent some of his money making the team competitive. If everything worked out as planned, both of them would be very well taken care of down the road.

"He told me later that, at that moment, he knew I was the right guy," McNall says. "It wasn't like I'm an owner and he's a player. We were almost in a partnership." And partners they would become, figuratively and literally—in racehorses, in antique baseball cards, in the Toronto Argonauts of the Canadian Football League. Now, Wayne Gretzky and Bruce McNall were joined at the hip.

On July 17, 1988, Wayne Gretzky and Janet Jones were married at St. Joseph's Basilica in Edmonton, the city's grandest church, which left a few local Roman Catholics with their noses out of joint (neither the bride nor groom were of the faith) but which seemed to please just about everyone else. Seven years earlier, Prince Charles and Diana Spencer had been wed at Westminster Abbey, an event attended by the rich and famous and those of noble birth that lifted the hearts of romantics around the world. Of course, this would be dubbed Canada's own royal wedding, our humble hero boy marrying his own beautiful princess surrounded by as much glamour and splendour as the Alberta capital could deliver. Every detail of the preparations would be lovingly captured by the press—Janet's $40,000 designer wedding dress, 1,500 hours in the making, with its detachable train; the rumoured $1 million tab for the ceremony and reception; the $250,000 Gretzky was supposed to have spent on the wedding ring (he denied it); the Rolls Royce convertible that Wayne was giving Janet as a wedding present; the six video cameras and three editing suites set up in the church basement, allowing Gretzky's friend, filmmaker Don Metz, to fully document the great event. The identities of those in the bridal party, especially Wayne's groomsmen, were of great interest: his best man, Eddie Mio, the old goalie who had been traded with him from the Indianapolis Racers, who shared the fateful flight to Edmonton when no one was really sure where they were headed; his brothers, Brent, Keith and Glen; his Oiler "brothers" Mark Messier, Kevin Lowe and already departed Paul Coffey. Rumours flew about the celebrity-studded guest list. Prime Minister Brian Mulroney was invited, but couldn't make it. *Playboy* czar Hugh Hefner, whose magazine had featured Janet in a semi-nude pictorial, also sent his regrets. But there would be plenty of famous faces from the hockey world—Gordie Howe, Vladislav Tretiak, Alan Eagleson, John Ziegler—and a few from the entertainment world as well. (In a move that was either endearingly inclusive or calculated, depending on the interpretation, Gretzky also invited members of the sports press, the same guys who would remain remarkably protective of him and his interests throughout his career, to the ceremony.) Alan Thicke, Gretzky's first L.A. pal, would be on hand to emcee the reception.

(Contrast all of that with Canada's last great hockey wedding, when Bobby Orr took the hand of Peggy Wood at the Presbyterian minister's house in Parry Sound, with only his sister and brother-in-law in attendance. He didn't tell his teammates, didn't invite the press—though a few of them showed up anyway—and the small reception afterwards at the local curling club was by definition a private affair. Different times, different guys, very different levels of comfort with the business of being a star.)

When the happy day arrived, three thousand people gathered outside the church to gawk at the invitees and bridal party, and the *Edmonton Sun* and *Edmonton Journal* both printed special sections in honour of the occasion. In other circumstances, there might have been an undertone of resentment. But in Edmonton, no one complained about the excesses. He was their adopted son; he had brought them so many moments of pride and joy that he deserved everything that was coming to him, including his beautiful bride. And Janet, though they didn't really know her, though he'd split with a local girl when they met, seemed like a perfect fit. The couple was looking for a house in Edmonton, it was reported. She was perfectly happy to settle there, and to start raising a family. "We plan on having kids right away," she said. "I don't think that we will stop at one. I come from a family of seven. Wayne comes from a family of five. I think that says it right there." That sure didn't sound like one of those Hollywood types. That didn't sound like some flashy movie star who would never be satisfied so far from the bright lights. That sure didn't sound like Yoko Ono, arriving to break up the jolly band of brothers. That sounded like their kind of girl, like Wayne's kind of girl.

The uncomfortable subtext, the knowledge of the great shock to come, was exclusively the burden of the bride and groom and an extremely small circle of their intimates. Even Thicke, when he made a joke during the reception about Peter Pocklington scalping tickets to the wedding, didn't know that his crack had extra meaning for a few people in the room, that it might have made the Oilers' owner stir a bit uncomfortably, and made the happy couple smile double-edged smiles. For all the world, for all appearances, here was the Canadian Horatio Alger story writ large: a boy from humble working-class beginnings, blessed with a strong family and a strong work ethic and a tremendous natural gift, rising to fame and fortune without ever losing touch with his origins. He is rewarded with wealth, with adulation, with success, and finally with a woman so blonde and beautiful, so in love with him, in love with his hometown, ready to settle down and make a family and live happily ever after. It was the stuff of fairy tales.

Chapter Eight

THE ART OF THE DEAL

THINK OF IT FOR A moment not as hockey, or as a business. Think it of it as theatre, as drama, and especially as propaganda. There would be a stage, there would be lights and props and actors, there would be audiences, both live and through television. There would be two separate performances in two different countries, requiring different aesthetic sensibilities and different cultural sensitivities, and at least three players trying to get their largely contradictory messages across. While the fine points of the Wayne Gretzky deal were being worked out behind the scenes, a select few in Los Angeles and Edmonton were being let in on the great secret. It would be their job to help explain it, to exploit it, to deflect it, and, in the case of Bruce McNall's loyal retainers, to pull together all of the funds necessary to make it happen. Only when each piece was in place could the curtain rise. And in the end, for all the planning and forethought and rehearsal, it would still wind up being a rush job, and it showed.

Roy Mlakar had paid his dues in the less-than-glamorous environment of bush league American hockey, serving ten years as president and general manager of the New Haven Nighthawks of the American Hockey League, learning the ins and outs, filling seats, selling popcorn, coming up with clever promotions designed to lure paying customers to watch a product that probably wasn't all that close to their hearts. (Most famously, to spur on a faltering season-ticket drive, Mlakar climbed to the roof of the arena and announced that he wouldn't come down until the team had achieved its modest goal. It did; otherwise, presumably, he'd still be there.) The Nighthawks had been independently owned, and were affiliated with the New York Rangers, who played not far down the road in Manhattan, before becoming part of a shared farm-team arrangement with the Los Angeles Kings. In the late 1980s, Mlakar thought they would function better with a single parent/owner, and helped broker the sale of the franchise to the Kings, who needed their own solid, well-run minor-league club to help stabilize their hockey operations. The Kings' owner, Dr. Jerry Buss, agreed with that reasoning, and was more than happy to have Mlakar running the Nighthawks on his behalf. But it was clear to Mlakar from the very beginning of their relationship that his new boss had lost whatever modest passion he might have had for the game. Buss was never much of a hockey fan, and hated paying what he considered outrageous salaries to his players. His Lakers, he loved. His Kings, he (barely) tolerated.

By then, Buss had taken a minority partner on board, one about whom Mlakar knew precious little. Obviously he was a keener, though, because he kept badgering Buss to allow him to increase his 25 per cent ownership stake, and because he had decided all on his own to make the trip across the country to see how a farm team worked. Mlakar liked Bruce McNall. (Heck, who didn't like Bruce McNall?) He enjoyed his enthusiasm, appreciated his obvious love of hockey, admired how he operated from a posture of humility despite his position of authority, asking all kinds of questions and then honestly listening to the answers. Buss might have gone sour on the sport, but here was a fresh-faced true believer and a professional sports virgin who hadn't been around long enough to become cynical and bottom line–obsessed. He was in many ways just a fan, and the two of them hit it off instantly. "He was happy-go-lucky, gregarious," Mlakar remembers. "He just wanted to be one of the boys. He was impressed with how everything worked. He wasn't an 'I'm going to woo you with my money' kind of guy. He was just very inquisitive, and excitable."

Soon enough, McNall persuaded Buss to sell him the rest of the Kings, and soon enough, the parade of talent from New Haven to Los Angeles began, including the Nighthawks' coach, Robbie Ftorek, who was promoted to work behind the Kings' bench. It stood to reason that Mlakar would eventually be called to the big time as well, and so it wasn't a complete surprise when McNall summoned him to a meeting at a neutral site—Caesars Palace in Lake Tahoe—where Mlakar went through the Kings' operation piece by piece and talked about what could be done to improve both the product and the balance sheet. Rogatien Vachon was the Kings' general manager, in charge of the hockey team on the ice, but McNall needed someone to handle the off-ice business, which was beyond the old goalie's capabilities. He laid out for Mlakar the essential marketing challenge: the Kings operated in the Lakers' shadow; they lacked a presence in a crowded sports marketplace; there were enormous limitations to what they could sell in their own arena because of the terms of their lease. But it wasn't as if McNall lacked for ideas. He knew that in L.A. they had to somehow turn hockey players into stars. He knew they had to market the young talent on the roster. He decided early on that they needed a different look, a different uniform—that by playing in the same gold and purple as the basketball team, they were all but begging for unflattering comparisons. In 1988–89 the Kings would don black and silver, cultivating the same edgy, outlaw image as football's Los Angeles (né Oakland) Raiders. It was a bit risky, but they had precious little to lose.

From Tahoe, McNall and Mlakar flew by private jet to Los Angeles, then were whisked to the posh offices in Century City that housed McNall's coin, memorabilia, horse racing and movie businesses. There Mlakar was introduced to McNall's inner circle—most notably an attractive young woman named Susan Waks, an accountant by training, and Steve Nessenblatt, a lawyer. The two worked as McNall's right and left hands, and would continue to operate at the upper levels of McNall's empire, of which the Kings were just one small part. Mlakar wasn't privy to any of that, and was in the dark about their methodology (as evidenced by the fact that, when the walls came tumbling down and people started going to jail, he was left untouched). His job was to make the Kings profitable while also making them relevant, making them front-of-the-sports-page news in Southern California. On the face of it, it was a daunting challenge, bordering on the impossible. But soon enough, he'd get some help.

In the early summer of 1988, not long after the conclusion of the Stanley Cup playoffs (in which the Kings, following a rather encouraging regular season, had been eliminated in the first round by the Calgary Flames, and in which the Edmonton Oilers, led by Wayne Gretzky, had won their fourth Stanley Cup), McNall invited Mlakar to lunch at Joe's, the kind of high-end, high-profile joint he tended to frequent. Mlakar was expecting the usual post mortem and look ahead—talk about the new uniforms, talk about how they might make Luc Robitaille or Jimmy Carson household names, maybe even kick around a new movie idea that McNall was pitching.

Instead, McNall leaned across the table and said something that was previously unimaginable.

"I think we can get Wayne Gretzky."

"You think you can what?"

"I think we can get Wayne Gretzky."

Out the remarkable story spilled. McNall had done his homework. He knew that Peter Pocklington's non-hockey businesses were underperforming, that he needed a quick cash infusion, and that he was now apparently willing to part with his most precious asset. Gretzky was for sale; the issue was who could pay the price, and to a lesser degree who could make Gretzky feel most comfortable, most welcome, so that he would give his blessing to a trade. It was clear to Mlakar from the way McNall told the story that he must already have been talking to Pocklington—and probably to Gretzky as well. McNall explained that Gretzky was spending plenty of time in Los Angeles, that his new wife lived there, that just maybe the Kings already had a leg up on the competition for his services. But still, it certainly wouldn't be easy to close the deal, and it certainly wouldn't be cheap. "It's going to cost us, and it's going to cost us big time," McNall said.

For a start, the Oilers wanted Luc Robitaille, the Kings' best player (Vachon was vacationing in Hawaii, so Mlakar acted as counsel on both the hockey and financial aspects of the deal), plus other players, plus draft choices, plus a huge sum of money. And it all had to happen fast. McNall told Mlakar that Glen Sather was still in the dark, and that the minute he found out, he would surely try to kill any trade. McNall's role would be to employ his considerable charms on Gretzky, persuading him that Los Angeles should be his new home. "I've got to make sure he wants to come here," McNall said. "I've got to make sure Wayne is onside." Mlakar's appointed task was to come up with ways they could make extra money with Gretzky on the Kings, to help justify the massive investment. At the same time, he'd have a more immediate challenge: helping McNall raise the cash to pay off Pocklington. It was an astronomical figure, a ridiculous price to pay for a hockey player—or just about anything or anyone else. Somehow, they were going to have to find fifteen million dollars. There would be the usual sweet-talking of bankers for the bulk of it, but that was Waks and McNall's job. While Mlakar was finding those new sources of revenue that might open up if Gretzky came to town—ideally, without actually spilling the news that it might happen—he would also try to unlock a bit of that money in advance, so that it might be thrown into the pot.

He put his thinking cap on.

Jeffrey Goodman certainly wasn't the first Canadian sportswriter to opt out of the life of the ink-stained wretch in favour of a career in public relations, but unquestionably he was one of the most successful. By 1988 the former *Globe and Mail* staffer, who had written about the Canadian Football League and World Hockey Association, was already running his own company in Toronto and had cut his teeth both in the corporate world and in politics, where among other things he had provided communications advice for Prime Minister Pierre Trudeau. In the early summer of that year, he received a call from a fellow corporate flak—in fact, the senior vice-president of public affairs for R.J. Reynolds tobacco—who had just been in Edmonton, summoned there to a meeting with a local luminary who was seeking full-time guidance. He couldn't take the job, but he had recommended Goodman for the task, and was now giving him a heads-up. "Jeff Goodman will tell you the truth," was his endorsement—which behind closed doors is exactly what's required from someone charged with the business of buffing and polishing an image, of highlighting the good news and mitigating the bad.

The potential client was Peter Pocklington.

"He's quite a character," Goodman's friend offered, in what was perhaps an intentional understatement.

Goodman got on the phone right away and made his pitch, and Pocklington, not being one inclined to long courtships, invited him to fly out to Edmonton the next day. They met at Pocklington's office, where Peter cut immediately to the chase. The tone was cordial, the jibes more friendly than confrontational.

"How could you work for that socialist Trudeau?" he asked.

"He paid his bills on time," Goodman fired back. "Do you?"

On that note began their relationship. Pocklington seemed to like the cut of Goodman's jib, the fact that he wasn't intimidated, and moved to strike an agreement. And Goodman liked Pocklington—he found him charming, quick-witted and, of course, just a touch egomaniacal. As a private chef prepared lunch, Pocklington laid out what he was looking for: someone to take on an advisory role, both for him personally and for all of his corporate holdings, including the financial, food and real estate businesses and, on a big-picture level, the Edmonton Oilers. A lawyer was summoned, and the broad strokes were agreed upon right there, with Goodman signing on the dotted line.

That done, the deal sealed, Pocklington cleared the office of any bystanders, then closed the door. It was just the two of them now.

"I need to talk to you privately," Pocklington said, his tone becoming dead serious for the first time in their conversation. "I have a first assignment for you."

"What's that?" Goodman asked.

"I'm trading Wayne Gretzky and I need you to handle the trade."

It was a tight circle that, in the time around the Gretzky–Janet Jones nuptials, understood what was in the works: Pocklington; McNall and his closest confidants; Gretzky, his father, his agent and his new wife. And now Goodman, charged with the unenviable task of explaining the inexplicable, taking what would be considered very bad news by just about everyone in the city and province and country where Pocklington did most of his business and spinning it into something reasonable and palatable and perhaps even positive. That was the magic PR guys were supposed to perform, but Goodman knew that spinning this one might be beyond anyone's powers.

"If I would have known this morning, I'd be charging you a lot more than what we just agreed to," Goodman said.

"That's why I'm on this side of the desk," Pocklington fired back, "and you're on that side of the desk."

Mlakar wouldn't actually meet Wayne Gretzky until the day he arrived from Edmonton for his introductory press conference in Los Angeles. But he understood that, somewhere along the way, McNall had been granted permission to talk to him, and he assumed that before that ever happened, his boss had found a way to make contact on the sly. That was the way Bruce operated. Little details started to leak out in their conversations that confirmed his suspicions, hints that the relationship between the owner and the hockey star was already in full bloom. McNall said that, one way or another, they had to get Marty McSorley from the Oilers as part of the deal. That had to have come directly from Gretzky–McNall wouldn't have known he was Gretzky's buddy and personal protector on the ice unless he'd been told.

As the hockey stakes got higher—Edmonton was asking for five first-round picks now, and were insisting on Robitaille—McNall never flinched. "Bruce was not going to say no to anything at that point, because he knew he had Wayne," Mlakar says. "It wasn't going to matter. It wasn't going to matter what Rogie thought. It was all about getting in that Learjet, getting to Edmonton and getting this over with." Still, there was the worry that Pocklington might get cold feet, or that Sather might somehow find a way to intervene. While Waks and McNall started to work on their favourite bankers, trying to beg or borrow the necessary cash, Mlakar turned his attention to the Kings' previously woeful broadcast contracts. Interest in the team had diminished to the point that it had no over-the-air television presence at all. Anyone who wanted to see the games on television had to find them on Prime Ticket (the early regional all-sports service co-owned by Jerry Buss and cable pioneer Bill Daniels), and anyone who wanted to hear them on radio—well, that was complicated as well. For awhile, the Kings were on the same station that broadcast the Lakers, and any time the two teams' games conflicted, hockey was tape-delayed, with games finally airing only after the basketball was done. That obviously was far from ideal, so Mlakar had come up with something marginally better: a station in San Diego which actually transmitted out of Tijuana, Mexico, which was happy to take the Kings' money in return for airtime—a time buy, the same refuge occupied by evangelists, infomercials, and sports desperate for exposure and short of a dedicated audience or advertisers. "Nobody else wanted us," Mlakar says, "so we had to be clever."

Mlakar went out in search of better deals, including cash up front—doing his best not to say the word "Gretzky," but promising something magical in the offing that would sell out the Forum for hockey every night. He was, naturally, met with considerable skepticism, if not ridicule, but had to keep plugging. The announcement of the trade was now supposed to be just days away, and they still didn't have the money.

—

The first principle of telling his story, Jeffrey Goodman explained to Pocklington, was that the Edmonton public had to be convinced Wayne Gretzky was leaving of his own free will, that he had agreed to the deal, perhaps even that he had engineered it for his own selfish purposes. Otherwise, it was game over. "If there is even a hint that he isn't on board with this," he told Pocklington, "you might as well move to the moon." Pocklington assured him that was already taken care of. Gretzky understood his role. He was fully informed. He knew the script. When the time came, he would say exactly that. He would explain to the fans that he had a hand in the trade, that it was what he truly wanted, that it was in his personal and professional interest to leave Edmonton. ("Peter never lied to me," Goodman says now. "He didn't tell me everything. But he didn't lie to me.") He believed then, and he believes now, that Gretzky had indeed agreed to those terms long before the famous press conference, though he had no idea that there was any tension between Pocklington, Sather and Gretzky until the day of the press conference.) There were still details to be worked out. Pocklington and McNall needed to finalize the financial arrangements, as well as whatever players and draft picks were going to be sent from the Kings to the Oilers, but according to Pocklington that was all but a fait accompli. Once the final t's were crossed, the news would be broken in measured, choreographed fashion, which was where Goodman came in.

Though no one from the tight inner circle had leaked the story, rumours were somehow percolating in the hockey world that a Gretzky trade might be in the works, and a few actually made it to print. But the story had been floated in the past, as far back as 1983, when Pocklington had experienced his most serious financial troubles, and every time it had been easily shot down by the owner or Sather, or some combination of both, because it wasn't true. If absolutely necessary, Goodman figured they could fire off another four-square denial, but otherwise would leave well enough alone. As for the announcement of the trade when the time came, Goodman was already working on a scenario.

He had learned that, every summer, Pocklington made two separate trips to a remote fishing lodge in the Northwest Territories—

the first, accompanied by Sather and members of the hockey crowd, usually including the Boston Bruins' longtime president and general manager Harry Sinden; the latter accompanied by the top executives of his companies and a few of his cronies. Up north, Pocklington was absolutely unreachable. There wasn't even a phone. Understanding that, when given an opportunity to talk, his client would talk, and not necessarily to his own advantage, understanding that however well the press conference went, emotions in Edmonton would be running high, Goodman saw the second trip to the Arctic as the perfect cover. They'd hold the press conference. They'd make the announcement. There would be the predictable gnashing of teeth. And then they'd spirit Pocklington away to the airport, get him on a plane and get him the hell out of town, disappearing—as far as the press and the fans knew—to parts unknown, and remaining there long enough for things to cool down. Barring something unforeseen, the announcement that Wayne Gretzky had been traded to the Los Angeles Kings would be made on August 11, and on the twelfth, Pocklington would be dealing with nothing more contentious than the odd Arctic char. In the meantime, it was essential that nothing get out. The flimsy rumours they could deal with; but any real evidence, circumstantial or otherwise, that the wild suggestion of a Gretzky trade might well be true would send the story spinning out of their control and make it much more difficult to get their intended message across.

Pocklington and McNall were going to have to get together face to face at some point soon to hammer out the final terms, and Goodman realized that that meeting couldn't happen in Los Angeles, where someone might notice, and it absolutely couldn't happen in small-town Edmonton, where someone would undoubtedly notice. He suggested that they could meet in relative anonymity in Toronto, and that he would take care of the details. For all of the back and forth, the occasional chats at NHL board of governors meetings, and the long series of phone calls over Gretzky, it would be the first time McNall and Pocklington had really talked to each other, face to face. Both flew to Toronto in their private jets, transferred to their limousines and connected at Goodman's office. He remembers exactly how, after the initial pleasantries, their conversation began—two lines of dialogue that would never be part of the accepted version of what was about to happen, that would fly in the face of nearly everything Canadians have come to believe about the Gretzky trade.

"You were absolutely right," McNall said to Pocklington. "I told him I'd give him another million dollars, and he felt much better about it."

"I told you so," Pocklington said.

The suggestion: that it wasn't just about hearth and home and country and team, that for Gretzky—just as it was for McNall, and for Pocklington—it was at least in part about the money.

The two tycoons, with Goodman maintaining a discreet distance, continued their discussions over lunch at a fine local restaurant called Il Posto, where they went unrecognized. There, McNall and Pocklington really began to get acquainted, telling each other their how-I-got-rich, self-made-man stories—Pocklington spinning tales about selling cars and buying real estate, McNall once again explaining the mystery and allure of ancient coins. Goodman says they hit it off famously, in many ways birds of a feather. When the meal was finished and the deal all but complete, they rose and headed off for their limos, to be taken to their jets, to fly to their western homes, to plan for the day when the world would be let in on their great secret.

Goodman followed them out the door. Only later, when the restaurant called to settle accounts, did he realize that he'd been stuck with the cheque.

There remained one loose end to be tied up: Pocklington still hadn't informed the president and general manager and architect and guiding spirit of his championship-winning hockey team that he was trading away his greatest player for money. A minor detail. Glen Sather had heard stories before, heard rumblings that Pocklington was going to do something with Gretzky, but he never believed them, because if there was any truth there, surely the owner would have told him, surely he would be among the first to know. "I knew that Peter was having some trouble with finances. He always seemed to have trouble with that," Sather says. "But I just sort of fluffed it off, and thought it was just conversation. Peter was the kind of guy—there was always stuff flying around with Peter. But most of it was hypothetical or fabricated by the media or just out there. I never seriously thought he was going to do something about it. Peter had talked about what he could do to raise some money. But I never thought that he was seriously going to consider trading Wayne."

Sather certainly wasn't naive. He understood Pocklington's growing financial challenges with his other businesses, and he understood how the Oilers were becoming a have-not franchise in the NHL's evolving class system, as player salaries spiralled ever higher, driven by wealthier teams. And better than anyone, he understood the implications of the contract Gretzky had negotiated with the owner. They were on the clock. In a free market for Gretzky's services, they simply couldn't compete with New York or Detroit or Toronto, unless Pocklington was willing to reach deeply into his own pockets—and there was little chance of that. The diminishing asset thing, Sather had figured out. He might have even been the person to first put the phrase in Pocklington's head. But during the happy weeks after the fourth Stanley Cup triumph, he never dreamed that any of that was actually in play. "It was a pretty quiet summer," Sather says. "It was enjoyable."

Off they went on that first fishing trip—Sather, an avid, expert fly fisherman, as enthusiastic as any of them—and it was there that the rumours of a Gretzky deal seemed to gain traction. Sinden told Sather that he'd heard them, and that he'd told Pocklington he would be making a terrible mistake if he followed through. Sinden was in Boston when ownership allowed Bobby Orr to leave for the Chicago Blackhawks. It was a notoriously murky chapter in hockey history, in which the Bruins might well have been absolved of blame. But whatever the logic behind the move, whatever the rationale, whatever the truth about who had been offered what when, the Bruins' season ticket holders and sponsors deserted the team en masse after Orr changed uniforms, and the fans blamed management entirely for letting an icon leave town.

Sather still couldn't wrap his head around it. He still couldn't believe that Pocklington could be up to something so significant without telling him. But neither did he immediately press the issue with his boss. After their return to Edmonton, Pocklington invited Sather to accompany him to a charity golf tournament in Beaver Creek, Colorado, where the former president Gerald Ford (one of Pocklington's favourite trophy acquaintances) would be the featured attraction. They travelled with an Italian friend of Pocklington's. The first night, Pocklington opened a bottle of wine—a very good one, of course—poured each of them a glass, and then dropped his bombshell.

"Well, I've sold Wayne," he told Sather, just like that.

"You've got to be fucking kidding," Sather said.

"Yeah, I made the deal. I had to do the deal."

"You're crazy," he said. "We can't do that."

In the heat of that moment, Sather acknowledges that he was tempted to deck Pocklington, but he calmed himself, held his fists and settled for an extremely agitated conversation. He was an employee, after all, and a loyal one, and his relationship with Pocklington had been long and productive. Better to get to the bottom of this than blow everything on the spot. Better to go to the source and kill this crazy deal before it went any further.

His first call was to Gretzky's agent, Michael Barnett, which Barnett recalls sounding something like this:

"Mike, all of this bullshit about Wayne getting traded. Let me tell you, I'm managing this hockey club and he's not going to get traded. When Peter gets back, I'm going to meet with him, and it's not going to happen."

"Okay Glen, whatever you say," Barnett said. "But as far as Wayne is concerned, he doesn't want to play for Peter again."

The next day, Sather phoned him back.

"I'm meeting with Peter tonight. It's not going to happen. It's going to die. Tell Wayne not to talk to anyone."

In the meantime, Sather got on the phone to Los Angeles, where soon enough he located Bruce McNall.

"He was furious," McNall remembers. "He hated the whole idea. He was pissed at everybody. It was, 'Fuck that. Fuck Pocklington. This isn't going to happen. Go fuck yourself.'"

In the face of that, McNall replied with a series of cold, hard facts. He and Pocklington had already agreed to the deal in principle, he explained. It wasn't just the money—they'd already talked about other players. Marty McSorley and Mike Krushelnyski were coming to the Kings, with a series of draft picks going the other way. Echoing the thoughts of others, Sather says that that was the moment when he realized Gretzky must have been part of the process. There's no way McNall would have known enough about the Oilers to ask for those two. That had to be Wayne's doing.

Pocklington had agreed to those conditions, McNall said. And if he backed out now, if the Oilers got cold feet, they could expect the mother of all lawsuits.

Sather hung up the phone and considered his options. By the time he called McNall back, he had cooled off and turned on the general manager part of his brain. If this was a trade, then he'd better make the most of it. He asked for Robitaille. McNall made it clear that there was no way the Kings were going to part with him. Jimmy Carson was offered instead.

The next morning, Sather phoned Barnett again.

"I can't believe it. Peter has been talking to Bruce. There are players involved. It looks like Pocklington is insisting, and it's his hockey club. If Robitaille's not involved, it's not going to happen."

Robitaille wouldn't be involved. It did happen. From a hockey standpoint, Sather hated the deal. He knew that the team he had so carefully constructed would react as though there had been a death in the family. But beyond hockey, he knew that this would have even greater consequences. Perhaps he couldn't have anticipated all of them, perhaps he couldn't have processed just how much of a pariah his boss would become, how his hockey team, the object of so much unconditional love, would suddenly inspire cynicism and distrust. But Sather sensed that the world as they had all known it would irrevocably change.

"I like Peter," Sather says. "I had a lot of fun with him, I enjoyed his company. He was exciting to be around. He was a dynamic guy. But it was never quite the same after that. I knew Peter was capable of doing a lot of things. I'd been with him and seen him do a lot of things. But I never expected this one."

He was pissed. He would stay pissed. He is still pissed, more than twenty years later.

They were already planning the party in Los Angeles, working with the William Morris Agency, lining up the stars, making sure that when Wayne Gretzky arrived, even if some of the celebrity crowd wasn't quite sure about what he did for a living, they'd be there to welcome one of their own. McNall had his raw materials now. He had something to sell, something more potent than any simple hockey player. He had his *idea*. This was hockey's Babe Ruth, its Joe DiMaggio, its Johnny Unitas—or, to be more local and more current, its Magic Johnson. They wouldn't need to know which end of the stick you held to understand that they were in the presence of greatness—The Great One. The ultimate. But there was still the matter of closing the deal, which required actually coming up with the fifteen million dollars. Mlakar was certainly doing his bit, making headway on the broadcast front. He had approached Bill Daniels, and was working especially hard on Jerry Buss—who would receive the most direct benefit, because it was his arena (for Kings games, under the terms of the lease, Buss still controlled the best seats in the house). There's something coming, Mlakar told them, that's going to sell out the Forum for hockey every night. He tried not to say the word "Gretzky," but with the hours ticking away, he finally spilled the beans. Immediately, Buss and Daniels agreed to kick in five million dollars, up front.

Craig Simpson had become an Edmonton Oiler in the same trade that sent Paul Coffey to the Pittsburgh Penguins in the fall of 1987. He scored 56 goals that season between the two teams, and had been with the Oilers for their glorious Stanley Cup run. At the end of a successful season, it was customary for the Edmonton players to get a little something extra from Pocklington, a little token of his appreciation. Following the Cup win, he handed each of them two tickets to anywhere Air Canada flew. Simpson was single, 21 years old and at loose ends as to what to do; Gretzky stepped up, and invited him to use one of his tickets to visit him in Los Angeles. He remembers arriving at Los Angeles International Airport on August 6, where Gretzky picked him up. Rumours had been floating around back home, wild stuff about Gretzky being traded, and making small talk, he asked about it on the drive back to Janet Jones' condo (they would actually be staying at Alan Thicke's house while the actor was away in Europe). "It's been a wild week," was all Gretzky said. When they got to Jones' place, the light on the answering machine was flashing. Gretzky pushed the button. "Hi Wayne," the voice said. "It's Bruce. I think we've got a deal done."

After that, Gretzky laid out the whole story. "I was flabbergasted," Simpson says. "I didn't know what to think." The only person he told was his mother.

Two weeks after the meeting between McNall and Pocklington in Toronto, three days before the secret scheduled date for the press conference, the phone rang at Jeff Goodman's home in Toronto. It was late—after midnight. The person on the other end of the line was clearly agitated.

"Jeff," Pocklington said, "it's getting out."

A Canadian radio report was the start of it, originating in the Ottawa area (Robitaille, who played his junior hockey in Hull, had appeared at a charity event there with Gretzky, and the inner circle assumed that Gretzky must have tipped him that the trade was coming, that he had in turn told a friend in the media, and it had gone from there—though Robitaille denies to this day it ever happened). Next, there was a story out of Vancouver, and the details were suspiciously close to the truth. Goodman told Pocklington to sleep on it, that the *Globe and Mail* would be on his doorstep at five in the morning, and if there was something in the newspaper, they would have to start revising their plans. Pocklington was temporarily satisfied with that, and hung up.

Forty-five minutes later, an extremely flustered Bruce McNall was on the phone. "I just got a call from a radio station," he said.

There was no putting this genie back in the bottle. Somehow the story was breaking on several fronts. At 2:30 in the morning, Goodman, McNall and Pocklington convened a conference call. They all agreed that they couldn't spend the next two days denying what, on the third day, would be confirmed as true. They'd have to hold press conferences the next day, both in Edmonton and in Los Angeles (all parties agreed with Goodman's suggestion that announcing the news first in Edmonton—which certainly wasn't the norm when a player left one team for another—would serve as a gesture to the city, a way of softening the blow ever so slightly, rather than having Gretzky simply appear in a new town wearing a new uniform).

Goodman started working on the press release. Pocklington and his people took care of the local arrangements. McNall left to track down Gretzky in Los Angeles—at that moment, he wasn't entirely sure where he was staying that night—and tell him to be ready to get on a plane first thing in the morning.

At the tail end of a sleepless night, before heading for the Toronto airport, Goodman began working on the speech that Pocklington would deliver later that day. His client might have imagined that his address to the Progressive Conservative leadership convention back in 1983 was the oratorical high-water mark of his life, but this message would in fact be far more important to far more people. The tone would have to be just right, the argument plausible, the explanation airtight. As Goodman imagined it, it was almost like a commencement address, a sad but fond farewell to someone moving on to another stage of life. Gretzky's departure was inevitable. He needed to be in California for personal reasons, and he needed to be there for the greater good of hockey, as a shinny apostle. Pocklington would express his love for Gretzky, express his profound sadness that he was leaving Edmonton and leaving the Oilers behind, but would make it clear that he felt it would be selfish in the extreme to stand in the way of what Wayne wanted, to stand in the path of his larger destiny, to stand in the way of hockey's progress.

At Thicke's house in the posh Toluca Lake neighbourhood of Los Angeles, there was a driveway, and at the end of that driveway there was a basketball hoop. His son Robin, the future pop star, liked to play there with a handful of his buddies—pickup games and H-O-R-S-E and the usual stuff. Above that driveway, within clear sight of the basketball players, was a large picture window, and behind that window was a large Jacuzzi tub. The kids shot hoops, and as the sun dipped in the California evening, they began to notice that when the light was just right, you could see through the window and right inside. The reason they noticed was that one of Thicke's house guests, the newly married Janet Jones-Gretzky, who was staying there with her husband and his teammate Craig Simpson, enjoying a safe, quiet retreat while waiting for the deal to be consummated, had gotten into the habit of using the whirlpool at precisely that time of the day, and was under the mistaken impression that the window she was standing before, gloriously naked, was a mirror.

The basketball crowd grew from a smattering of kids to a full-scale crowd of adolescent boys, drawn by the show; but aside from them, no one—including McNall—was certain that Gretzky was there. (Thicke himself was vacationing in Norway, where in a few days he would see front-page headlines he couldn't read, above an image that he immediately understood: it was a picture of his friend, the hockey hero, crying.)

It was late when the phone rang. Robin Thicke picked it up.

"Is Wayne there?" It was Bruce McNall calling.

"I think he's asleep," the boy said.

"Well, I think you'd better go wake him up."

Chapter Nine

GRETZKY'S TEARS

S O MUCH FOR METEOROLOGICAL omens. Don Metz and the rest of the crew from TSN rolled up to Molson House on what was a sunny and glorious Alberta summer morning. The weather made their lives that much easier. Had it been raining, had the ground been wet, they would have had to leave the satellite truck out on the street and schlep their gear back and forth through the mud. But now, they could drive almost to the front door of a place that looked like it had been misplaced from a movie studio backlot. Molson House, attached to the brewery of the same name, was built of logs to resemble an old fur trapper's fort, a kitschy homage to Edmonton's frontier past. It was meant to look ancient, in a pioneer village sort of way, but in fact it dated only to 1961, when it had been originally conceived as a place where Molson employees could entertain customers over a frosty mug of their fine product and admire the various dead animals hanging from the walls. The brewery would occasionally lend the building to others for receptions and special events, and since beer and hockey were commercially and culturally linked, it made some sense that, however oddball it appeared, this was where Peter

Pocklington chose to summon the gentlemen of the press at the stroke of noon on August 9, 1988, for an announcement of great consequence.

August was a dead zone on the hockey calendar, and until the past twenty-four hours, the last local Gretzky sighting had been at his wedding nearly a month before. But now the story of the trade had exploded, just as Pocklington and Bruce McNall and Jeffrey Goodman anticipated it would, and that morning it was all over the papers. Wayne Gretzky was leaving town, and the faux fort suddenly became the focus not just of Edmonton but of an entire hockey-loving country. Reporters from around the continent scrambled to the closest airport to grab flights, and arrangements were made to broadcast the proceedings live by satellite, the first time in Canada that that had been done for a mere press conference. By the time the big show started, there would be a couple of hundred spectators crammed into the new/old log cabin, understanding what they were about to witness, though battling disbelief until they saw Gretzky and Pocklington in the flesh and heard them say the fateful words.

Metz, who had documented just about all of Gretzky's career with the Oilers, staked out a spot at the front, near the table set up in front of a huge stone fireplace for the guests of honour. He'd get the close-ups, while another cameraman at the back would handle the wide shots. Inside, Metz noted that sunlight was streaming so brightly through the windows that it threatened to cause havoc with his shot. He made a point of walking over and closing a few of the blinds.

After waking Gretzky with the news that the deal was finally done, Bruce McNall asked him to meet early the next morning at the suburban Van Nuys Airport, the closest runway to Alan Thicke's digs in Toluca Lake. From there they'd fly in McNall's private jet directly to Edmonton, then turn around immediately after the press conference and head back for a similar (though in tone, very different) event at an airport hotel in Los Angeles. It figured to be a long, tough day.

McNall's staff, along with Gretzky's agent, Michael Barnett, took care of the arrangements at the other end, lining up a car and driver to meet the plane on arrival. There was still the pressing business of getting fifteen million dollars into Pocklington's bank account, but happily the combined hustling efforts of Roy Mlakar and Susan Waks, along with McNall's own silver-tongued work with some of his favourite bankers, had borne fruit. Pocklington, though, wasn't about to take anyone's word for it. Until the money was actually in Edmonton, there would be no deal, and because everything had been done in such haste, the bank transfer had yet to be completed by the time McNall and Gretzky took off. But at least the hockey part of the transaction, with enough moving parts to make it look less like a straight sale and more like a trade, had been settled. Glen Sather had failed in his efforts to land Luc Robitaille for the Oilers, and so was forced to settle for 55-goal scorer Jimmy Carson, along with the Kings' first-round draft picks in 1989, 1991 and 1993 (staggered, as per Gretzky's suggestion, to prevent hobbling the franchise in the short term). He also acquired a blue-chip prospect, Martin Gélinas, the Kings' first round pick, chosen seventh overall in the 1988 draft. Coming to Edmonton along with Gretzky were the two players he had specifically requested, Marty McSorley (who would continue to act as his personal protector on the ice, the same way Dave Semenko once had) and Mike Krushelnyski.

Gretzky arrived at the airport, bleary-eyed from lack of sleep, and realized immediately that he'd forgotten something. The gravity of the announcement required a certain formality. He needed to look his best, but in his haste he hadn't remembered to pack a necktie. With the jet warming up on the tarmac, McNall called Goodman in Toronto, who had been up most of the night, and who was still in the process of putting the finishing touches on Pocklington's speech before heading for the airport and his own flight to Edmonton. Now, as if he needed it, the big day's stage manager was given one more task.

"Wayne doesn't have a tie," McNall told him. "Can you do something about that?"

"Don't worry," Goodman said. "I'll take care of it. There will be a tie waiting for him at the airport in Edmonton."

The flight north, as McNall remembers it, was quiet, subdued and "a little surreal." It was just the two of them on the jet, and neither was in much of a mood for conversation. Both were sleep-deprived, and both were a bit nervous about what was to come. Gretzky spent some time trying to contact a few of his teammates in order to break the news personally, with limited success. He talked to McNall about making changes with the Kings, about the new uniforms that they would soon be unveiling, about creating a winning attitude around the franchise, about how many tickets they were going to sell.

"What do you think it's going to be like in Edmonton?" McNall asked him at one point during the trip.

"It's going to be a zoo," Gretzky said, because he knew.

Mike Barnett met them at the airport with a car, and they then picked up Gretzky's financial advisor, Ian Barrigan. There was talk of heading to Pocklington's office, but Gretzky asked to be taken to his condominium instead. Though time was short, he wanted to contact some people—foremost among them his teammate Mark Messier—and explain to them personally what was happening and why before heading to their date at Molson House. (Pocklington had, in fact, phoned Messier the night before to tell him about the trade.) En route, Barnett relayed a phone conversation he'd had with Pocklington. As Barnett remembers it, the Oilers' owner had called him at his office and asked if he had a fax machine handy. "I've got to fax you Wayne's speech," he said.

"I don't think he needs a speech, Peter," Barnett said. "He's going to speak from his heart."

"Well, he's got one, and we'll give it to you when you get there because there are some points he's got to touch on, points that Bruce and I agreed on."

Those points? That the trade had been all Gretzky's idea, that Pocklington was merely acceding to his wishes, that for personal and professional reasons, Wayne wanted to leave Edmonton and the Oilers for Los Angeles. Barnett says that during the negotiations he had caught sight of a document in Pocklington's possession detailing the particulars of the trade. Written across the bottom in ink were the words, "Wayne will take the heat." He believed Pocklington and McNall had agreed to a strategy that would provide public-relations cover in Edmonton by casting Gretzky against type as the bad guy.

(Here we enter a historical grey area, more than twenty years after the fact. Gretzky, in his autobiography, mentions being asked to read from a script, and says he became infuriated when Goodman—whom he refers to only as a "public-relations pest"—tried to coach him on what to say. McNall tells the same story. When the time came, Gretzky certainly seemed to be working from a prepared text. But it was Goodman who wrote Pocklington's speech. It figures that if Pocklington had demanded a script for Gretzky, Goodman would have been asked to write it. Goodman says unequivocally that he wasn't. "I never wrote a speech for him, I never wrote a draft for him. I never gave him anything.")

Whatever he had agreed to, whatever the truth of the phantom speech, something stoked Gretzky's emotions that day. Perhaps it was that one last twist from an owner whom he had once liked and admired very much, and had now come to despise. Perhaps it was also the sentimental return to familiar ground, the final realization that Edmonton and everything it had represented in his life was finished. Perhaps it was talking to teammates, and knowing that the old gang was splintering, that graduation day loomed.

By the time he phoned Pocklington's office from his apartment, demanding to talk to Goodman and no one else, Gretzky was angry and upset, and Goodman's plan for a calm, neat and tidy announcement was already headed off the rails.

"I don't think I want to do this news conference," Gretzky said. "I want to hold my own."

Goodman, though he had never met Gretzky, understood immediately how agitated he was—and understood that instead of managing the carefully choreographed event he had imagined, he was now in fact in the business of crisis management. He tried to calm Gretzky down, reminding him that the joint press conference was part of the agreement between McNall and Pocklington, suggesting that maybe he ought to come over to the office and talk it over in person. Gretzky flatly refused.

How about if we meet you at Molson House a little bit early? Goodman suggested. We'll sit down there and work it out. With Barnett and McNall and Barrigan encouraging him at the other end, Gretzky reluctantly agreed on one condition: if he wasn't going to be allowed to hold a separate news conference, then McNall had to be right there on the stage with him. It wouldn't just be him and Pocklington and Sather.

Everyone agreed that would be fine.

Goodman had a potentially volatile situation on his hands. Gretzky, with words or gestures, by simply raising an eyebrow at the right/wrong time, could make things extremely uncomfortable for Pocklington. If there was any hint that the Oilers' owner was driven by his own selfish motives, the entire city—the entire country— would have their villain. That was one ticking time bomb. Then there was the issue of Glen Sather's state of mind. It didn't take Goodman long to understand that here was another extremely unhappy camper.

What was eating Sather wasn't just that he hadn't been consulted from the beginning—that he been caught at least partially unawares by the trade, and that he hadn't even been able to make the best hockey deal possible in a very bad situation. There was also the question of the future—his future, his team's future—which for the Edmonton Oilers wouldn't be the storybook tale of the recent past.

The perfect hockey team was starting to fray at the edges even before Pocklington made the decision that Gretzky had to go. Now that process would accelerate. It had as much to do with larger forces in play, with the evolution of the National Hockey League in particular and professional sports in general, as it did with the owner's personal financial challenges. For years, the Oilers had lived something of a charmed existence. While player salaries increased around the league, while agents and the Players' Association pushed as hard as they could to allow a limited free market for talent, in Edmonton there wasn't much talk about money in the dressing room. As they were wrapping up a fourth Stanley Cup in five years, nearly all of the players—including Gretzky—had to know that they could be making more money elsewhere, that in a larger city with a wealthier owner they might be able to sign a contract for something approaching their true value and spin off extra income through endorsement deals. There was certainly some grumbling about that, and growing signs of rebellion. But with the exception of Coffey, who played out an ugly contract dispute with Sather before finally being traded to the Pittsburgh Penguins in 1987, the boys' club remained intact. By and large, the rest of the Oilers liked playing in Edmonton, they liked winning, and for the most part they liked each other. They were in a bubble, really, a sort of shinny Shangri-La. And now that bubble would surely burst.

Sather was going to lose his best player—not to mention the best player in the world—and even if the draft picks and talent coming back from the Kings proved useful, it wouldn't be the same. There would be disenchantment in the room. They'd all want to get paid now. They'd grow cynical. They'd see the owner for what he was. And when it came time to compete for their services, Edmonton couldn't—or at least it couldn't if Pocklington used that fifteen million to enrich himself and solve some of his other problems rather than reinvesting it in the hockey team. Sather had started to see all of that writing on the wall, and now seemed on the verge of boiling over, of telling the world exactly what he thought. Though he said he was prepared to swallow hard and stick with Pocklington, stick with the team he'd built and play the good soldier, Goodman felt there was every possibility that, at some point during the press conference, he might be provoked and go off—which wouldn't be in anyone's interest. Better to let him say his piece in a controlled situation, then get him off the stage.

"I think Glen should speak," Goodman suggested, "just so that everybody is protected here. Peter speaks first, and then Wayne, and then Glen." But not for long. And there wouldn't be any lingering afterwards, there wouldn't be any free-form conversations with reporters. They'd get the message across, smile their forced smiles and then get the heck out of there before the story they were trying to tell began to unravel.

Goodman, Sather and Pocklington arrived at Molson House first and, seeing the crowd of reporters and cameramen beginning to assemble, understood immediately that this was a level of media madness they had never experienced before. They slipped into an adjoining building, safely out of sight, and waited for Gretzky to arrive. When he rolled in, with Barnett, McNall, Barrigan and his brother Glen in tow, the temperature of the room instantly dropped several degrees. McNall pulled Goodman aside. "I didn't realize it was going to turn into what it turned into," he said apologetically. (In fact, McNall says that he felt uncomfortable throughout the entire process—or at least until the roadshow returned to his home turf in Los Angeles. "I was the man cheating with another guy's wife," McNall says. "I always felt a little bit guilty.")

Sather took Gretzky into a back room, away from the others. It was there that he made his final pitch. He said that he'd be happy to kill the deal then and there. That if Gretzky wanted to stay, he'd make it happen, he'd threaten to quit and force Pocklington to back off—and if Pocklington said no, they could walk out on the Oilers together. (McNall, standing outside, says that he was worried that Sather might somehow succeed—at least until Gretzky emerged and gave him a reassuring wink.) It was a fraught conversation, and the first tears flowed, but the truth was, Sather and Gretzky had their own issues as well, a growing-apart that perhaps was a natural offshoot of Gretzky's maturation, of evolving from boy to man. Both, whatever romantic thoughts might have crossed their minds about pulling back from the brink, had to understand the inevitability of what was about to take place. Pocklington eventually chimed in as well, though perhaps not entirely sincerely. He told Gretzky that he'd call it off if that was what Gretzky really wanted. Things

Gretzky, age 13, meeting Jean Beliveau at the Quebec City peewee tournament. (1974: *Journal de Quebec*/The Canadian Press)

Gretzky in Brantford jersey on the backyard rink. (Gretzky Family/ Hockey Hall of Fame)

Gretzky, 17, with Nelson Skalbania, owner of the WHA's Indianapolis Racers, after signing his first professional contract, June 1978. (1978: The Canadian Press)

Gretzky playing with Ontario jun¡ All Stars in 1978. (Robert Shav Hall of Fame)

Gretzky during his short stint with the Racers, 1978. (Graphic Artists/Hockey Hall of Fame)

Signing away his hockey life to Peter Pocklington via a twenty-one year personal services contract. (*Edmonton Journal*)

Gretzky with the Oilers in the early 1980s: note his eyes are not on the puck but where he wants the puck to go. (O-Pee-Chee Hockey Hall of Fame)

Vikki Moss with Gretzky. (The Canadian Press/Dave Buston)

Gretzky surrounded by fellow Oilers after winning the 1988 Stanley Cup, the last time that team would be together. With him are Glen Sather, Charlie Huddy, Peter Pocklington, Mark Messier, John Muckler and Grant Fuhr. (Paul Bereswill/Hockey Hall of Fame)

Gretzky in action on the ice during his first Stanley Cup finals in 1983, with Butch Goring of the New York Islanders. (Paul Bereswill/Hockey Hall of Fame)

Gretzky married his girlfriend Janet Jones on July 16, 1988, just weeks before he was traded to the L.A. Kings. (The Canadian Press/Dave Buston)

Gretzky's tears. (The Canadian Press/Ray Giguere)

Jeff Goodman, Peter Pocklington and Gretzky at the press conference that changed everything, August 9, 1988. (Doug MacLellan/Hockey Hall of Fame)

The reaction in Edmonton: Gretzky following Janet out of town. (*Edmonton Sun* cartoon, August 10, 1988)

Gretzky with L.A. Kings owner Bruce McNall on August 10, 1988, the day after the trade was announced. (The Canadian Press/Reed Saxon)

The Last Perfect Moment (II): the captains, Gretzky and Doug Gilmour.
(HHOF)

John Candy, Gretzky and McNall,
the new owners of the Toronto
Argonauts football team, in 1991 with
Raghib "Rocket" Ismail.
(The Canadian Press/Hans Deryk)

Bruce McNall leaves a California
courthouse after pleading guilty to
four federal felony charges that he
defrauded banks in a criminal
conspiracy, 1995. (The Canadian
Press/Brennan Linsley)

Gretzky and Mark Messier on *Late Night with David Letterman* just before Gretzky's first game as a New York Ranger in 1997. (The Canadian Press/Alan Singer)

Gretzky retires, but no tears this time, on April 18, 1999. (The Canadian Press/Paul Chaisson)

The 1909 baseball card picturing the legendary Honus Wagner bought by Bruce McNall and Wayne Gretzky for $451,000 in 1991. They sold it four years later for $500,000. (CP photo/AP photo/Kathy Willens–files)

Gretzky is inducted into the Hockey Hall of Fame in November 1999. In the middle is former referee-in-chief Scotty Morrison, and on his left is referee Andy Van Hellemond. (Dave Sandford/ Hockey Hall of Fame)

Gretzky as coach and part owner of the Phoenix Coyotes with the team's GM—and his former agent—Mike Barnett and draft pick Peter Mueller in 2006. (The Canadian Press/Chuck Stoody)

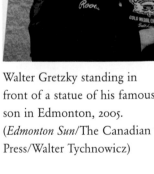

Walter Gretzky standing in front of a statue of his famous son in Edmonton, 2005. (*Edmonton Sun*/The Canadian Press/Walter Tychnowicz)

Gretzky coaching in Phoenix. (The Canadian Press/Ross D. Franklin)

could just go back to being the way they were. Those words had to ring particularly hollow.

They couldn't. It was all over. The die was cast.

"It's too late now," Gretzky said. "I can't come back."

Meanwhile, the crowd at Molson House was starting to get a bit restless. Forty-five minutes had elapsed since the announced start time. They hadn't heard a thing, hadn't seen any of the principals, hadn't even been handed a press release as would have been the standard practice. That was in part because of the last-minute histrionics, because of Sather's final plea and Gretzky's final acceptance of his fate, followed by everyone taking a few moments to put on their game faces and putting on the show as planned. But it was also because Pocklington was still waiting for a phone call. There would be no press conference until the money was in the bank. Only when the call came did he give Goodman the go ahead. The group walked outside, into the bright sunlight, and then into Molson House proper with all of the solemnity of a funeral procession.

(It felt, *Edmonton Journal* writer Jim Matheson remembers, "like someone was about to take the *Mona Lisa* off your wall.")

In Brantford, Walter and Phyllis Gretzky sat in front of the TV, anxiously waiting for the press conference to begin, while at Alan Thicke's house in Los Angeles, Janet Jones and Craig Simpson were trying to find some way to follow the events in Edmonton. (Simpson had awakened that morning to find Gretzky already gone. "It's done," Janet told him. "He already left.") Canadian television would be going live, but any American coverage would wait for Gretzky's arrival in California later that day. Jones called the Gretzky family home in Brantford, and there Walter held the phone up to his television set so that she could listen in while sitting outside by the pool.

Goodman sits down in front of the bank of microphones and immediately apologizes for the delay. Before Gretzky, Pocklington and Sather settle in at the table (with McNall, Barnett, Barrigan and a few others tucked in behind them), he explains how the event will proceed. "You have to appreciate that unfortunately we're under a time constraint because people have to get back to Los Angeles," Goodman says. He is wearing big, wire-rimmed aviator glasses, the style of the moment. "So we will not be allowing any scrums afterwards."

There is a grain of truth in that: they did have to take the whole roadshow back to Los Angeles later that day. But the time constraints are mostly arbitrary, designed to control the message. They'd get in, get out, limit any possibility for improvisation, severely curtail any questions from the floor, keep everyone on message and on schedule and hope to escape a very difficult day unscathed.

Gretzky takes off his jacket, leaving him in shirt and tie. He looks directly into Metz's camera and gives him a quick, though somewhat forlorn, thumbs up. For a guy who has been in the public eye so long and so often, who has learned to live under the brightest lights, he seems remarkably uncomfortable. He runs his hand through his hair repeatedly, bites his lip, sighs, stares at the ceiling, fidgets.

Pocklington moves to the microphone. He looks impossibly well groomed, every whisker in place, seems appropriately sombre, projects an air of gravitas. He speaks extemporaneously for only a few seconds.

"Ladies and gentlemen, first of all thank you kindly for coming out to this conference. Before I begin, it's been an emotional two or three days—possibly two or three weeks, but mainly in the last two or three days for Wayne and myself and Glen. . . ."

Then Pocklington looks down, starts reading Goodman's script and begins the performance of his life.

> . . . and it's with mixed emotions, a heavy heart for our community and our hockey club, but I guess with delight and sincere best wishes for Wayne Gretzky, that I announce—and I guess, more important, confirm—that the Edmonton Oilers have agreed to trade Wayne Gretzky to Los Angeles.
>
> Glen Sather will discuss the specifics with you in a few moments. However, since this hockey trade is of such magnitude, I felt it

imperative for me as the owner of the Oilers to explain to our city and the many devoted Oiler fans in this city and across Canada the reasons behind it.

First, I would like to tell Wayne on behalf of the Oilers how we appreciated all that he has done, not only for the hockey club but for our city. Because of Wayne, the Oilers have been compared to a dynasty. Our city has been known throughout North America. Wayne, you have served Edmonton as a model citizen and especially as a role model for our young people and as our city's greatest ambassador. Your natural instincts and talents and skills on the ice have thrilled and awed us. We are not replacing Wayne Gretzky in this trade. You cannot replace Wayne Gretzky.

I'd like to clarify that some of the details of this trade were not completed until the wee hours of this morning. And the media can take credit for forcing us to move more quickly than anticipated. Although the speculation has been going on for the last two or three weeks, it was impossible to confirm anything to any of you. You have been friends of Glen and mine for the past twelve or thirteen years. So rather than trying to confirm or deny, we tried to stay at a distance. Because of this, I have been unavailable for comment and wouldn't respond to any media calls. I do not believe in misleading the public and I would not have been able to answer the questions in a forthright manner until now.

As well, I'm sure you appreciate this, so many people are affected by this trade, it would have been inconsiderate if not foolish to reveal any facts until the appropriate people were notified and all of the details finalized. This deal was consummated by the owner of the Los Angeles Kings, Bruce McNall, and myself. And I had the expert advice of our president—in fact, my best friend, Glen Sather—in putting it together.

Perhaps he feels Sather's eyes burning a hole in the back of his head, perhaps he understands that he's now cast Sather as his willing accomplice, which surely raises Glen's hackles. Pocklington pauses for a moment, looks up from the sheets of paper in his hands and tries to make it right.

"Glen denied knowing anything of the deal as far as was it completed or not. In fact he was telling the truth. He did not know until roughly a day or so that in fact the deal had been 99 per cent completed."

So his team president and hockey guru/"best friend" had been left in the dark? Some smart guy in the audience would have jumped on that revelation immediately, had it not been for the high drama to come.

Pocklington then returns to his script . . .

As all of you are aware, Wayne was married this summer to a very special young woman. Anyone involved in a committed relationship who wants to have a family knows that changes and change are brought about by marriage. This is why, despite a tremendous amount of trepidation, I truly understood when Wayne approached me and asked to be traded—asked himself to be traded—to the Los Angeles Kings. He wants to spend more time with Janet and begin their family life under one roof and one city and be able to call it home.

Let's face it. Despite the obvious pluses, it is not the easiest thing in the world to be Mr. and Mrs. Wayne Gretzky. There are numerous encroachments on time and tremendous outside pressures to start a new marriage. As well—being a hockey player involves a lot of time and travel. The best comparisons I can draw to this situation are these. What to do when an outstanding, loyal employee approaches you as an employer and asks for an opportunity to move along for logical and understandable reasons. In an emotional sense, you know you don't want to lose him. But at the same time, you don't want to stop him from pursuing his dreams and achieving his goals. Wayne has given so much to our hockey club and to this city for the past decade I believe he has earned the right to determine his own destiny in the National Hockey League.

The situation also might be compared to a son or daughter advising their parents of their desire to leave the house to go to university or to take a job. Your heart says no, but at the same time your head understands and says yes. This is not the first time there have been trade discussions involving Wayne. The Los Angeles Kings and numerous others have been trying to acquire him for years, first through Jerry Buss and later through Bruce McNall. As well, a few months ago the Vancouver Canucks, through a Vancouver business-man, offered to pay many times as much as we are receiving from the Kings. The deal was refused. But situations, circumstances and directions have changed dramatically. Wayne has a new life and Bruce McNall's sincerity has convinced me that Wayne would be welcome, received and treated with the same warmth he received in Edmonton. Taking all of this into consideration, I have put aside my emotions, and out of deep personal respect for Wayne I made a decision based more on Wayne the person than Wayne the hockey player. I believe this is why this trade has taken so much longer to complete than most. And I don't mind telling you that when Bruce McNall approached me and asked what it would take to get Wayne to Los Angeles, I asked for the entire Kings franchise and an option on Jerry Buss's Lakers.

Therefore, if my fellow Edmontonians are upset about this, I understand. But I ask you to view this trade the same way Wayne asked me to view his request to be traded. I will conclude by expressing to Wayne in no uncertain terms my personal gratitude for the eleven tremendous and glorious years he has played hockey for the Oilers in the city of Edmonton. I believe I know the people of Edmonton well enough to say that they will join me in wishing you, Wayne, the best of luck. Except, of course, when you come back to play the Oilers. I know that there are millions of Canadians across this country, Wayne, who also wish you the best. Your move to Los Angeles will not only be a tremendous boost to hockey in that city but in the entire United States—but of long-lasting benefit to the National Hockey League as well. Wayne, good luck. You've made an awful lot of friendships in this city.

Pocklington, through Goodman's words, has hit the important talking points. It was all Gretzky's idea. He had resisted overtures to trade him in the past, but this time could not stand in the way of his loyal employee's wishes for self-improvement and advancement

—and, of course, family happiness. By implication, he suggested that perhaps Janet was pulling strings behind the scenes, delicately tossing her under the bus. There was an acknowledgement of the broken-hearted fans, whom he'd soon enough be asking to buy tickets for his Gretzky-less team. He made the kid-leaving-home analogy, and attempted a bit of levity with the line about the Lakers. And not a single mention of money. Down the road, sports owners, when it suits them, will feel no shame in pleading poverty with the fans, but Pocklington can't play that card right now.

He finishes up in his own words, off the cuff, adding a personal touch, one from the heart, and sounds very much like he means it.

"I told Wayne earlier—and that's why we were late—it was an emotional parting with Wayne and also with Glen. It's like losing a son. He's been more than a hockey player to me. It's with deep emotion that I had to have this press conference. Thank you very much."

Now it is Gretzky's turn to talk, though he seems surprised when summoned to the mike. "I didn't know I was next," he says, which is supposed to come off as a light-hearted aside, but because of his grim countenance seems nothing of the sort. His hair is very blonde, his eyes very blue in the glare of the television lights. There's less of the kid about him than there was in those Stanley Cup–winning moments a few weeks back. Gretzky is outwardly calm as he begins speaking.

> First of all, I would like to thank everyone for coming. The last three weeks have been a whirlwind for myself and for my new wife. I think, first of all, I want to apologize to my friend Jim Taylor in front of everyone. He's been more aware of the situation than probably I have. But as Mr. Pocklington says, circumstances forced things to be moved up and hurried along. I approached Mr. Pocklington and talked to Mr. Pocklington about the possibility of playing for another hockey club. I felt at the time that my career now, after ten years in Edmonton, that at this point in time I was still young enough and capable enough of helping a new franchise win a Stanley Cup. I talked to Mr. McNall when Mr. Pocklington

met my request and let Mr. McNall talk to me directly. And I chatted to Mr. McNall. After spending some time with him, I decided that for the benefit of Wayne Gretzky, my new wife, and our expected child in the new year it would be beneficial for everyone involved to let me play with the Los Angeles Kings. I'm disappointed about having to leave Edmonton. I truly admire all of the fans and respect everyone over the years.

Aside from the slight detour of the Jim Taylor reference, Gretzky certainly begins as though happy to play along. (Taylor, the long-time Vancouver sports columnist, was especially close to Gretzky's father, Walter, and through him—they were collaborating on a book—had stumbled onto what could have been the scoop of his career. But, out of loyalty to the Gretzkys, Taylor chose to sit on the story instead, spurring plenty of debate among his journalistic colleagues about whether that was the right thing to do.) It was all his idea. The trade was driven by his ambitions. And there is a bit of personal news there, heretofore known only to true Gretzky intimates: Janet is pregnant.

It couldn't have been as striking in the moment as in hindsight, but contrast all of those Elvis-like, über-humble "misters" with the fact that Gretzky speaks about himself in the third person.

He continues. The mention of leaving Edmonton obviously strikes an emotional chord. Gretzky isn't visibly weeping at first, though he begins dabbing at his eyes.

But . . .

More eye-dabbing. You can hear the camera shutters whirring like a swarm of cicadas in the background, and see the flashes lighting his face again and again. Gretzky's tears. The money shot. He is drying his eyes. He takes a drink of water. He beckons to Goodman, asking for a tissue. More shutters, more eye-dabbing, more water.

Smiling through the tears.

Coming back . . .

That is, coming back emotionally, ready to go on. . . . A deep sigh.

So, as I said . . .

A big sniff. Wiping his eyes. Wiping his nose.

I promised Mess I wouldn't do this . . .

The absent Messier. There's not another hockey player in the room. Just a bunch of guys in business suits. The end of the band of brothers.

But, um, as I said, there comes a time when, when, uh . . .

He is crying now. Barnett walks up behind Gretzky, leans in and whispers in his ear. Tells him he doesn't have to continue, that he can stop if he wants to. "You don't have to do this. You don't have to put yourself through this." Pocklington looks on, as though paralyzed. "I made a terrible mistake by not going over and putting my arm around him and saying to the press, 'Wayne, if you don't want this to go ahead, the deal is off,'" he will say years later. Would that have changed anything? Not a chance.

The image carries more weight than anything any of them says. It is the picture that will appear in newspapers all around the world, the video that will pop up on every newscast. In other places, it's a curiosity—that famous hockey player got traded, and apparently isn't too happy about it. In Canada, those images speak to far more than that: to innocence lost and birthright sold, American imperialism and a fragile national culture, cold-hearted capitalism trumping shinny idealism.

Gretzky says he wants to go, and they're all saying it is for the greater good. So many others have headed south for fame and fortune, so it can't be such a shock.

Why, then, is he crying? Why this sinking feeling that we just got fooled again?

Gretzky stands up without saying another word, leaves the table, moves to one of the seats set up behind it, sits head in hand, weeping, and the audience breaks into spontaneous applause (Goodman vigorously, visibly, is doing his best to lead the claps). Journalists aren't supposed to do that; no cheering in the press box, no rooting interest allowed, but here that line is crossed.

Now it is Glen Sather's turn to speak. He is grim and to the point.

I don't want to try to philosophize on what's happened, because I don't think we can justify the reasons why this has happened. But we're all trying to do something that's good for Wayne, the Edmonton Oilers, for the National Hockey League. We all would like to be proud of what we do for a living. I think you can see here today the reason we won four Stanley Cups is because of the emotion we displayed for each other. It's genuine, and in a couple of days I know that we'll adjust to it. And I'm going to work my hardest to try and find a way to kick the hell out of the Los Angeles Kings. But right now I feel a lot of empathy for Wayne and what he's going through. I guess I've seen him play more than anyone and gone through all of the ups and down with him more than anyone alive. It's tough. That's what sports are all about.

We think what's happening here is going to keep us where we have been for a long time—at the top of the National Hockey League. It's not going to be easy. I know that the fellows that are coming here are going to try and work and the fellows that are remaining are going to try and work as hard as they can. We'll all make some adjustments and we'll get on and we'll be successful. But it will be a hell of a lot tougher than it has been in the past playing against Los Angeles with Wayne and Mr. McNall.

Everything changes. We all get older. We all have more demands on our lives. It's a boy's game that men try to play. This is the tough part of it. So I think from my staff and the Edmonton Oilers and everyone that's involved with our hockey club, we wish Wayne well and Bruce well, and like Peter said, only until they play against us. It's going to be one hell of a season.

That last line doesn't come off as a call to arms. There's not a hint of excitement or expectation. The anger, the bitterness, the resignation in his voice is unmistakable.

And that is where most memories of the fateful day begin and end, with Gretzky's tears, of course, and perhaps Pocklington's attempts at self-justification, but not much more, beyond the shock of it all. Largely lost to history were the moments that immediately followed.

Goodman steps forward to direct the question-and-answer session, making it clear again that it will be short, that no one will be lingering afterward, that the press will be escorted out at the conclusion, and so this is it, their only chance to ask a question, in a stilted, public forum, eliminating the possibility of any quiet asides to trusted pals.

It is a very different show than what preceded it, featuring a very different Wayne Gretzky. Just moments later, he is no longer crying, no longer despondent. His eyes dry, he stares straight ahead. His answers are assured, his intent clear. He is not a pawn, but a player. He is focused in a way that great athletes are when, following a moment of adversity, the game must go on.

Sather begins by laying out the details of the trade—the hockey part, not the money part—which, in the belated haste to get the conference started, had never actually been discussed. Now the probing begins.

First question: Mr. Pocklington, didn't you once use Wayne Gretzky's contract as collateral for a loan, and is this deal somehow linked to your personal finances?

"First of all, it isn't correct, and second, it's basically private business."

Second question, from a reporter at the *Edmonton Sun*, Graham Hicks, whom Gretzky obviously doesn't much like (he has always been extremely aware of what was written about him, and by whom): Could Janet not have moved to Edmonton? (The first invocation of the spirit of Yoko Ono.)

Gretzky, in answering, is absolutely composed—if anything, a little chilly.

"Sure. That would have been no problem at all. I think it was your article that said we weren't going to have kids. I guess we've proved that theory wrong. Janet was and is one hundred per cent behind whatever I decided to do. After playing nine years in Edmonton, to meet someone—no one was going to tell you to leave a Stanley Cup team four years out of five, a place that you really enjoy, a community you're involved with and in. Her ambition now is to raise a family, and she would have had a tremendous amount of fun raising a family in Edmonton. This was my decision that I made. I probably had some people that work with me that I kept in the dark a little bit too much. But this was my own gut feeling. This was my decision. This wasn't Mr. Barnett's or Mr. Barrigan's or Janet's or my father's. It was something that I felt would benefit myself and as I said my family now. The Oilers are a great team with or without Wayne Gretzky. We need the Los Angeles Kings in the NHL, and hopefully I can go down there and inspire and get some enthusiasm and a winning attitude that I don't think they've had in twenty years—with Marty and Krushelnyski, and put that in their locker room. Hopefully, we can be a contender for the Stanley Cup. I told Slats I'd tell those guys to make sure they finished first because we don't want to play them in the first round. That was why I made the decision. But if I wanted to stay in Edmonton, that was totally up to me also."

Third question: Pocklington is asked directly if there was money involved in the deal.

"Yes, there was some financial consideration."

Would he care to specify how much?

"No, I wouldn't."

Fourth question: How important was the money in his decision? (Now it's getting interesting.)

"I guess when we were faced with the fact that the inevitable might happen, it then becomes a business transaction. I had to do what was best for the Edmonton Oilers in the short term and in the long term."

The reporter follows up. Surely that unspecified amount of cash wouldn't just be good for the Oilers? Wouldn't it also improve your overall financial health?

"I guess it would allow me to buy another company or two. But it has nothing to do with the financial success, or lack of it, with the Edmonton Oilers."

Another company or two. There's Peter Pocklington in a nutshell.

Goodman, sensing that his client is being forced into an uncomfortable corner, tries to move things along, to change the direction by intervening, looking for a different interlocutor.

Fifth question: Wayne, you have four years left on your Oilers contract. Would you like to renegotiate your deal when you get to Los Angeles?

Gretzky looks back at McNall, and for the first time during the proceedings, laughs out loud.

"Yeah. I just want to say that . . . how awfully disappointed I am at leaving, as I showed. But the great news is I'm hooking up with a great man and an outstanding individual. I'll let him answer that.

"Right now, my contract is four years. I guess I get an automatic raise because it's American money now. Other than that, we're going to sit down with Mr. Barrigan and myself and Mr. Barnett and Mr. McNall. We'll worry about that bridge. But right now I'm happy with what I have."

McNall steps to the microphone and speaks for the only time.

"Obviously, this series of events came about rather quickly. We haven't had the opportunity yet to really get into that issue. I'm happy with Wayne's present contract. I would like to consult with Wayne and his associates about what they would like. We're going to accommodate whatever Wayne would like to have in that respect and see if we can make everybody happy."

Sixth question: When did Gretzky decide he wanted to move to L.A.?

"I'm not exactly sure when it came into my mind. Everyone likes to be there when everything is rosy and nice. Right now, the Edmonton Oilers are sitting pretty nicely. They have the best team in the National Hockey League. As I said, because of my contract only lasting for four more years and knowing that at the age of thirty-one, I may test the free-agent market. At the age of thirty-one is a lot different than twenty-seven. I felt in my own heart that maybe I could help a team achieve a Stanley Cup or help them get to a Stanley Cup at twenty-seven. I felt if I was ever going to make that move it had to be now and not at thirty-one."

Seventh question: Did McNall offer him a piece of the Kings?

"I hope." He's laughing again. "No. As Mr. McNall said, when I talked to Mr. McNall and he advised me that there was a deal pending, that I said to him that right now the four years, we'd have to sit down and talk to my business people and go from there. Really, a whole lot has not been said."

Eighth question—well, not a question at all, really. One of the photographers in the room thanks Gretzky for all those great pictures he's provided over the years. Jim Matheson remembers a moan from the reporters at that point—understanding that one of their precious opportunities had just been squandered.

Ninth question: What does Gretzky think he can do for the NHL by playing in Los Angeles?

"Well, first of all let me say that I was very disappointed to hear that the NHL lost the agreement with ESPN. I think ESPN was a tremendous backer of the National Hockey League. I think that we have taken a step or two backwards. I think that the Los Angeles Kings are important to the National Hockey League and to this division. This division with Edmonton, Vancouver and Winnipeg and Calgary—we need Los Angeles, we need Seattle, we need San Francisco. We need hockey in this part of the world. Hockey is strong in Canada. It will always be our number one sport. We need to help create that interest and that atmosphere in the United States. Hopefully I can be a small part of that. And hopefully, as I said, with Marty and Mike Krushelnyski, who are great role players and great team players—who I feel this team are going to miss as much as Wayne Gretzky–can bring to that Los Angeles Kings locker room and to that team and hopefully help make that a winning atmosphere."

(The NHL losing a contract with ESPN? Funny that: the more things change . . .)

Goodman advises that only two more questions will be allowed.

Tenth question: How does it feel leaving his Oiler teammates behind?

"Well, that will be the hardest part. You can't replace the talent that they have and the friendship that we all have as a group. But as Slats said, players come and they go. It's the hardest part of hockey. We were all devastated to see Paul Coffey go last year. We were all devastated when Willy Lindström left. When Lee Fogolin left it was tough. It's tough for everybody, but life goes on. This team is too good not to stay strong. With leaders like Messier and Lowe and Fuhr, they're fine. What I have to do is stay positive and go down with those other two guys to L.A. and make hockey special to those players and make those players have a winning feeling and a winning attitude. Hopefully, for what I think is the good of hockey, we can bring a Stanley Cup to Los Angeles."

It was the subject of his teammates, the thought of breaking up the old Edmonton gang, that had brought Gretzky to tears a few minutes before. Now he is calm and rational and business-like.

Eleventh question: more about Janet's pregnancy.

"We are definitely going to have a family in the new year. My family and Janet's family are the only people that knew during the wedding. But we are definitely going to have a family in the new year, which we both wanted extremely badly since we got engaged last January. Sometime in the new year–we don't know officially, we'll know in a couple of weeks. We're both extremely excited. We both have had pretty happy and successful careers. I think we're as much excited about this as about this as anything we've done in our lives."

Goodman, a softie–or at least, showing his roots as an ex-reporter–breaks down and allows one final question, the twelfth. What does Gretzky consider the highlight of his Edmonton career?

Earlier in the day, that kind of inquiry surely would have sent Gretzky's emotions spinning. But he's gone now. He's all gone.

"Oh, I've got a flight to catch."

It feels like he's already on that plane.

"We had a lot of great memories. To say one would be too hard. I think the first Stanley Cup."

The final answer, Wayne Gretzky's final statement at his farewell press conference in Edmonton, is absolutely perfunctory.

Goodman has planned for the question-and-answer session to last for ten minutes. It stretches to just over twelve. The whole show has been wrapped up inside a half-hour. All things considered, he figures it's gone awfully well.

A single, stray, angry black cloud sailed over Edmonton that afternoon. It blew over the Northlands Coliseum, stirring up winds so strong they knocked down tents set up outside for a trade show. Dan Craig, who would go on to a job supervising ice making for the entire NHL, was working at the nearby Agricom that day and had taken a break to watch the press conference on television. He saw the strange little storm fly by, and remembers that it was as if the wind was blowing right into the rink just as Gretzky began crying.

Don Metz had stopped telling the story. People kept looking at him like he was crazy. But then one day, years later, he was talking to Craig and they compared notes, and it all made sense.

When Gretzky moved to the microphone, when the tears started flowing, Ken Chilibeck, the TSN reporter, looked over at Metz and asked, "Are you rolling?" Of course he was rolling. By reflex, he looked at the second camera, shooting wide from the back of the room. Everyone in the place was staring forward, fixed on Gretzky—everyone except Metz. He made eye contact with the other cameraman, gave him a nod to indicate that they both had the shot, then looked past him, through the open door.

Outside, rain was pelting down, and the bright blue sky had turned dark as night.

What he thought about in the moment was the fact that their satellite truck was now likely mired in mud. It would be a mess now, hauling the gear back and forth.

What he thought about later was the poetry of it all. When Gretzky, too distraught to continue, stepped back from the microphone and dried his tears, Metz looked outside once again. Now the sun was shining, as brightly as before, and whatever rain had hit the ground was evaporating into thin air. It was as if the storm had never happened at all.

Chapter Ten

BREACH OF FAITH

N o, NOT EVERYONE CRIED along with Wayne Gretzky—at least not in the beginning, at least not in the first twenty-four hours after it happened, at least not outside of Edmonton. In other places, with other agendas, even in other hockey-loving Canadian cities, the citizens didn't automatically rise in a great rebellion. Instead, a lot of people believed what Gretzky said, because why would The Great One lie? They reasoned that Los Angeles might indeed be a better place for him, for his wife, for his child on the way. And, being human, they also thought about themselves, their teams, how it might not be such a bad thing for the best player in the game to be somewhere other than with the powerhouse Oilers. *Gretzky Heading for Hollywood? Great!* That was one of the headlines in Vancouver (as was *Canucks Were Used to Raise Gretzky Ante—Griffith Says*, a reference to Nelson Skalbania's failed scheme to bring Gretzky there, which was slowly becoming public knowledge). In Winnipeg, the papers said *Trade Benefit to Jets' Bankroll* and *Jets Lost Bid to Land Gretzky*. So it could have been better—we could have had him (as if). And it could have been worse—he could have stayed in Edmonton and stood in the way of any chance we had of winning the Stanley Cup for many years to come. (That the forces the Gretzky deal had set in motion would eventually cost Winnipeg its NHL team naturally hadn't dawned on anyone, and wouldn't for quite some time.)

In Calgary, the great rival down the road, where the Oilers and their Stanley Cups, the Eskimos and their Grey Cups, and Gretzky himself represented the only bragging counterpoint to the money, the glitz, the postcard mountain backdrop *and* the Olympics, the city's glee could hardly be contained:

> *Tearful Gretzky Now a King*
> *Edmonton in Shock; Flames Fans Rejoice*
> *Flames Cup Hopes Are Given a Boost*

In Ottawa, New Democrat member of Parliament Nelson Riis issued a press release, suggesting with tongue at least partially in cheek that the government ought to do something to prevent Gretzky from leaving Canada: "Wayne Gretzky is a national symbol like the beaver, Pierre Berton and Harold Ballard. It's like the *Wheel of Fortune* without Vanna White. . . . They may as well have sent him to the moon as to L.A. Everybody knows that Los Angeles isn't a hockey town—they wouldn't know a hockey puck from a beach ball."

Back east in Toronto, the self-styled centre of the hockey universe, there was a range of reactions. The Gretzky loyalists in the media, such as wedding guest Al Strachan, puzzled over their hero's self-professed choice to leave Edmonton for California. But if Wayne said it, it must be the truth, and it must be for the best— and having witnessed the whole press conference, including the question-and-answer session, that conclusion seemed all the more reasonable. "At his own request, Wayne Gretzky, the greatest player in National Hockey League history, has been traded to the Los Angeles Kings," was the dead-straight lead on Strachan's *Globe and Mail* story from the news conference in Edmonton, in which he unknowingly quoted all but directly from Peter Pocklington and Jeffrey Goodman's script.

For those who existed outside the orbit of the Friends of Gretzky, this was a rare opportunity to fire a salvo at St. Wayne, a chance to suggest that even he had feet of clay, that he might not have been entirely honest with his fans when it was in his own interest. Hockey culture in Canada, and by extension hockey writing in Canada, had been remarkably free of cynicism, especially given the ways in which the curtain had been pulled back on the dirty, profit-driven workings of all professional sport. There was still a real rooting interest—not for teams, so much, but for the sport itself, and by extension for the NHL. Hockey was good and hockey players were good guys, and all that money stuff was somehow beside the point. There were only a few exceptions who didn't tend towards the romantic, who boiled the deal down to its commercial essence and then went for the jugular—foremost among them William Houston, writing the morning after in the *Globe and Mail*:

But guess what? The joke, apparently, was on us. And what a laugher it was. Gretzky has told us repeatedly how much he loved playing hockey in Edmonton, how he wanted to end his career as an Oiler despite the periodic trade rumours.

But now, suddenly, it was time to move on. We have not been told why, except that Wayne wants to be with wife Janet Jones, whom, he revealed, is pregnant. He said it was time to play for another team, time for a new challenge. He would miss Edmonton, of course. He said this with tears, and at one point could not continue, moving away from the microphones to regain his composure.

The point is, who's kidding whom?

What can we really believe when words come out of Gretzky's mouth? Perhaps the Great One really is smitten, and can't bear to be away from his bride. But didn't Jones and Gretzky, plus Gretzky's friends, tell us that she had made no demands? Wasn't she going to live with Wayne in Edmonton during the hockey season? "Janet has never questioned Wayne's decision to stay in Edmonton," said Walter.

There is talk that Gretzky will get 10 per cent of the Kings as part of his new deal in Los Angeles, and that his contract will be renegotiated, putting his salary up near $2-million (U.S.) a year. Maybe that was part of the incentive. Maybe in L.A., he will be a big star.

The Oilers, too, will prosper. They should remain strong and they might even repeat as Stanley Cup champions. In addition to the millions of dollars, the club will receive young, highly rated players over the next five years, through first-round draft choices. Jimmy Carson is already a star and will replace Gretzky between Jarri Kurri and Esa Tikkanen.

And perhaps Gretzky will rise to the challenge of L.A. and transform a sickly, poorly-managed West Coast franchise. But it struck others yesterday that the most exciting and glamorous years of the Gretzky story are in the past.

Perhaps, too, Gretzky's credibility.

The feelings in Edmonton were, understandably, both rawer and more complicated. In the wake of the announcement, a gut-punch shock for the town, there was a struggle simply to understand what had happened. "It's like ripping the heart out of a city and saying put it back together," the mayor, Laurence Decore, said. No one there would dare call Gretzky a liar, or suggest out loud that his had been crocodile tears. The most reasonable Edmontonians tried to get past their hurt and disappointment and broken hearts and see it all through Gretzky's eyes, tried to understand why it was that he had made the obviously painful decision to leave them, and their city, behind.

Maybe once the initial hurt wore off, it wouldn't be so bad. Maybe, even for the hockey team, it was really all for the best. Maybe the players they received in the trade, and the draft choices and the cash, would help the Oilers keep right on winning. Gretzky might have retired young in any case, as he'd hinted in the past, or left as a free agent, or simply lost a bit of his magic. Better to part company with him today, however wrenching it might be, in the interests of a bright, sustainable tomorrow. They had Carson, who'd scored plenty for the Kings, and they had all of those draft picks. It wasn't as if they'd traded him away for a handful of magic

beans. "It is a good trade for the L.A. Kings right now," the emi-
nently sensible Cam Cole wrote in the *Edmonton Journal*. "It will be
a good trade for the Edmonton Oilers in three years."

Some fans were also comforted by an age-old Canadian instinct
when it came to the national sport: if this was good for hockey,
then it must be good, period (the line between the business of the
National Hockey League and the game as an aspect of national culture was blurred once again). There was a sense of inevitability.
Hockey had begun to outgrow our borders. The natural appeal of
the sport was beginning to make inroads with Americans. And so,
what could really be done in the face of those larger forces? Better
to sacrifice our genius son, better to offer him up for the sake of
the sport. It would be sad, certainly, there would be an enormous
sense of loss, but that melancholy would be mitigated by a calling
of higher purpose. Wayne Gretzky had gone to America on a holy
mission, and it was our duty to wish him well. (A few years later,
when franchises left Winnipeg and Quebec City for bigger, wealthier U.S. homes, there would be considerable gnashing of teeth, but
also more of that same sentiment, that same sense of resignation
that this was evolution in play, that no one, no humble Canadian
city, could stand in the way of the NHL's progress.) As the *Edmonton
Journal*'s lead editorial put it the day after the trade, "Hockey's gain
is city's loss." (The *Journal*, the city's long-established broadsheet
newspaper, maintained a similar tone throughout its early coverage
of the story, soberly taking the long view.)

Naturally, not everyone in Edmonton was so sanguine. Naturally, there were those who blamed Pocklington, who smelled a rat
from the start, and figured that whatever Gretzky may have said
for public consumption, it was the owner—known for his fast-
buck wheeler-dealerism—who was pulling the strings in his own
interests. Rich bosses aren't often cast as sympathetic figures in
morality plays.

In other circles, an even older sentiment kicked in—one that
began with the talking snake and the apple, and continued in
variation after variation through human history, through Jezebel
and Delilah and Yoko Ono: the honourable man led astray by a

beautiful woman, led away from his proper destiny, from his friends, from his home, a slave to his baser instincts, to his primal nature, to his lizard brain. Janet Jones was never one of us. Just look at her. There weren't a lot of girls like *that* in Edmonton. And though, when Wayne chose her, it might have been easy enough to embrace the fairy tale, to believe that one of the world's more beautiful women (Hollywood being the natural arbiter of such things) would fall for a handsome, humble hockey god whose heart was in the right place, the suspicions lingered, even through the euphoria of the wedding. Then, when the deal was announced, when Gretzky looked so helpless, so neutered, weeping in front of the microphones—surely that couldn't have been the work of another *man*. He must have must have been seduced away from Edmonton, he must have been made temporarily irrational in the face of this object of desire. *There* was the one explanation for the otherwise inexplicable that made perfect sense, because who hadn't felt similarly weak and helpless at some moment in their mating lives?

The *Edmonton Sun*, the local tabloid, saw sex at the root of the story and understandably played it hard, beginning with a remarkable day-after column under the byline of Graham Hicks (remember him from the press conference). Gretzky confidants would suggest later that of all that was written in the wake of the trade, this was the story that most got under his skin—especially the "Jezebel" line: "Now in cold blood he walks away without giving a damn about how much we cared, how much his teammates cared. . . . That wasn't a wedding. It was a swan song. Jezebel Janet has busted up the Oilers dynasty. If only Wayne had stuck with Vikki or found himself a decent Edmonton girl. Sigh." The *Sun* also ran a cartoon depicting the Janet character, complete with sunglasses, a tight dress, a suitcase packed for California and great, heaving bosom, headed for L.A. with an emasculated Wayne literally clinging to her apron strings, hollering "Coming, dear!" The *Sun* also managed to track down Vikki Moss, the aggrieved ex, reduced to an afterthought around the time of the royal wedding, who opined that Janet must be behind the move, that Pocklington would never have traded Gretzky of his own free will. "I think it was Wayne's wish," Moss said. "Peter loved Wayne and I don't think he would give him up for a few million dollars." Moss then slipped the knife in a little deeper, with a parting shot about how Gretzky had "got bitter" because she had gone to Los Angeles herself to become a singer. "He was opposed to the idea of me pursuing a career. That's why it bewildered me when he chose to marry a career woman." There was even a story about her brother, Joey, about how his world had crumbled with the announcement of the trade.

Best of all was the interview with Anglican canon John Munro, who had officiated at the Gretzky wedding. How did he feel, the *Sun* wondered, when he found out by way of the press conference that Janet was pregnant—that she was pregnant on her wedding day? "It seems that's the way things are being done these days," Canon Munro said, "to check the field to see if it's fertile." Not much of a stretch to understand what was implied, what was written clearly between the lines: that becoming pregnant had perhaps helped Jones tighten the snare.

It was all playing out pretty much as Goodman had hoped it would— or at least as well as could be expected, given the haste, given the rush job that was the press conference, given the underlying tensions. As long as the focus of the anger remained divided, as long as what had really happened remained a debating point, everyone had cover. Gretzky was in Los Angeles now, in heart and mind and body, and perhaps not quite so distraught. The hockey season would start soon enough, and the Oilers would still be pretty darned good—strengthened over the long term, many believed, by the hockey part of the exchange. Broken hearts in Edmonton would mend, eventually; new bonds would form. Gretzky's inevitable return in a foreign uniform would be painful, and there would always be a lingering nostalgia for the glory days. But players came and players went, heroes changed uniforms all the time, sports dynasties inevitably crumbled, and somehow life went on. Peter Pocklington was one bad guy among many, for now. He'd take his lumps and watch himself hanged in effigy, but in the confusion he had escaped the worst of it. Now, he could get away on that fishing trip, let everyone calm down, count the money and be pretty damned pleased with himself.

They were sitting in Pocklington's office early that evening, performing a bit of a post mortem on the day's events, when Harry Sinden, the crusty longtime boss of the Boston Bruins, called. Once upon a time, he'd had to explain to his paying customers why their team was parting company with Bobby Orr, and it hadn't gone so well—as he'd told Glen Sather at the fishing lodge a few weeks before. Now he was offering congratulations, telling Pocklington that he couldn't believe how well he'd pulled it all off. Pocklington demurred, giving credit to his PR wizard. He said that if he ever tried to become prime minister again, Goodman was going to be his right-hand man.

"I don't think that's going to happen," Goodman said, cutting in.

They were exhausted, but it was a good exhausted. They had survived. A third of the people hate you, Goodman told Pocklington. A third of them hate Gretzky's wife. A third of them are questioning Gretzky and Sather. And you have fifteen million bucks in the bank. Surely, those were numbers he could live with. Goodman was planning to fly home the next morning, then fly right back for Pocklington's second fishing trip (all of them were given jackets for the occasion with nicknames on the lapel; Goodman's, in honour of his Trudeau connection, was "Grit").

"Don't do any interviews," Goodman told Pocklington. "Don't talk to anyone. Even if they say stuff about you, let it go. Think like you're already up in the Arctic."

In plainer terms, which Goodman would have never used with his client, he was saying, *Please, shut the fuck up.*

Back at the hotel in Edmonton, Goodman phoned home. His son, who was seven, got on the line and asked him if he'd heard the news, asked him if he knew that Wayne Gretzky had been traded, asked if he knew Gretzky had shed tears.

"You see," Goodman said to his boy, sensing a chance to impart a life lesson, "it's okay for a grown man to cry."

He got home the next day, packed his bags, prepared for the return flight to Edmonton and then on to the Northwest Territories.

The following morning, before heading to the airport, his phone rang.

"Jeff. It's Peter. We've got problems. I did an interview."

Jeffrey Goodman's heart sank.

Everyone remembers the press conference, everyone remembers the tears, but it was Pocklington who sealed the deal, who writ the myth large, all by himself. He woke up the morning after, opened up the local papers, and temporarily lost his mind. Had he been seeing straight, had he retained even a modicum of perspective, he would have understood that not all of the vitriol was directed his way—that he was cast as a villain, certainly, but not the only one in town. Instead, as vain as he was, so high and fragile was his self-regard that he took every slight, every shot, every criticism personally. He got mad, and then he decided to get even. All that fuss over Gretzky boo-hooing. Hadn't he just given Wayne what he wanted, hadn't he made him a whole lot richer, hadn't he done what was best for his hockey team (and best for himself, best for his bank account, though that was beside the point)? It was personal now.

The truth was, Gretzky—bawling aside—had so far taken the high road and stayed on the agreed-upon message (though there was that one subtle shot, delivered at the press conference in Los Angeles, where he said that he was the first hockey player ever to be "forced to be sold twice in his career," a clear message to the folks back home). But that didn't matter to Pocklington. He was going to set everybody straight about what a prick, what a phony, their hero was. Still raging, he put in a call to Jim Matheson, the *Edmonton Journal* hockey writer, and handed him one of the best scoops of his career.

Afterwards, predictably, Pocklington would claim to have been misquoted, or at least taken out of context. He'd blame Matheson for writing the story, and refuse to speak to him for the better part of five years. But his protests seemed a touch hollow—especially because, later the same day, he'd done another interview with another reporter, Gordon Edes of the *Los Angeles Times*, and said almost exactly the same things, in almost exactly the same words.

And his quotes, even now, stand up all by themselves, without any spin, without any help.

"Wayne has an ego the size of Manhattan. I understand that, though. If people had told me how great I was day in and day out for ten years, I'm sure my ego would be a pretty generous size, too."

"This has nothing to do with Janet having a baby. All of a sudden he figures, gee, I'll go out and conquer that market. Not only that, but he'll conquer the United States. Wayne believes he can revive hockey in the U.S. or make it a sport to be watched by millions more."

"He's a great actor. I thought he pulled it off beautifully where he showed how upset he was. I think he was upset but he wants the big dream. I call L.A. the land of the Big Trip and he wants to go where the trips are biggest."

"It doesn't matter if [Edmonton fans] buy it or not because that's the truth. . . . All you can do is what Mark Twain says: when in doubt, tell the truth. If they don't buy it that's their problem. If they think their King walked the streets of Edmonton without ever having a thought of moving, they are under a great delusion."

"Maybe it'll never pass, not until the fans realize we've done this for the long run. I think people will come to their senses and realize we're still one big team."

"I'd swear on a court document, anything you wish, that Wayne wanted to be traded. It was his idea."

"If Wayne has the integrity I think he has he'll back up what I said. He had the ability to back out of the deal, to say he didn't want to do it, just before the press conference started."

"I made a billion and a half in food sales. I have over seven thousand people working for me and all my companies are very healthy financially."

Pocklington had drawn a moustache on the Canadian icon. He had called Wayne Gretzky a liar, a fake. Even if he believed it in his heart, he had started a battle he could never win. And he had solidified in the minds of anyone who read the story, or heard of it second-hand—which, by the time the dust had settled, would be just about everyone in the country—what the real truth was here. A national treasure, a natural resource, had been sold to the soulless Yanks because of greed. Wayne Gretzky had been exiled from Edmonton against his will. It was all Pocklington's doing, and all Pocklington's fault.

"Are you serious?" Goodman said to Pocklington, his voice raised. "You have to be kidding. You and I had an agreement and understanding. No media. This has got to be one of the biggest screwups I have ever seen. Have you flipped out? Are you crazy?"

Pocklington didn't really have an answer.

Of course, there would now be other shoes to drop. The Gretzky inner circle, always sophisticated in the ways of the media, began fighting its own rearguard propaganda action, spreading the word through trusted sources—though never, of course, with Gretzky's name directly attached. Strachan, who had taken the press conference at face value two days before, came out with a completely different interpretation of the events, one that certainly sounded as though it had come straight from The Great One's mouth.

> Now that you've had a day to digest all the alleged facts concerning the trade of Wayne Gretzky to the Los Angeles Kings, does it make sense to you? If it does, give it a second look.
>
> At first glance, the story seemed plausible. Gretzky had initiated the trade for the good of his family, his career and his sport. But as the day rolled into evening and other facts were collected, it became apparent that Gretzky did not initiate this trade. Edmonton Oilers owner Peter Pocklington did. . . .
>
> In typical Gretzky fashion, he tried to make the best of a bad situation. He did what he thought was right for those around him even though Wayne Gretzky, who hates to fly, now plays for a team that spends more time aloft than the space probes.
>
> He does truly believe that the success of the Kings is important to the league, just as he believes, and justifiably so, that he can help their cause appreciably.

But his sale—which Pocklington likes to call a trade—was not Wayne Gretzky's idea. In terms they'll understand in L.A., this was a Peter Pocklington production. Technical assistance was provided by Wayne Gretzky.

Janet Gretzky was more direct in making sure that her side of the story got out. She tracked down the *Edmonton Sun*'s star columnist, Terry Jones, and unloaded.

"I never intended to talk—but let's talk. . . . The story of the trade as presented by Peter Pocklington is false. Pocklington is the reason Wayne is gone. I know the real story. I know the whole story. I know Wayne didn't deserve any of this. He wouldn't let Edmonton fans, Canada and most important, his teammates, down without good reason. . . .

"Wayne speaks from the heart. People who aren't good at lying aren't good at lying. The tears that came out were not all an act. To see Wayne hurt like this hurts me. That's why I'm making this call to you. . . .

"Peter Pocklington is the reason Wayne Gretzky is no longer an Edmonton Oiler. . . . The key to everything that happened was an event five days after our wedding. Pocklington gave Bruce McNall permission to take Wayne if he could do it. And that did it!"

At the same time, Gretzky, always aware of appearances, was extremely careful to do nothing to suggest that what Pocklington had said about him just might be true. Craig Simpson, still visiting in California in the days after the trade, remembers Gretzky telling him that they had been invited to a party at the Playboy Mansion—not just any party, but a pyjama party. Immediately, Simpson's twenty-one-year-old imagination went into overdrive. "I can't go," Gretzky said. If he was seen there, he explained, if someone took his picture living the wild, decadent Hollywood life so soon after the departure scene in Edmonton, the people back in Canada might take it the wrong way. Gretzky offered to get Simpson into the party without him, but Simpson said he wasn't interested (though he acknowledges now that it may have been an opportunity missed).

—

Damage control, by now, was pretty much beside the point. Goodman phoned Gretzky's agent, Michael Barnett, and apologized for Pocklington's words. ("Your job was mission impossible," Barnett said.) Then, along with a group of loyal Pocklington employees, he flew off to the Northwest Territories, to Plummer's Lodge on the Coppermine River, where they could fish for giant Arctic char and forget the troubling events of the past week. Except they couldn't really forget. On or off the river, it was the natural topic of conversation—though, because almost everyone on the trip owed their existence to Pocklington, he wasn't likely to hear a lot of challenging or dissenting voices. But over drinks one night, one of his friends, a doctor, had the temerity to suggest that perhaps Pocklington ought to offer a public apology.

"All right, Mr. Professional, what do you think?" Pocklington said, passing the buck to Goodman.

Apologies worked in Canada, Goodman believed—personally and professionally. It was, by nature, a forgiving culture. Not now, though. Not after the fateful interview.

"It's too late," he said. "No one is going to believe you anyway. You did what you did. You brought it on yourself."

So, what now?

"My advice to you is to sell the Oilers and buy another hockey team," Goodman said.

Pocklington's thirteen-year-old son Zach, who had been quietly following the conversation, piped up.

"Listen to him, Dad," he said. "He's giving you the right advice."

In the end, it's all about faith. Though spectator sport shares elements in common with other forms of entertainment, with show-biz in all of its permutations, it is also fundamentally different because at its heart can be found the makings of a modest church.

At the movies, the theatre, the opera or a concert, all that's required to make the experience satisfactory to the audience is that there is a willing suspension of disbelief once the lights go down (which can be easy or not, depending on the quality of the picture and whether you've chosen seats close to read-the-credits-aloud, candy-wrapper-crinkling, short-attention-span-when-nothing-is-exploding morons). When the show is over, when the lights are back on, everyone can decide for themselves whether it was worth the time and money invested, whether they were moved or excited or annoyed or bored, whether the artistic experience was profound or perfunctory or fell into the great gulf between. But that's it. There is no other investment necessary. A favourite actor or musician might be involved, one who inspires a cultish devotion, but, outside of Deadheads in the good old days, there is no fantasy of shared purpose. They aren't playing for you, they aren't acting for you, there is no rooting interest. It's a straight cash equation: money offered up in exchange for pleasure, for diversion, for keeping the harsh realities of mortality temporarily at bay, and everyone understands the mercenary nature of those whose names are up in lights. That's why, when an actor's paycheque or a band's amassed fortune is trotted out in the popular press, there tends to be little or no righteous indignation from the little people who are the source of that wealth, ten, twenty or a hundred bucks at a time. Everyone understands what they're buying and why they're buying. Everyone understands that it's a matter of free will, a take-it-or-leave-it proposition. Rarely—well, perhaps at La Scala, or Carnegie Hall or CBGB's—is the venue treated as a temple, as sacred ground partially worth the price of admission in itself. ("The movie stunk, but it was worth it just be able to eat a five-dollar bag of popcorn at Silver City!") You might come back the next time the star is involved, or you might decide that it's time to stop pretending that Eddie Murphy will ever make another film worth watching. But there are no added values in that judgment. It is in no way a repudiation of home or family history or of some great shared experience in the distant past. You pay your money and you take your chances, and then it's on to the next show.

Sport is different. It delivers spectacle in bite-sized chunks, but the quality of the pure entertainment experience varies widely and can't be guaranteed. There are walk-off home runs and overtime championship-winning goals, but there are also games that simply play out with no real dynamic or dramatic tension, that begin and end with a whimper. (Those who created professional wrestling tried to correct that small problem, by staging something that looked and felt like sport, by distilling its essence but eliminating the uncertainty along with the authenticity, scripting the action to guarantee a payoff every night. For a certain crowd, it worked.) For the fan, though, it isn't just about making a one-time commitment. Teams are followed over the course of a season that might be as short as sixteen games, or as long as 162. Allegiances can, and often do, last a lifetime, passed down from parent to child. That long-term buy-in from the spectator is essential to the equation. And it is built, in large part, on affiliation, on identification, on belief.

Without something or someone to cheer, sport loses almost all of its meaning (which is why anyone tuning into a game as a neutral observer is immediately tempted to adopt one team or another, one athlete or another, to root for the underdog, a favourite city, even the ones with the best-looking uniforms). In its original, organic form, that allegiance would have been based in hearth and home—supporting the people you know, the place where you live, the country of your birth. You cheered them on because they were playing for you, they were affirming who you were and where you came from, which is a powerful, comforting, necessary feeling. As sport was professionalized and athletes commodified, as it became possible through radio and television to follow teams in faraway places as easily as those that played down the street, the relationship became more abstract, became transferable, but became no less passionate. Even if the connection between fan and team was less direct and obvious, to have that connection was still intensely desirable

By the late twentieth century, spectator sport had become a more significant cultural force than at any time in human history since the fall of the Roman Empire, and there were reasons for that—not just the growth of the great sports–entertainment complex to manipulate tastes and demand, but a desire, in an increasingly fragmented world, for community. In a culture in which face-to-face connections were made less necessary by technology, in which organized religion or mass political movements were less likely to bring people together in the same place, at the same time, caring deeply about the same thing, spectator sport filled a void. To be a fan meant becoming part of a larger whole. To be a fan provided the opportunity for collective expression, for joy and sadness shared with a multitude of others. It provided a sense of belonging, of inclusion, which is something nearly all of us desire—even if that connection came through a television, a radio or a computer monitor.

Intrinsic to that sense of loyalty, of commitment, was the need to believe in the athletes, believe in the teams, believe that somehow fans and players and coaches and owners are all in this together, that they care about the city, care about the team, care about the uniform. Once upon a time, when athletes' private lives were off-limits in the popular press and the business behind the games was rarely discussed, it was relatively simple to cheer wholeheartedly for heroes whose virtues as human beings were equated with their athletic feats on the field of play, who were perceived to be out there giving their all as much for joy as for money. It was possible to think of owners as paternalistic curators of local cultural institutions, more concerned with winning silverware than turning a profit (and in any financial dispute with players, those owners would automatically be given the benefit of the doubt, because it was a game, because players played, not worked).

That is a more complicated process in the modern world, requiring large doses of fantasy. Fans now understand that professional athletes are flawed, that they play for money, that they have agents and are represented by unions, that owners care most about turning a profit, that sport is an entertainment business. But the belief system remains, still. It is unbreakable. It isn't rational. It is about faith.

In that context, consider what it meant to have Wayne Gretzky sold by Peter Pocklington to the Los Angeles Kings, what it meant if you lived in Edmonton, what it meant if you lived in Canada. What it meant to hear him cry. Had he been an actor or a comedian or a musician, Gretzky would have been simply the latest in a long line of Canadian talent that has successfully taken its act south, from Mary Pickford through Neil Young and Jim Carrey. His departure would have inspired melancholy, but would also have been completely understood. And when he succeeded there, on the big stage, Canadians would have felt a certain pride in his accomplishments, a certain vindication of his talent, because however nationalist the spirit, to make it in America is still regarded as the great validation, the affirmation that what people appreciated here was for real, that it was world-class, that it wasn't just a Canadian thing. Even if he had been a professional athlete in a different sport—one of those rare Canadian players who excels in the National Football League; a basketball player like Steve Nash, who was for a time the best player in the National Basketball Association and therefore the best in the world; or a baseball player like Larry Walker or Ferguson Jenkins or Justin Morneau, whose career path inevitably led to major-league fame and fortune in the U.S.—there would be no wringing of hands.

Hockey, though, was ours. Hockey players were natural resources, born of the land, pure products of the elusive national culture. They were different than young men from other places who happened to play the same game, because they understood it differently, they felt it differently. Hockey coursed through their veins in a way that it simply couldn't for a non-Canadian. A Canadian forced to play outside Canada because of the realities of the NHL surely pined to one day be given the chance to return to a real hockey city. A Canadian lucky enough to play in Canada, to captain a team in Canada, to win Stanley Cups for a Canadian city, could not be lured away by money or the love of a good woman or the allure of a better climate, because nothing could possibly mean more, nothing could possibly be more important. That, all of it, was the gospel.

Sell them our water and our oil and our trees, sell them our fish and our wheat, gradually erase the great unguarded border, gradually break down the real and imagined differences. But sell the greatest hockey player in the world, sell Jesus of Brantford, and it cut to the heart, to the core, to the essence of belief.

THE TRADE THAT SHOOK THE HOCKEY WORLD

When Gretzky went to L.A.
my whole nation trembled
like hot water in a tea cup when a train goes by.

Something about Hollywood and hockey.
Something about Canadians in Babylon.
Something about gold and the gilded blades of grace.
Something about kings and the great republic.
Something about titans and the golden gods.
Something about the myth of boys and the truth of men.
Something about beer in the holy grail.
Something about the commodity of the human heart.
Something about the fast life . . .
Fast food, fast cars, fast women, and a fastness.
But mostly something about moving too fast in time.

John B. Lee

Chapter Eleven

THE MIRACLES OF LOS ANGELES

I T WAS A CALM FLIGHT BACK to California. The traumatic parting was over now, and Gretzky's new home beckoned. He had quietly slipped away with McNall after the press conference at Molson House without having to say another public word. Now there would be a similar, yet very different, event arranged for a hotel near Los Angeles International Airport. Gretzky fretted a bit about what kind of a reception he would receive there, perhaps flashing back to his first, failed crack at being a hockey prophet in America: the trip to Indianapolis with Nelson Skalbania, when almost no one showed up to greet him and next to no one cared. McNall reassured him. On those kinds of details, in *his* town, he and his minions were all but infallible, and of course he was right. After landing, Gretzky and McNall were hustled to the Sheraton La Reina and taken to a back room in advance of their grand entrance. The hall in which the press conference would be held was packed—nothing like the tiny smattering of reporters who would normally attend a Kings event in mid-summer. There were even more cameras and reporters than had covered the departure from Edmonton. When the show started, local television and radio programming was interrupted for live, breathless coverage of the arrival of . . . a hockey player . . . in California. It seemed a small miracle.

Gretzky was worn out from his roller-coaster day. But peering out at the crowd from behind the curtains, like any great performer, his batteries were recharged.

"Don't worry," he whispered to McNall. "I can handle this."

("Wayne understood what L.A. meant," McNall says now. "The problem with Canadians and hockey is that hockey's not a form of entertainment for them, it's a form of religion. If you don't have stars and you don't produce something entertaining—people have alternatives, especially in L.A.")

McNall decided to have a bit of fun to kick things off. He came to the microphone alone, leaving Gretzky backstage to build some suspense where, in truth, none existed. "Now, the reason we're here, and the moment you've all been waiting for . . ." he began, ". . . the introduction of our new team colours and uniform!" A short, theatrical pause. "May we have our model please?"

Out stepped Gretzky, the euphoric Janet beside him, to join his beaming new boss and an extremely jolly Jerry Buss. This time, Gretzky's speech was uninterrupted by tears. There would be only passing reference to the past, to the broken-hearted town he had departed. "This morning it was very difficult for me to leave the city, to leave some of the people who have become my greatest friends," he said. "As is your basketball team down here, they are in their own category as far as winning, as far as sportsmanship and entertainment. . . . Tonight, it's all uphill. It's very exciting. I'm sure it's something that will not only be good for Wayne Gretzky and the L.A. Kings, but also for the game of hockey. It's a disappointing day to have to leave Edmonton, but it's a great new challenge for me."

He was on top. He was in control, eyes forward. He might still have a lot of Brantford and Edmonton in him, but for all intents and purposes he was now fully in and of *this* place. He carried off the press conference with a seamless mix of aw-shucks Canadian humility and quiet but apparently supreme self-confidence, a combination that stood out in what had become a sea of swaggering professional athletes and pampered, shallow stars. Gretzky was different from what they were used to in Los Angeles. In Edmonton, some might have felt he'd become a bit full of himself, but here, in this context, he seemed all humble pie, a throwback, the kid next door. Of all the reasons that his celebrity would come to far transcend his sport, for all of the clever marketing and packaging, that would be the single greatest key: people *liked* him, and so they were willing to cut him plenty of slack and to give his alien game a fresh look. In the local press the next day, the news of Gretzky's arrival was greeted with much wide-eyed enthusiasm, and hardly a hint of cynicism. There were a few suggestions that it might not be the greatest hockey deal in the world for the Kings—as if that mattered to the masses—and there was one slightly cautionary note struck by someone in a unique position when it came to the city and to the sport. "Anybody that hires a man because of his personality or his popularity needs his bloody head read," the former Kings owner Jack Kent Cooke said. "In this instance here, McNall is getting an unquestioned great, if not the greatest hockey player that ever lived, and may ever live. So, that's the reason for all of this. . . . I think that McNall deserves all the credit in the world for his derring-do, for his spirited, adventurous move, but I have no idea [if it will work]. My name's Cooke. It's not Cassandra."

Beyond Cooke, only a tiny Los Angeles subculture greeted Gretzky's arrival with even the slightest reservations—and strangely enough, they were among the few people in the city who actually understood what the Kings were getting. The team's hard-core fans were a small, committed group, united in their cultish passion. Now, suddenly, their cozy little planet was about to become a whole lot more crowded, thanks to a player who for years had been one of their greatest tormentors. "I was mad when we traded for him," says Mike Altieri, then a Forum usher and superfan, now a Kings vice-president. "Because I hated him as a fan. I knew the Oilers were incredible. It was like a sixty-minute power play when they played the Kings, like they had a sixth guy on the ice. But as a Kings fan, they were the hated Oilers. And I didn't like Gretzky.

I was one of the fans waving the pink hankies whenever he came to play in L.A. . . . It kind of tore out that cult feeling that had grown and developed. Now all of a sudden there were all of these fans who never cared about the Kings, who all of a sudden cared. It kind of bothered me. They hadn't invested what I had invested in the team."

But that community of actual, committed hockey fans was the least of McNall's concerns. They'd continue to show up—and if they didn't, early returns suggested that it wouldn't be much of a problem finding someone else to fill their seats. The day after the trade, would-be ticket-buyers formed a lineup that stretched nearly around the Forum. Roy Mlakar sat there with a tin box full of cash, selling just as fast as he could. The phones rang all day and into the night. Famous people called—those who had never before expressed the slightest interest in hockey—asking for the same kind of seats they held for Lakers games. (Though one of the worst places to watch a hockey game is from directly behind the glass, McNall and company found those tickets easy to unload to the Hollywood crowd, who were accustomed to watching basketball courtside and intent on being seen.) The transformation of the City of Angels into a hockey town seemed all but instantaneous. Everything McNall had thought, had dreamed of, was magnificently, perfectly right. They were responding to Gretzky's star power. They had bought into the *idea* of Gretzky—faster than anyone could have imagined. No one dismissed the phenomenon by suggesting it was just the Kings, it was just hockey, so it couldn't possibly matter. He had arrived, and now the team and the sport *did* matter, at least here, at least now. Conventional wisdom had been turned on its head. It was as McNall would have scripted the scene, as though it was a movie about a previously forlorn sports franchise transformed overnight by the arrival of one magical player.

Later that week, McNall arranged, with the help of the William Morris Agency, to stage a party at Chasen's in Gretzky's honour, featuring the cream of Hollywood celebrity: not just the faithful old hockey crowd like Tom Hanks and Kurt Russell and Goldie Hawn, not just displaced Canadians like John Candy and Alan

Thicke and Michael J. Fox, but a whole range of old guard and new guard big names, including Milton Berle, Neil Diamond and Barbra Streisand. When he had tried to do the same thing for Luc Robitaille and Steve Duchesne and Jimmy Carson, hardly any of the invitees even knew who they were. This time, that wouldn't be an issue; and this time, the guest of honour certainly wouldn't go unnoticed. McNall remembers Gretzky expressing initial unease in the surroundings, intimidated by all of those famous faces. A few minutes later, McNall noticed that Gretzky had quietly slipped away, and wondered if he'd made his exit—only to find him happily signing autographs for a lineup of people who were used to signing their own. "In Edmonton, he was a star in Mudville," one of Gretzky's buddies says. "In L.A., he became a star in Starville."

The challenge now was to maximize the return, to make sure that McNall's crazy fifteen-million-dollar investment could be justified by fresh cash flow. That wasn't the only game, of course—for McNall, pulling off the Gretzky deal enhanced his reputation as a modern Midas, helped build confidence in whatever other schemes he brought to the table and kept his bankers happy, all extremely important in the big picture. The value of the Kings franchise immediately shot up, allowing him to claim huge—though largely theoretical—gains in equity, which could be used as leverage to borrow more money. Still, in the short run, he had to pay the bills. The Kings' Forum lease favoured their landlord, Buss, who controlled the building, the signage and the best "club" seats between the blue lines, for which he paid a flat fee. So even with Gretzky, new revenue streams from the arena were severely limited. McNall and Mlakar could renegotiate the Kings' broadcast deals upward, which they did; they could sell the place out every night, which they did; and they could charge considerably more for those tickets. They could try innovative stuff like flying a miniature radio-controlled blimp, decorated with advertising, around the inside of the rink—a gimmick then unique, now commonplace. But to really make the Gretzky deal pay required a great deal more than that. (In hindsight, McNall thinks that one of his biggest mistakes was not convincing other NHL owners to subsidize the cost of acquiring Gretzky for the Kings, because it would benefit the overall health of the league to have him in Los Angeles. "What I should have done, which I didn't, because I didn't have the courage, was go back and say to my partners in the league, 'If I do this Gretzky trade, here's the new deal,'" McNall says. "'I get half of your gate when I walk into the building. You charge extra, do whatever you want to do. But this is a new road show. This is not just Wayne Gretzky—this is entertainment. If I have a concert, I can charge more money for someone big.' They would have said no. And I would have said, 'Okay, see you later.'")

Mlakar remembers that it was from the desperate drive to find more ways to make money from Gretzky that the biggest and best idea emerged: a plan to take the Kings on the road during the preseason, flying into mostly non-hockey cities, selling games like rock concerts and reaping the benefits. It was far more lucrative to play those meaningless exhibitions outside of Los Angeles, where they could simply rent a building and then control every dollar that came in. McNall spent five million dollars to get the Kings their own plane—a Boeing 727 that had formerly belonged to the president of Mexico—and the Great Gretzky Tour began, to Dallas and Portland and St. Petersburg, Florida, and Miami and Sacramento, to nondescript B-markets and to the parking lot at Caesars Palace in Las Vegas, where they managed to build a rink despite desert heat. At each stop, the cash registers would be ringing, which was Mlakar's main concern. But as much as McNall loved and needed the money, he also had a larger game in mind.

Gretzky in L.A. wasn't an end—it was a beginning. Once he had proven that you could sell hockey in one sunbelt market, it was time to bottle that formula and use it to transform the entire sport. The NHL had tried and largely failed with expansion schemes in the past, but that was because the owners were a backwards, conservative group, caught up in the past, in their antiquated ways of doing business. They were hockey guys and arena operators, not entertainment guys, not movie and music promoters, and had fallen far behind the times. McNall at least had their attention now. "It was a reactionary league," he says. "It was dominated by guys like Bill Wirtz [the owner of the Chicago Blackhawks, who famously refused to televise his team's home games lest it hurt his live gate] and Jeremy Jacobs [the tight-fisted owner of the Boston Bruins]. But they saw this and they knew somehow this would be a good thing. With the exception of one or two people, I think they were all excited about it because it would help boost everything across the board." McNall rode that growing trust, rode the warm, happy feelings that were generated when Gretzky filled up arenas around North America, rode his new image as a sports marketing genius all the way to the chairmanship of the NHL's board of governors, which made him the single most powerful figure in the league. He had effectively seized control of hockey's destiny, and was free to enact his own wildly innovative plans. Building confidence, making friends, selling others on his dreams and schemes, had always been his greatest gift.

Though McNall's thinking was in many ways revolutionary, at least for hockey, his blueprint was relatively simple. The plan went like this: leverage Gretzky's impact in Los Angeles to expand the sport's presence—and its value—on American television; begin the task of expanding the game's footprint; go into those cities where the Kings had filled arenas for exhibition games; pitch prospective owners—not the modestly rich guys who used to be the best that hockey could attract, but real high flyers, the über-wealthy, now convinced of the NHL's upside, of the possibilities for rapid, exponential growth. It didn't matter if they weren't in traditional hockey cities. It didn't matter if they were in places where no one played hockey, where no one had grown up watching the game, where there was never a hint of snow and ice. Gretzky in L.A. had proven that you could sell the NHL to anyone, anywhere, if you did it right. Tell potential investors that, show them the numbers, introduce them to a few movie stars, and then sell them an expansion franchise. For how much? How about fifty million dollars for a start? Sure, no one had ever paid that price for an NHL team before. But once you got over that hump, once you sold the first one, then everyone's team was worth *at least* fifty million dollars.

You could take that instantaneous equity to the bank—or at least to your banker. And if you created the right kind of buzz, the right kind of chatter, if you could attract the right kind of partners— movers and shakers who, it would be assumed, were on the cutting edge—then other prospective owners would be lining up, desperate to get into the NHL before the price went up, desperate to be part of the new sports in-crowd.

If any of that in hindsight is suggestive of a Ponzi scheme, it's worth remembering that it sure didn't sound that way at the time. The proof was in the pudding. The proof was in those full houses at the Forum, the celebrities fighting to get tickets, the U.S. endorsement deals that were making Gretzky wealthier than he could ever have imagined. Bruce McNall had discovered a secret formula that had eluded everyone else in hockey, the world was beating a path to his door, and the rest of the NHL was only too thrilled to share in the benefits.

While most of that was still but a glint in McNall's eye, back at the rink the two hockey teams involved in the deal of the century began the task of redefining themselves, with, and without, Wayne Gretzky. In the fall of 1988 in Victoria, British Columbia, the Kings gathered for a very different training camp than had been their norm. In other years, they could prepare for the season in happy anonymity, but now a huge media contingent was along for the ride, analyzing their every move and every mood.

There was no arguing that, for some of the players, perhaps even for its head coach, the new presence in the dressing room was a bit intimidating. Luc Robitaille remembers how he felt when he first heard news of the trade. "As a fan, it was the greatest day of my life," he says. "I was a fan of Wayne. I had his picture in my closet. To me, he was perfect. He was Wayne Gretzky. It almost took me a year and a half to adjust, because I was so enamoured with Wayne. Wayne couldn't swear and Wayne couldn't say a bad thing because that was my idol—my ultimate idol. They say, 'Who is the one person you'd like to meet?' That was Wayne. Then you get so close to him and you don't even know how to act." Gretzky arrived determined to change the culture of an organization, to erase what he perceived as a losing tradition, to upset a soft, country-club atmosphere that wasn't conducive to success. Of course, that wasn't the only thing standing between the team and greatness— the Kings also didn't have Mark Messier or Jari Kurri or Glenn Anderson or Kevin Lowe or Grant Fuhr. "Any change from what he had in Edmonton wasn't going to be any good," Mlakar remembers. "Because he walked into the dressing room and didn't have near the talent, near the Hall of Fame lineup, near the friendships. So that was going to be a bridge to cross. They all realized who he was. And it was going to be Wayne's way. He didn't come in and try to run the dressing room. But you knew there were going to be changes." It was going to be a tricky adjustment on both sides—and it seemed inevitable from the start that Gretzky would have a difficult time co-existing with the Kings' coach, Robbie Ftorek, who had a reputation for being no-nonsense, principled and a tad inflexible. You could play the role that way with a bunch of players who had never won a thing. You could be an uncompromising authoritarian, as Glen Sather had been with the young Oilers in the beginning. But the minute Gretzky walked in, Ftorek's became the second most important voice in the room, and that would eventually become untenable.

The other players realized immediately that Gretzky was still driven to succeed, that he had something to prove. His mission in Los Angeles wasn't merely a marketing exercise. He had to make the team better. The Kings had to win something. Eventually, he had to bring the Stanley Cup to California, justifying McNall's faith and investment. It may have been true, as Mlakar suggests, that "the biggest thing he wanted was to stick it up Peter Pocklington's butt. That was the driving force right there." Getting even was part of what motivated Gretzky. Looking back, though, which he had always resisted, wasn't going to help him achieve that goal. His new team, as constituted, simply wasn't good enough. And even the best players on the roster would have to learn to play with a genius teammate who, on the ice, did things his own unique way. What had become second nature for the Oilers would have to be learned from scratch by the other Kings. "All I wanted to do was please Wayne Gretzky," Robitaille says. "In the first game there was a two-on-one, and I wanted to hold the puck and give him the perfect play. It didn't work. He came back to the bench after and he just says nonchalantly, 'Lukey, give it to me and I'll give it back to you.' From that day on for the next month or two months, every time I got the puck I just literally threw it to him. I was so nervous. That's how much I wanted to impress him. It got to a point where I almost literally couldn't play with him, because I just wanted everything to be perfect."

Getting it right would take some time, and the Los Angeles Kings, even with Wayne Gretzky in uniform, would start the 1988–89 season as a work in progress.

In Edmonton, the Oilers reassembled in an angry, bitter, heartbroken city. The players had been shocked to receive news of the trade. Kevin Lowe remembers that he was playing in *Hockey Night in Canada* broadcaster Bob Cole's golf tournament in St. John's, Newfoundland, in the same foursome with Marty McSorley, when McSorley was called off the course to take a phone call in the pro shop, informing him that he'd been dealt with Gretzky to the Kings. "Everyone was kind of walking around like the president was shot or the prime minister was shot," Lowe remembers. "Cole was just devastated. He kept saying, 'That's not right. That's just not right. That can't be. What the hell is going on?'" Personally, Lowe says, he "kind of took it in stride. That kind of thing happens. We were going to be all right. The Oilers will still be good and we're going to carry on." But that sentiment was hardly universal among his teammates. Messier and Kurri, in particular, were furious at what had happened, and naturally focused their anger on owner Peter Pocklington, and to a lesser degree on Sather. "They were pissed off at the team," Lowe says. "Whereas for me, it was kind of like mourning a loss. You have to get on with your life, move on here. You're bringing everyone else down."

The Oilers' veterans had already come to view Pocklington with a jaundiced eye. They might have respected his success in business, and admired his wealth, but incidents far removed from hockey, especially the Gainers strike, had begun to reflect badly on the team, as did other trivial but telling stories, like those circulating locally about Pocklington cheating on the golf course. For every generous gesture he'd made—chartering a plane during the playoffs, for instance—there were examples of the petty and penurious, most notoriously the time he substituted zircons for real diamonds in the Stanley Cup rings presented to assistant coaches and trainers after the Oilers' first championship (once he found out, Gretzky took it upon himself to have them replaced with the genuine article). As owners go, Pocklington wasn't particularly intrusive. Stanley Cup celebrations aside, he'd drop into the dressing room once or twice a season to deliver an inspirational speech. (A particular favourite—the greybeards had all heard it at least two or three times—was a fable about encountering a man in Europe chiselling rock, who saw himself not as a stonemason, but as a cathedral-builder. In other words, you are what you believe you are. Self-actualization was a big part of the Pocklington gospel.) Now, in the wake of Gretzky's departure, Messier and Kurri and some of the others weren't in any mood to humour him anymore, and Sather, who had deftly played good cop/bad cop with his boss when the occasion demanded, could no longer be an effective, credible intermediary. The Oilers started more and more to look around the league, look at what others were making in other places, to imagine themselves in different settings and different uniforms, cashing in. (Even other players on other teams weren't immune. Craig Simpson remembers many a conversation with those from opposing clubs, shocked that the greatest star in the game could simply be sold. It was, he believes—and there's ample evidence to suggest that he's correct—a watershed moment in the history of hockey labour relations. The last romantic attachment to teams and uniforms and owners vanished with the Gretzky trade. Players understood their true function in hockey's economic system, and hardened their attitudes. "We were stunned to believe that a guy like Wayne in the best part of his career on a team that was destined to win and keep winning and be great could ever be gone," Simpson says. "Hockey had been built on the idea that you stay and you play for less and you're loyal because you want to win. I really do think the trade changed the way players felt about their own positions and their own place in the game. They understood that they were a poker chip that could be thrown into the middle of the table." It was a message that union boss Bob Goodenow, who had succeeded Alan Eagleson in the role, would do his best to pound home in succeeding years.)

At the same time, the great prize the Oilers had received in return for Gretzky, Jimmy Carson, did little to ease those feelings of unrest. He would wind up scoring 49 goals and recording 100 points in his first and only full season in Edmonton, but his discomfort with his teammates—and theirs with him—was clear almost from day one. "I know that the guys weren't very accepting of him," Lowe says. "He was kind of a strange cat. It had to do a little bit with his personality. To be fair, he was close to Bruce so he felt betrayed. His preference would have been to go to Detroit and not to go to Edmonton. But I know Mess wanted to strangle him a few times." (Jim Matheson remembers that Carson seemed acutely aware of the fact that he'd been traded for Wayne Gretzky, and never felt comfortable in Edmonton. Though he came from Detroit, the winter climate seemed especially to bother him: the other players noted the sheepskin covers on his car seats, and had fun winding him up about the dangers of black ice on the local roads. "Any little thing got him upset," Matheson says. Early the following season, Carson was traded to the Red Wings in what turned out to be a magnificent deal by Sather, who acquired Adam Graves, Petr Klíma and Joe Murphy. Carson never again scored more than 34 goals in an NHL season.)

All of that discontent produced a hangover season in Edmonton in 1988–89, the first time in a long time that the team would play below its potential. Resentment hung too thick in the air.

On October 6, 1988, Wayne Gretzky played his first regular-season game in a Los Angeles Kings uniform. The setting was the Forum, the opponent was the Detroit Red Wings, and the atmosphere was full-blown Hollywood. The team skated out in their new jerseys, famous faces were sprinkled throughout the crowd, and with his first shot Gretzky scored his first goal, as though it had been pre-ordained. He eventually added three assists in what finished as an 8–2 L.A. victory. The newly minted hockey fans who made up the vast majority of those in attendance got exactly what they had been promised. And up in the cheap seats, Altieri and the other old-school loyalists, who had greeted Gretzky's arrival with skepticism and a touch of bitterness, were instantly converted. "I'll never forget being at that first game and the feeling in the building," he says. "I was hooked. It immediately changed the dynamic of what the franchise was all about." Mike Downey, a columnist for the *Los Angeles Times,* captured the moment perfectly, giddily, in a piece that seemed to have been drawn straight from Bruce McNall's dreams.

Slash me, trip me, rough me. Ice me, slice me, dice me. Slide me through a crease. Face me off. Put me inside a box for 2 minutes and leave me there. I am Hockey, and I am here. I am a puck; I am an Islander. I am an Oiler, a Red Wing, a North Star, a Whale. I am, proud to say at last, a King. The Kings are dead; long live the Kings.

Good day, L.A., eh? Welcome to the first hockey game ever played in Los Angeles. Anybody who's anybody is here. Roy Orbison is here, to sing the anthem. Mercy. Neil Diamond also is here, somewhere. He'll sing for the King family some other time. And John Candy is right there behind the bench, and so's Michael J. Fox, and Kurt Russell with Goldie Hawn, and the Pointer Sisters, and, uh, Mary Hart, I think. There definitely will be entertainment tonight. Everybody has come to see. . . . The New Guy. It's hockey night in California.

Forget that stuff about the National Hockey League already having been in Los Angeles for more than 20 years. Hockey has never been here. Hockey has no more been here than the Ice Capades have been here. All hockey ever did was visit the Forum every year, same as the rodeo. Hockey was a ticket you bought to kill an evening, once every couple of years. Hockey was something your daughter played in school, with a stick.

Not now, though. Now that The New Guy is here, ice hockey is hot. Ice hockey is cool. Ice hockey is hip. Hockey is right up there with October baseball. Hockey is right out there on Page 1, with the other big guys. It's no longer stuck in the back with the mud-wrestling ads. We don't even care who the Kings are playing. We will pay attention to them even if they are playing . . . oh, heck, Winnipeg, even.

All because of The New Guy. The Gretz. King of Kings. Lord of posts.

He blew into town like Gilbert blew into Jamaica. Bang. Zoom. The hockey gods had sent down their thunderbolt. People ran to their telephones to order tickets as if the Shubert Theater had just announced that Les Miserables would star Eddie Murphy. "Hello? King season tickets? Gimme four at rinkside." Knowing Jack Nicholson, he probably bought out the penalty box. Sit there all season and yell mean things at the Canucks.

It was only August when Bruce McNall, like a Mountie, went into Canada and got his man. "Six weeks ago, or something like that," the man who owns the Kings said Thursday night at the Forum, an hour or so before the grand opener. "Seems more like six months. Like six years, sometimes. People stop me on the street and say, 'Thank you.' Look over from their cars and yell out, 'Hey, thanks for getting Wayne.' Incredible."

McNall left Canadians sadder than Ben Johnson did. It was like he went up and shot their national bird. Or worse. It was like McNall got elected prime minister, and immediately declared prohibition. Declared Molson's and Labatt's illegal. Took away their reasons for living. Bruce McNall is the man who left Canada dry.

Not that Los Angeles took the big trade too seriously. Naw. Los Angeles only went nuts, is what it did. It discovered hockey, as if it had never even been there. Which, as a matter of fact, it hadn't. The Forum had two tenants now. Two teams, the Lakers and the Kings. All over the Coast, husbands and wives began discussing hockey, asking their neighbors if they knew how long it took the Forum crew to flood the basketball court and freeze it so there'd be ice all over it.

This wasn't just any old trade. This was the Trade, with a capital T. This was buying Manhattan from the Indians. This was the Louisiana Purchase. This was Fritz Peterson making a straight-up swap with Mike Kekich. Play-by-play announcer Bob Miller, the voice of hockey in Los Angeles—bet you didn't know there was a voice of hockey in Los Angeles—stood at center ice Thursday with a spotlight trained on him, introduced the rest of the Kings, then shouted out to a full house:

"They called it the Trade of the Century!"

Yeah?

"The man who holds 49 NHL records!"

Yeah?

"No. 99: Wayne Gretzky!"

Yeah!!!

The new guy. Man of the hour. Man of the season. Bring him on. Let's have a look at him. Oooh, nice, new white and black uniforms. Formal wear. A pucksedo. Yeah, the Gretz looks good, don't he? Yeah, sure does. Looks as though he belongs here. Tell me again—who'd he used to play for?

OK, on with the show. Let's see if the guy still knows how to play this game. Let's see if he can play L.A.'s kind of hockey. No. Check that. Let's see if L.A. can play his kind of hockey. Yeah. Let's see how great the Kings can be with Gretzky. Let's see if you can play winning hockey with a tan.

Ninety-two seconds gone—Hey, the night's first fight! Hockey is back!

Five minutes 22 seconds gone—Hey, shot and a goal! For the Red Wings! The Kings are back!

Eleven minutes 14 seconds gone—Hey, somebody tripped the Gretz! Go into the box, Tim Higgins, you Detroit criminal, you! Thug! Goon!

Twelve minutes 54 seconds gone—Hey, shot and a goal! Who got it? Anybody see who got it!

Public-address announcer: "Kings' goal scored by No. 99, Wayne Gretzky!"

Don't slash me, push me or high-stick me. Pinch me. I must be dreaming. Wayne Gretzky is already scoring goals for the Kings. All this, and the Lakers, too. The Forum has never been so fabulous.

Back in Canada, hockey was, of course, still front of mind, though the ecstasies of Los Angeles certainly didn't cross the border. There was also some serious, nation-defining business that had come to the fore. In the fall of 1987, the government of Progressive Conservative Prime Minister Brian Mulroney completed negotiations on a free trade agreement with the United States, which was signed in October 1988 and would become the central issue of an election campaign in the autumn immediately following the Gretzky trade. Mulroney—who seemed awfully comfortable with the American empire, once famously singing a duet with President Ronald Reagan on "When Irish Eyes Are Smiling," to the chagrin of cultural nationalists—sold the pact to Canadians as a natural evolution, as a necessary step to protect the Canadian economy, more an acknowledgement of a pre-existing relationship than the start of something new. The opposition Liberals and New Democrats suggested otherwise, that it represented an immediate, tangible threat to the country's sovereignty, and in the campaign that followed they wrapped themselves in the flag and in protectionist rhetoric, decrying the Americanization of Canada. "We reject this deal because it turns us into little more than a colony of the United States," Liberal leader John Turner said during an impassioned speech to Parliament. "Let the people decide—between a Conservative government which is willing to sell Canada's soul for a deal which gives us virtually nothing in return, and this [Liberal] party, which will advance a trade strategy . . . but without shredding our political independence or yielding on the sovereignty that has made this a unique nation."

Today, there is a wealth of academic literature devoted to the ensuing crisis of national identity—some of it questioning whether it was really a crisis at all. But what it was, certainly, was one of those rare moments when sport naturally intersected with politics, when there seemed to be continuity between the playing field and the real world. And it wasn't just Gretzky. A month or so after the trade, there was also that unfortunate incident at the Olympics in Seoul, when the most recognizable Canadian on the planet, immediately following the moment of his greatest triumph, tested positive for the use of performance-enhancing drugs. Ben Johnson's fall set off a profound, wrenching period of self-criticism that in many ways is still going on, an examination not just of what he did and why, but of how Canadians reacted to him. The shame of having so celebrated a cheater was matched by the shame at how quickly we cast him aside.

Almost simultaneous were two of the greatest hand-wringing exercises in national history, both involving sport. When it was revealed that Carl Lewis, the American who finished second to Johnson and was then handed the gold medal, had also been guilty of drug use in the past, but that those results had been suppressed to protect his interests and U.S. interests, it played to the same age-old theme as the Gretzky trade. Canadians, intellectually, understood their relationship with their southern neighbours, understood that they were huge and mostly happy consumers of American culture and American products, that they were a little fish swimming next to an often genial but always intimidating whale. But when Americans decided that they had to get their way, that they wanted what we had—even though it meant everything to us and just about nothing to them—the relationship was immediately cast in different, far less benign terms, with someone surely invoking a history of conflict dating back at least to the War of 1812. What to do when the Yanks coveted one of our greatest natural resources, when they just reached in and took, by virtue of their economic might, what was by birthright ours? Gretzky's old man, Walter, summed up the sentiment as well as anyone. "He's a Canadian institution and what's Canadian should remain Canadian," he said of his boy. "It's a son-of-a-gun when Americans can take away something like that. . . . You Americans think you can buy anything we have. That's not the way I feel. That's reality."

At least one sports sociologist, Steve J. Jackson, in a paper entitled *Gretzky Nation,* argues that what followed was merely a case of
opportunistic politicians and other parties with vested interests
exploiting the emotions kicked off by the Gretzky trade in their
anti–free trade campaigns, aided and abetted by a compliant
media. (" . . . [T]he media, for whatever reason and intent (if any),
articulated the Wayne Gretzky scenario within the discourse of a
culturally based Canadian identity, which they suggest, is constantly and increasingly under threat from its overbearing southern
neighbour. Gretzky is characterized as portraying the supposed
plight of Canada, with Janet Jones representing the American
threat even though her influence on his move was really never
substantiated. Although the Gretzky saga was overwhelmingly
articulated within the framework of a discourse of crisis, it would
be foolish and inaccurate to presume that this representation
guaranteed any influence upon the Canadian populace.")
Certainly, a whole lot of people made hay with it–none more
than Turner, who enjoyed some of his finest moments as a passionate opponent of free trade, more than happy to link the Tories and
Mulroney with Pocklington, the least popular man in Canada.
When he was accused in Parliament of anti-Americanism, Turner
shot back: "That is another Conservative myth. We are not anti-
American; we are pro-Canadian, and we don't like being sold out.
Sold out! Like what happened to Wayne Gretzky. What Peter
Pocklington is to Edmonton, our prime minister is to Canada."
And there were also others outside the fray who at the time took
the connection between the Gretzky deal and the anti–free trade
movement very seriously. "The deal could hurt the pending
U.S.–Canada trade agreement," sports sociologist Neale Snarr
told Kevin Allen of *USA Today.* "I'm not saying the Gretzky trade
to Los Angeles will kill [the agreement]. But I wouldn't be surprised to see it happen. . . . [Canadians] view it as another example of the U.S. flexing its big-money muscle to get something
from Canada."

Of course, in the end the Gretzky trade did nothing of the sort.
It didn't kill the free trade agreement, nor did anything else. The

Conservatives won a reduced majority in Parliament, with less than half of the popular vote, and the agreement became law. It would later be expanded into the larger North American Free Trade Agreement, bringing Mexico into the fold, with precious little protest. Politically, it was Turner's last stand. He would soon be supplanted as Liberal leader by Jean Chrétien. Life went on, hockey went on, franchise fortunes rose and fell, Gretzky's life and career continued in Los Angeles, and Canada remained a sovereign nation, culturally distinct in many ways, including its all-encompassing passion for the national game.

But were Canadians really wrong to feel like the sky was falling the day Gretzky was sold to the Kings? Soon enough, they would see the business of big-league hockey apparently begin to outgrow Canada—or at least the smaller markets in Canada. All of that money, all of those super-wealthy owners suddenly taking an interest in the game, skyrocketing player salaries, all conspired to make it difficult to compete on a level playing field. In 1995, the Quebec Nordiques moved to Denver, after their ownership, unable to finance the construction of a new arena, finally threw in the towel. A year later the Winnipeg Jets, following a prolonged death spiral during which fans demonstrated in the streets (and after absorbing significant government subsidies), were sold and moved to Phoenix, Arizona, where they were rechristened the Coyotes. Soon enough, there would be talk of how the Oilers would inevitably be forced out of Edmonton, with Houston cited as the most likely destination. Even the NHL's one concession to Canadian fans during the years of Gretzky-driven expansion, establishing a franchise in Ottawa in 1992, seemed for years doomed to failure as the Senators teetered on the brink of financial ruin.

Call it what you like—a cultural crisis, an identity crisis, the simple inevitability of market economics in play. The Gretzky trade signalled a change in direction for the NHL, which for so many Canadians was the same thing as hockey culture. The league was headed south, for what appeared to be the land of milk and honey. It was following the money, and there was nothing anyone could do to stop it. Any Canadian hockey fan who, on the day that Wayne Gretzky was sold to the Los Angeles Kings, imagined that a piece of their heritage had been sold along with him, would in the coming years have every reason to believe that was so.

Chapter Twelve

A LONG GOODBYE

O N THE DAY THAT WAYNE Gretzky was traded, Glen Sather set his anger aside just long enough to give Bruce McNall some sound advice—consider it a little throw-in for his fifteen-million-dollar investment, courtesy of a great hockey mind. Go out and get yourself a goalie, Sather said. You need one. In February of 1989, the Los Angeles Kings finally did just that, acquiring Kelly Hrudey by trade from the New York Islanders, a necessary piece for a team that had been lifted considerably by Gretzky's presence, but still wasn't as good as it might be. With Hrudey playing well between the pipes and the team growing in confidence in front of him, the Kings sizzled down the stretch and wound up finishing second in their division behind Calgary, but with the fourth-best record in the entire NHL. By kismet and by the rules of seeding, their opponents in the first Stanley Cup play-off round would be the Edmonton Oilers.

Gretzky's old team had struggled to get its act together that first season without him, and every time the Oilers and Kings played, it was as though the unsettling drama of his departure was being played out again. Former teammates kept an awkward distance in the hopes of maintaining their competitive focus. "It was tough even to look at him," Kevin Lowe says. "It was the elephant in the room all of the time, as much as you try to move on," Simpson says. "If Peter had dealt with it properly and just said, look, it was my decision and it was a business decision, I think the guys would have maybe respected that. But there was the innuendo that it was Wayne asking and all of the stuff that Peter did at the press conference—I think that soured everybody a little bit."

But all of them knew who it was in the other uniform, even if it seemed that the Edmonton fans had become colour-blind, cheering Gretzky when the Kings came to town the way they had cheered him when he was one of their own. "Those games fuelled the fire for him," Lowe says. "All of the attention was on him. We looked at some of our fans like they were jumping ship, becoming Kings fans for a night. It was one of the few times that ever happened, because Edmonton fans are notorious for booing anybody who came back, no matter if they wanted to leave or not."

There were also problems with the Oilers that extended beyond the emotional: Grant Fuhr had reported to training camp overweight and struggled all season to find his form, joining other stalwarts like Glenn Anderson, who seemed never to have regained his balance following the trade, and Messier and Kurri, who were still mad at the owner and mad at the world. Though Jimmy Carson piled up points and Simpson enjoyed another fine season, the Oilers finished seventh in the league, convincing just about everyone that the dynasty was over, that without Gretzky, the supporting cast didn't add up to much. Something essential had changed for the team, on the ice and in the dressing room. "We accepted defeat more easily than ever before," Fuhr said. "It took awhile for us to regain that fear of losing." The team seemed to have a hole where its heart used to be, and it didn't take a hockey genius to understand why.

"It's been a beauty of a season," Sather said sardonically before the playoff series against the Kings began, still in a sour mood. He understood by now that Pocklington wasn't going to be pumping much of his windfall back into the hockey team, where it might have made a huge difference in a pre-salary cap world. He couldn't have been thrilled with the matchup, either, with the scene set for humiliating playoff elimination at the hands of the departed hero.

But his Oilers weren't quite dead yet. Through the first four games of the series (with Hrudey missing the opener with the flu, then fighting to regain his health), it seemed as the though the old champions had merely been sleepwalking, had been biding their time, understanding that when it mattered they could turn it on at will. Edmonton built a three-games-to-one lead, which historically had been nearly insurmountable in the Stanley Cup playoffs—only five other teams had ever come back from that deficit. Given the wealth of experience on the Edmonton squad, given how few of the Kings had ever been called upon to really show their mettle, the hockey world outside of Los Angeles felt secure in its belief that balance was finally being restored eight months after the deal that shook the world. The Oilers might not be as great as they had been, but they could still be very good without Gretzky after all, and the Kings had come so far, so fast, that it was only natural they would fall back. It happened all the time in professional sport—a reality check—and even Gretzky couldn't change that on his own. The Oilers were starting to feel the hangover lifting, finally. "We've got that fear back," Fuhr said after winning game four, "and now we'll be tough to beat."

The Edmonton fans seemed to be recovering as well, rediscovering their loyalty to the uniform, embracing their team—their different team—and now willing to cast Gretzky as the enemy, at least temporarily. Late in the season, he had taken potshots at both Pocklington (naturally) and Sather during a newspaper interview, suggesting that the latter had known more about the trade than he had let on at the time. There was clearly bad blood, enough that Sather felt compelled to fire back with a denial, to say that the only role he'd had in the deal was in trying to kill it when he had found out. Edmontonians were now being forced to make a choice between the glorious past and the less certain present. They decided to stick with their guys, to stick with the Oilers' players and their coach and even, by extension, to stick with the owner, whom a few months back they had wanted to tar and feather. Briefly, it appeared that their loyalty would be rewarded. After winning game three, with the series apparently in his team's control, Pocklington felt confident enough of the fans' affection to opine that the people of his city now supported his decision to sell Gretzky. Though he was wrong about that, they at the very least still loved their Oilers. They wanted desperately to beat the Kings, to reassert the franchise's dominance—and every time Gretzky touched the puck at Northlands Coliseum, they now booed him without reservation, a reminder, as if he needed it, that this was no longer his home.

That brief intimation of old glories turned out to be a mirage. The 3–1 lead evaporated. Hrudey felt better, the Kings rose to the occasion, Gretzky was magnificent and the Oilers, who in their championship years had been able to battle through any adversity, who had learned how to finish off a wounded foe, now found the well dry, their old killer instinct gone. "The guys just didn't have the heart," Lowe says. The climax came in a seventh game at the Forum in front of what had become the usual star-studded crowd, as Gretzky contributed two goals and an assist in an easy 6–3 win, the biggest victory in Los Angeles hockey history to that point. "Let Posterity note that the Edmonton Oiler dynasty expired last Saturday at 10:29 p.m., Pacific daylight time," Austin Murphy wrote in *Sports Illustrated*. "The mortal blow, though, had been struck eight months earlier, on Aug. 9, 1988. That was the day Wayne Gretzky became a Los Angeles King and the day a great team, the Oilers—winners of four Stanley Cups in five seasons—became merely good."

"He said after game three that the people of Edmonton had told him the trade was a good trade," Gretzky said of Pocklington, twisting the knife just a bit. "We'll see what they say tomorrow." He was a bit more conciliatory towards his old teammates. "I saw those guys every day, and yet we didn't speak," he said. "That's not what life is supposed to be about. You're supposed to be able to talk to your best friends. Those two, Kevin [Lowe] and Mark [Messier], are the ones I feel most sorry for. They are champions."

For public consumption, Sather paid the appropriate respect to his former captain. "If anybody thought for a moment when he was sold last summer to Los Angeles that he wasn't going to make a difference in that team, they must have been smoking dope. . . . He's the greatest hockey player in the world, and he'll stay that way as long as he plays. If you don't think that guy has an effect on a hockey club . . . you just have to coach him to find out."

But behind the closed doors of the Oilers' dressing room, listening as the Kings celebrated their victory and the Los Angeles crowd went wild, Sather delivered a rather different message to his players. "Look out there," he told them. "There's your little buddy out there dancing at centre ice after he just shoved it up your ass. Don't forget that. Don't ever forget that."

"We weren't the same team," Simpson says. "That was the lesson we needed to learn. We needed it. We needed it bad."

The Kings would lose in the next round to the eventual Stanley Cup champions, the Calgary Flames, but that playoff victory over the defending champs had provided more than enough confirmation of the miracle transformation, of Gretzky's magical abilities and of McNall's entrepreneurial genius in bringing him to town. Writing in the *Los Angeles Times* the morning after the seventh-game win over the Oilers, columnist Scott Ostler perfectly captured the joyous mood of the city and the way it had embraced both the player and the owner as stars.

It seems crazy now, but when King owner Bruce McNall made the trade for Gretzky, there were a lot of knowledgeable hockey people who said McNall was making a huge mistake, giving away too much, bankrupting the franchise.

All Gretzky did was jack the Kings up from the 18th-best team in the league to fourth best, instantly revitalize the franchise and convert about 100,000 L.A. fans to hockey.

"Bruce showed a lot of courage making that trade," Jerry Buss said Monday night in the Kings' dressing room. "You don't just step up to the line with $15 million of your own money like that, plus (Gretzky's) additional salary."

Buss, the former King owner, tried hard to make a trade for Gretzky two years earlier, at roughly the same price, and Buss and Rogie Vachon almost pulled it off. At the last minute, Edmonton owner Peter Pocklington backed off.

When McNall came calling, though, the timing was better, Pocklington was ready and was blinded by the cash.

In the dressing room after the Kings knocked Edmonton out of the playoffs, a reporter asked McNall, "Does this represent a triumph of money over tradition?"

McNall wasn't offended, because he does not offend easily.

"That's a good question," McNall said. "It (money) didn't hurt any, did it?"

They were already becoming all but inseparable in the public imagination: Gretzky and McNall, McNall and Gretzky, joined at the hip, joined at the wallet, not just employer and employee, but partners, soulmates, very different characters but still the best of pals. Certainly, McNall paid and Gretzky played, and both benefited enormously, but away from hockey, off the ice, their personal and business relationship flourished and expanded and took on an entirely different cast. "Of course, the minute I went after him with the Kings he became my business partner in a way," McNall told the *New York Times*. "Although he has no equity in the team, it would be naive of me to think he's not. Ninety-five percent of our success is due to him." McNall's interests became Gretzky's interests, and the owner became his star player's financial mentor, his social mentor, much as Pocklington had been during the early days in Edmonton. McNall's investment schemes would often involve Gretzky as a very visible co-investor, inspiring confidence among others who might come on board, since they knew McNall would be a fool to play his best asset for a sucker. He would use Gretzky—as Pocklington had—as an adornment, dragging him along to meetings with potential investors as a symbol of his success, as a sort of living, breathing Rolex watch, that might more easily loosen purse strings, make them think with their sports fan hearts as much as their heads. "Bruce kept him really, really busy," Luc Robitaille

remembers. "The first two years, I don't think Wayne had any time
to himself. He'd come off the plane and Bruce would take him in
the car somewhere." When Bruce bought a Honus Wagner baseball
card for the then unheard-of sum of $451,000, during a boom
period in the sports memorabilia business, Gretzky was his co-
investor. (The card was later sold, at a profit, to the Wal-Mart corporation, which used it for promotional purposes.) When McNall's
race horse Saumarez won the prestigious Prix de l'Arc de Triomphe,
or another, Golden Pheasant, won the Arlington Million, everyone
knew that Gretzky also owned a piece of the action and presumably was building his own fortune. Naturally, McNall brought
Gretzky into the world of coins—though, rather than the ancients,
Gretzky interests apparently tilted (fill in your own punchline here)
towards Canadian currency. (Asked by a reporter if coins were an
appropriate and conservative investment for professional athletes,
McNall said: "Yes. That's why I have a couple of hundred million
dollars.") When McNall purchased the Toronto Argonauts of the
Canadian Football League—an apparently moribund franchise in
an ancient, idiosyncratic loop, struggling just to survive, his co-
owners were Gretzky and their mutual pal, the comedian and movie
star John Candy, another expat Canadian and a die-hard fan of the
team. (McNall's influence on the CFL is worthy of a book in itself.
The short version: at a time when his plans for the NHL seemed to
be absolutely on course, he cast an eye at the league and imagined
a similar play. He could buy a team playing in a nearly new domed
stadium for next to nothing because the major market that was its
home had become largely indifferent to the sport. McNall would
then somehow infuse the Argos with star power, fill the house, and
then lead the entire league down a previously unimagined path to
American expansion, sending everyone's franchise values through
the roof. Sound familiar? And if that didn't work, McNall's lease
deal with the SkyDome assured him of football exclusivity, putting
him in an enviable position should the National Football League
ever hope to establish a franchise in Toronto. The Argos' Gretzky
was Raghib "Rocket" Ismail, a star kick returner and receiver from
the University of Notre Dame who would have been the first pick

in the NFL draft had the Argos not outbid the NFL and signed him first—generating headlines around the continent. At the team's opening game at the SkyDome, a near-capacity crowd of fifty thousand was entertained at halftime by the Blues Brothers band, and was joined by a cast of Hollywood celebrities McNall had flown north on the Kings' jet for the occasion. Sadly, the magic soon gave way to some grim financial realities. When it became obvious that there would be no Argo miracle and the losses piled up, Gretzky—whose heart was never really in the project—quickly let it be known that he wanted out. Candy hung on, and was a supporter of the league and the team until his sad, premature death.) The truth was, when it came to investing, Gretzky was, by nature, no risk-taker. He was Wally's boy—he liked to make money, he liked to keep it, and he had little stomach for risk. But with Bruce, it just all seemed so natural, so fail-safe, so much like he was riding the coattails of the cleverest guy in any room, that any instinctive doubts evaporated.

Soon enough, Gretzky would assume the same flashy Hollywood trappings as his boss, driving a Rolls Royce, building a mansion on a hill, become a Hollywood guy, an L.A. guy, doing what it took to fit in. He was of America now, and it wasn't as if he was ever coming home. The day Gretzky was sold to the Kings was the last day he'd really have a foot in Canada. He and Janet would settle in Los Angeles, raise their family there, and as his career path eventually took him to St. Louis (briefly), New York and Phoenix, it would be true that Gretzky had spent more of his life outside of Canada than in it. Canadians were familiar enough with the pattern, having watched as a long line of musicians and actors and comedians had moved to the United States out of necessity while pursuing their careers. It happened so often, and seemed so obviously necessary, that it certainly wasn't perceived as any kind of sell-out. Gretzky stands alone in one respect, though: the longer he was away from home, the more Canadian, in a kind of pure, mythical, cultural sense, he seemed to become in the national imagination.

In part, that was a reflection of the way he had departed, the way it appeared he hadn't left the country of his own free will. (Most any Canadian would continue to believe that, given his druthers, Gretzky would have played his entire career in Edmonton, with the Oilers.) Part of it had to do with a sense of pride in the way Gretzky was taking the national sport and making it matter on the biggest stage in the world, however much of a double-edged sword that might actually represent for Canadian hockey interests. Part of it was masterful packaging, especially when it came to Gretzky's carefully chosen endorsement deals, an unbroken line stretching to the present day. Twenty years after he left Edmonton, the Ford Motor Company could still use him as a pitchman, extolling the virtues of vehicles "Built for Life in Canada," and the audience didn't require any further cue. Wayne was Canadian, so he understood exactly what that meant.

By the time the day finally came for Gretzky to retire from the NHL as a player, a wave of nostalgia and affection engulfed his former homeland. It was as though Canadians could easily imagine him and Janet and the kids, after their forced exile in a foreign (at least for him) land, coming back and finding themselves a nice house in Brantford, up the street from Wally and Phyllis, where they could raise a family right, away from the corrupting influences of America, where Wayne could build his own backyard rink.

That wasn't him anymore, by a longshot, but it was what Canadians wanted him to be. Just as his arrival on the scene as a ten-year-old prodigy had instantly been adapted to fit the great shinny creation myth, Gretzky as an adult would be forever cast as the small-town Canadian boy made good, whose heart was always really in his homeland, who never really changed. It didn't matter where he lived, whom he hung out with, what were the details of his real life. In the national imagination, he was forever ours, because we required him to be that way. We find the heroes we need, we worship the gods we create.

When he temporarily returned to the fold in 2002, after three years away from the game, to act as the general manager of Canada's team in the Salt Lake City Olympics (a move that was equally beneficial to Canadian hockey, as the country captured its first gold medal since 1952, and to Gretzky himself; his profile and earning power, both of which had waned during his absence, were significantly boosted) it seemed a perfect fit. When at a press conference during the Games, with Canada's team floundering, Gretzky without prompting launched into a tirade–spontaneous or contrived–about how the whole hockey world wanted Canada to lose, it became a natural call to arms for both the country and the players. When it was revealed that a loonie had been buried at centre ice–on American soil–for good luck, it seemed a defiant nationalist gesture. And when, four years later, with his wife and one of his best friends embroiled in a gambling scandal, Gretzky's Olympic magic wore off in Turin, all was forgiven instantly, because the country understood that his beating Canadian heart was in the right place.

Gretzky would return to deliver one more painful reminder of how it used to be for the Oilers fans–this time on home ice. In the early part of the 1989–90 season he was closing in on Gordie Howe's career NHL points record, a stunning achievement given that it had taken Howe 1,767 games to reach 1,850 points, while Gretzky would hit the mark in just 780. He could have done it in Los Angeles, or he could have turned the trick in another rink. But as with the playoff matchup the previous spring, it was as though something larger was at play. On October 15, 1989, back at the Northlands Coliseum, the Edmonton crowd was once again cheering Gretzky on, and the Oilers wanted no part of the humiliation. Despite their best efforts, they were helpless to prevent it. "When he broke Gordie's record–that was just unbelievable," Kevin Lowe says. "We were playing such a good game. We had shut him down well. We had one last face-off–the draw went in the corner and I went in to grab it. I threw it off the glass on the short side. It was up high enough. It was getting out of the zone–except Larry Robinson was there, all six foot three of him. I couldn't believe that he kept it in. I remember watching the play–it was almost like slow motion in a dream. He put it down and corralled it and he got it on the net. Then Billy Ranford's kicking the rebound right onto Gretzky's stick. I'm watching the whole thing saying, 'You're shitting me.'"

Different names, a shifting cast. John Muckler, the longtime loyal assistant to Sather, was behind the bench now, leaving Sather to concentrate full time on his duties as president and general manager of the Oilers. Ranford had claimed the starting goaltending job that season from the injured Grant Fuhr—who after the season would admit to a substance-abuse issue, without specifying which substance was involved (his ex-wife said it was cocaine), and accept a year-long suspension from the league. Shortly after Gretzky broke Howe's record against the Oilers, Sather solved the Jimmy Carson problem, trading the unhappy player who had never really fit in to the Detroit Red Wings, part of a larger deal that would bring Petr Klíma, Adam Graves and Joe Murphy to Edmonton. The Kings, meanwhile, continued to add pieces, including bigname pieces like Robinson, who had been part of the great Montreal Canadiens teams of the 1970s and who would now cash in at career's end thanks to McNall's largesse. And they had also made one rather large subtraction: at the end of the 1988–89 season, despite the playoff win over the Oilers, Robbie Ftorek was relieved of his duties as head coach and replaced with Tom Webster. His failing, all agreed, came from engaging in a battle he couldn't win with the most important player in the dressing room, the most important player in the league. The final straw came during a game against the Detroit Red Wings, when after making a mistake that resulted in a goal against his team, Gretzky smashed his stick against the crossbar in frustration. "He was pissed off at himself," Robitaille remembers. "Me, as a player, I liked the fact that Wayne broke his stick. That's what you wanted out of your teammates." Things were otherwise going swimmingly for the Kings at that moment—they were in first place in their division. McNall had invited a group of people to the game who, for one reason or another, he was trying to impress, and had them sitting directly behind the team's bench. Ftorek decided on the spot to seize what he believed was a teaching moment, a way of asserting his authority, of preaching to the other players that all were created equal, and all were equally responsible for their failings. He became the first coach, ever, to bench Wayne Gretzky. Ftorek then compounded his sin. When asked by reporters after the game if the superstar had been hurt, he opted not to tell the traditional little white lie, and instead threw Gretzky directly under the bus. Was Wayne hurt? No, Ftorek said, he sat him down for displaying negative emotions and setting a bad example for his teammates.

Gretzky muttered something about how if a guy wanted to teach, maybe he ought to be teaching in the minors and not the NHL, and an always uneasy relationship was pushed beyond the breaking point. "From that day, it was just not the same," Robitaille says. Even if he'd gone on to win the Stanley Cup, Ftorek had essentially fired himself.

Under Webster, the Kings struggled to follow up on their break-through season, finishing a mediocre fourth in the Smythe Division. Gretzky enjoyed what would have been an exceptional year for anyone but him—his 142 regular-season points represented his lowest total since 1979–80. In the first round of the playoffs, the Kings upset the defending Stanley Cup champions from Calgary in six tough games, and then again drew the Oilers—who had fallen behind the star-crossed Winnipeg Jets 3–1 in their first-round series before storming back to win in seven. Craig Simpson remembers watching the final game of the L.A.–Calgary series on television with some of his teammates. "It was perfect," he says. "We get to play L.A. We had something to prove."

Many imagined a repeat of the spring before, with the Gretzky hex once more coming into play. Instead, they discovered an Oilers team that had, over the course of two seasons, redefined itself, with other players stepping to the fore, with Messier now fully emerged from Gretzky's shadow as its leader, with Esa Tikkanen shadowing and largely shutting down Gretzky, with the talent acquired in the Carson trade playing a key role, and with a new sense of mission. "It was a bit of an eye-opener for us," Kevin Lowe says. "The whole trade, and losing in '89. Winning in 1990 was a chance for the rest of the team to validate ourselves with the city. There was a lot of talk that year—it was all about Wayne and Wayne and Wayne. It's not like we were trying to prove anything. But you think to yourself privately, it takes a bunch of guys to win a championship. Not just one guy—as great as he is. I think it really motivated us to want to win a championship to prove [something] to everybody."

Whereas before, it had been awkward playing against Gretzky, to the point that the Oilers seemed reluctant even to hit him, to push him around, this time there was no hesitation. "I remember in one of the games he passed the puck, and I drilled him," Simpson says. "He chased me back up the ice, hollering 'Simmer, you cocksucker.' When I went to the bench, I remember saying to Mess, 'I feel awful.' But that's the way you play against any great player. And that's how we turned the page."

Backed by the brilliant goaltending from Ranford, who would win the Conn Smythe Trophy as the playoff MVP, Edmonton swept Gretzky and the Kings aside in four games, and swept aside every other obstacle in their path as well: they would lose only three more games in the entire playoffs, beating the Boston Bruins in five in the final to claim the franchise's fifth Stanley Cup—its first without Wayne Gretzky. Sather believes that the players still felt his absence. "They all missed him," he says. "It was something that they had to do, but I think that they missed Wayne more than anything, I think the whole team did. It was sort of the consolation prize. It wasn't the same." But there was also a deep sense of satisfaction in the dressing room precisely because they *had* done it without him. Gretzky was among the first to call with his congratulations after they won the Cup, and the old blood ties remained strong. This one wasn't *his* Cup, though. It was *theirs*. It belonged to a new Edmonton team, a new Edmonton champion, linked to but separate from those that had come before because of that one missing piece. Bittersweet, perhaps, but oh so sweet as well for all of those in the room who had been cast as second bananas, as add-ons, as spare parts. And for Sather, for Pocklington, here was affirmation that it hadn't all been about one guy, that it hadn't just been the luck of the draw. Pocklington had sold Gretzky, endured the wrath of the fans, and now here they were standing and cheering as the Cup was raised once more. Sather had taken his broken-hearted squad, endured a terrible, dispiriting year, made some savvy personnel moves without any great cash infusion from above, and then added another ring to his collection. In some ways, it was even better than the other four.

And in every way, it was also the end.

Glen Sather figures that the larger National Hockey League was never cheering on the Oilers dynasty. "I don't think they were always that excited about Edmonton winning the Stanley Cup," he says. "Most of the teams did whatever they could to try and stop us. The league made rule changes. They did all kinds of things to put the boots to us. A small market in western Canada. You get Wayne into a large market, it helps raise the profile of the team. It did a lot of good things for the league." But it wasn't a conspiracy that ended it. It wasn't a rule change. It wasn't even the Gretzky deal itself, but rather the forces it had unleashed, none of them good for Edmonton.

Peter Pocklington's financial problems, only peripherally related to his hockey team, would continue, and the fifteen million dollars he got from Bruce McNall—or at least, from Bruce McNall's broadcasters and bankers—could only staunch the bleeding temporarily. At the same time, player salaries in the NHL began to escalate dramatically, fuelled by expansion money and pushed by a clever union and player agents, who would exploit the league's labour agreement to their advantage, hoodwinking the owners time and time again. In one of the NHL's smallest markets, the Oilers had found it difficult to compete even before inflation really kicked in, and now the players certainly weren't about to offer Pocklington any hometown discounts. Messier would play only one more season in Edmonton before being traded to the New York Rangers, part of an exodus that quickly broke up the last remnants of the championship teams. "Players realized that the seventy or eighty thousand a year they were making wasn't a lot of money," Sather says. "They could all see that. These guys aren't fools. But the NHL wasn't ready for that. There wasn't enough television revenue to support it. Then the expansion came along, the owners started thinking they could build bigger buildings with more suites and create more revenue. All of the revenue that you created from those suites went to the players. So now, everything changed. All of a sudden you're not a family anymore. Your family has been fractured. Somebody has gone someplace else. He's living a different lifestyle, he's got a much bigger home, he's got a lot better home, he's making a million dollars. Things change. They did change. The economy was changing everywhere. But they hadn't changed in Alberta yet. . . .

"That team was a hell of a team. That team was in a position to win for a lot more years than it did. We didn't have anybody talking about making huge amounts of money or wanting to get out of Edmonton. Those players all loved Edmonton. They loved the team. They played hard. They worked hard. They had all kind of grown up together. They were at the right time to keep playing like that. . . . You think of what happened to Peter [Pocklington] after that. My theory was that his demise came from that."

In 1993, the Oilers missed the playoffs, and would miss them for the next four seasons. Pleading poverty and implying that the franchise might otherwise be forced to leave town (among the cities he flirted with was the perpetual bridesmaid Hamilton, Ontario), Pocklington cut a deal with the City of Edmonton in 1994 which gave him the right to operate Northlands Coliseum and to pocket whatever profits he could generate from the building in exchange for two million dollars a year and—most importantly—the promise to keep the franchise in the city until at least 2004. Three years later, he agreed to sell the team to Les Alexander, the owner of the Houston Rockets of the National Basketball Association. Pocklington pledged that Alexander would operate in Edmonton in good faith, that he would keep the team there while hoping to acquire an expansion team for Houston, but no one believed him, and the city moved to block the sale. In 1998, with the Alberta Treasury Board breathing down Pocklington's neck over a hundred-million-dollar loan that remained unpaid, and with Alexander still lurking in the background, a group of thirty-seven local businessmen cobbled together enough money to buy the Oilers and keep them in the city, though their long-term prospects still appeared bleak. But the Oilers would survive the low Canadian dollar, survive salary escalation and the 2004–05 NHL lockout (though there would certainly be tense moments along the way), and reach the Stanley Cup finals once more, in 2006, losing in seven games to another former WHA team, the Carolina Hurricanes (formerly the Hartford Whalers).

A year after selling the Oilers, Pocklington placed his main holding company into bankruptcy and lost his Triple-A baseball team, his private jet and his art and wine collections along the way. In 2000, Pocklington and his wife, Eva, left Edmonton and moved to Toronto. Two years after that, they shifted their home base permanently to their winter digs in posh Indian Wells, California, and Pocklington let it be known that he would be applying for U.S. citizenship, having soured on Canada, or perhaps having exhausted its possibilities for handouts. By all outward appearances, he and Eva still enjoyed the opulent lifestyle that had been their trademark during the years in Edmonton.

Trouble followed Pocklington to California. A civil suit filed against him in 2008, which included the Alberta government among the aggrieved parties, alleged among other things that Pocklington owed more than twelve million dollars to provincial taxpayers from bailouts and accrued interest—quite a number for such a champion of the free-market system. In August 2008, Pocklington filed for personal bankruptcy, claiming less than $3,000 in assets ($200 in his wallet, a $500 watch, a $500 set of golf clubs, $300 in clothing and shoes, $450 in appliances and furnishings, $500 worth of memorabilia and $450 in other personal goods) and more than $19 million in debt—soon after U.S. marshals raided his house to seize art, furniture, sports memorabilia and some of Eva's wardrobe on behalf of a group of his creditors, who claimed that he had bilked them. "They took everything that they could get their hands on, and it'll all come back," Pocklington told Brent Jang of the *Report on Business* magazine. "In the U.S., in some cases, it's a bit of a police state. It's sickening. California seems the worst in the country. They have so many lawyers per square inch, and they're all just trolling. It's sad."

On March 11, 2009, Pocklington was charged with two counts of felony bankruptcy fraud for allegedly misleading authorities about his assets. If convicted, he could be sentenced to up to ten years in prison. After appearing in court with his wrists bound in chains, Pocklington spent two nights in jail before being bailed out by his old pal Glen Sather, who put up a piece of property he owned in Minnesota to secure the million-dollar bond. Because he was viewed as a flight risk, upon his release pending trial, Pocklington was required to wear an ankle bracelet equipped with an electronic tracking device.

Still, unbowed, Pocklington planned to go ahead with the publication of his autobiography in the fall of 2009. The working title: *I'd Trade Him Again.*

The events in Edmonton—sad, then happy, then sad—didn't matter a lick to Bruce McNall, because the future he envisioned for hockey didn't include cities like that, or Winnipeg or Quebec City. It was unfortunate, perhaps, for the loyal fans up there, but this was a natural, evolutionary process that, with Gretzky in Los Angeles and Americans turning on to the game en masse, simply could not be stopped. It would be survival of the fittest—or, rather, survival of the richest—and the investors who got in on the ground floor would be swept along with the tide. His own financial empire was far more precariously constructed even than Pocklington's, but hockey was going to save him.

Around the same time that the Kings were regrouping from the 1990 playoff loss to the Oilers, over at the Walt Disney Studios, somebody had a bright idea, a movie pitch that might well have been scribbled on the back of a napkin. Nothing big. Just a little family-oriented film, a clichéd, triumph-of-the-misfit-underdogs story, absolutely by the book, a kind of *Bad News Bears* redux, except this time it would feature a hockey team instead of a baseball team, albeit with an equally goofy name. The sport seemed to be a bit more in the air these days, a bit closer to the zeitgeist. And everybody remembered *Slapshot,* the 1977 comedy starring Paul Newman. Among the motley, heart-warming crew that made up *The Mighty Ducks,* there would be a smart kid, a fat kid, a nerd, a misunderstood kid. And, cast as the coach, no big star, but someone marketable, believable as the crusty cynic who finds redemption through the unlikely, inspiring victory (of course) in the big game.

Michael Eisner was the boss at Disney at the time. He had inherited the Mouse Factory built by Uncle Walt and helped transform it into a modern, diversified entertainment giant. Eisner wasn't a hockey guy, but his two sons, Anders and Eric, happened to be among the relatively small number of kids then playing the game in Los Angeles, and were nuts about it. McNall knew Eisner from his forays into the movie business. Eisner at least knew *of* McNall. And though he'd never considered getting Disney into the professional sports business before, though he didn't know a thing about the National Hockey League, all of that would change soon enough.

Back in the days when everyone said he had a Midas touch, the world seemed to fall neatly into place that way for Bruce McNall all of the time.

Chapter Thirteen

THE LAST PERFECT MOMENT (II)
MAY 9, 1993

T HE IMPOSING YELLOW-BRICK edifice on Carlton Street, constructed as Conn Smythe's act of defiance in the face of the Great Depression, had in many ways become a hall of ghosts. Walking the corridors lined with black-and-white photographs of the glorious ancients, sitting in the uncomfortable colour-coded seats, it was still possible to imagine how it must have been, to imagine crowds of men in dark suits and fedoras, a few women dressed to the nines, hockey without advertising marring the perfect whiteness of the boards or the ice, and Maple Leaf Gardens alive with the sounds of a game that really mattered. It still looked like hockey and smelled like hockey, but how long had it been?

Since 1967, when the Leafs' Over the Hill Gang won the franchise's last Stanley Cup, defeating the hated Montreal Canadiens? Since 1972, when the Summit Series, then yet to become the mythical touchstone of Canadian culture, passed through town for game two—Canada 4, Soviet Union 1? During a few futile playoff runs in the interim? Mostly, on hockey nights the place had come to represent hopelessness, and cynicism, and forces far more troubling than those, unleashed in its dark recesses and backrooms during the years of Harold Ballard's reign.

Now, for a night, it shone with a brand new, old-fashioned light, the previously unimaginable just a single victory away: game seven of the conference finals, its victor going on to compete for the Stanley Cup. The Leafs were still in contention at this late stage for the first time in twenty-six years. They had awakened the echoes, finally, thanks to clever team-building by Cliff Fletcher, fine coaching by Pat Burns and just the right amount of good fortune. On the ice, the heroes were Doug Gilmour—undersized, dark-eyed, dangerous and compelling—and the brave, iconic, oft-injured Wendel Clark, the Leafs' lone beacon of dignity through some dreadful years, who, when asked a long set of questions, offered the same simple answer ("I'm just a farmer from Saskatchewan"), even as he was being cast as the franchise's ever-suffering St. Sebastian. A terrific team, gritty and talented and riding an emotional wave after winning each of the two previous playoff rounds over Detroit and St. Louis in dramatic seventh games—the former in a miraculous overtime finish on Nikolai Borschevsky's goal. Now, once more to the brink. The only thing standing between the Toronto Maple Leafs and a date in the finals against the Montreal Canadiens—the perfect way to end those years of wandering in the desert—was one game against a team with no glorious past, that had never won a thing, led by the greatest player in the world.

The truth was, Wayne Gretzky wasn't really the king anymore. Mario Lemieux had supplanted him as the sport's gold standard, and beyond that Gretzky had suffered through an injury-ravaged season in which he missed the first thirty-nine games with a herniated disc in his back. There were whispers that he might be done, that he might never play again. But Gretzky had come back and eventually returned to peak late-career form, and until the beginning of the Toronto series had thrived during these playoffs, his legs fresher than they might have been had he played a long, gruelling campaign. The Kings also seemed inspired by the leadership of their new coach, Barry Melrose, a larger-than-life character with an oiled-back mullet and a devotion to the positive-thinking motivational guru Anthony Robbins (a nice Hollywood touch, coming from a guy who grew up with Wendel in Kelvington). Not everyone among the players bought into Robbins's act, but by the semifinals he was travelling with the team, ready to provide a quick pick-me-up when needed.

During the first five games against Toronto, Gretzky looked like he was in need of just that. He was playing, as one Toronto writer described it, "as though he was carrying a piano on his back," and the L.A. sports press that had unconditionally adored him was now wondering aloud why he couldn't find another gear when it mattered most. Perhaps those shots across the bow inspired him—Gretzky was nothing if not media aware and sensitive on the rare occasions when he was criticized. For game six at the Forum, with the Kings trailing three games to two and their season on the line, he rode to the rescue.

In Toronto, they would tell you—and *will* tell you, will *forever* tell you—that it shouldn't have happened, that after Clark sent the game to overtime with his hat-trick goal in the dying moments of the third period, the Leafs would have triumphed in overtime had justice been done. Early in the first extra period, during a Kings power play, Gretzky struck Gilmour in the face with a high stick, drawing blood—accidentally, for sure, though still worthy of at least a two-minute penalty, probably a five-minute major, perhaps even a game misconduct. But the officiating crew, led by the remarkably coiffed Kerry Fraser, was suddenly stricken with ethical paralysis. The play stopped after Gilmour went down and then popped up rubbing his mug, while Gretzky skated away, looking very much like someone who realized he might have cost his team a victory and ended its season. The zebras talked and pondered and perhaps shat themselves at the thought of sending the icon, the NHL's number one meal ticket, to the penalty box or to the dressing room at such a crucial moment. Never saw it, they decided. Can't call what you didn't see. Fraser, looking extremely uncomfortable, conferred with linesman Ron Finn, and then they motioned the players back to the face-off circle. Gretzky scored the game-winning goal a few seconds later, and Leafs fans could argue—with real moral authority—that they had been jobbed.

Not a bad prologue for game seven, back at Maple Leaf Gardens, the already sky-high emotions in the city now heightened by that sense of grievance, by a still very much intact sense of hope, and also playing against a background of underlying dread, the residue of all of those seasons of failure. A great story was there to be written either way: the revival of a previously dominant, long-beaten-down franchise, reward for its faithful, their loyalty passed down through generations, or the triumph of the new NHL, the final confirmation of Gretzky's genius, the final act of deliverance following the events of August 9, 1988.

Once more, it is *Hockey Night in Canada,* with Bob Cole and Harry Neale looking on from their perch high above centre ice.

"Game seven," Cole says, setting the scene. "This . . . is . . . it. *Tonight.*"

All clichés aside, the atmosphere is electric. The building is thrumming—the entire city is thrumming. The Gardens is packed to the rafters, the golds, reds, greens, greys, end blues and standing room—though, emerging from the College subway station, you can still get yourself a very good seat, so long as you're willing to hand over a thousand bucks or so to one of those familiar faces hollering, "Who needs a ticket?" Farther downtown, at the SkyDome, forty thousand people have nearly filled the stands to watch the game on the big screen, to leave their homes and televisions behind and share in the communal experience, the great secular church that is spectator sport. At other times, the dome is the home of the Toronto Blue Jays, anointed champions of America's national pastime the autumn before, on their way to doing it a second time this year. The Jays are a star-studded group, a model franchise that at times has come close to usurping the Leafs as the true local obsession, with fans hanging on every pitch. When they were feted with a World Series parade, it was like nothing the city had seen before, but now, perhaps, that celebration will be topped by whatever crazy revelry a Stanley Cup might set off. Every playoff victory this spring has spawned spontaneous, rowdy street parties (they'd scoff at them in other Hogtown-hating places—only in Toronto do they riot after winning the first game in the first round), and now you can feel the first low rumblings of an eruption. Toronto, City of Champions. It has a nice ring to it.

The home team wears white. The visitors black. Wendel Clark comes close on his first shift, and then the Kings are handed the gift of a power play. It's not Kerry Fraser tonight—Andy Van Hellemond is the referee—but given the events of game six this is an unforgiving crowd, and the boos rain down. Felix Potvin in the Toronto net holds the Leafs in early, as the Kings buzz around. Then it's Toronto with a power play—a bad line change and the Kings are caught with too many men on the ice. If anyone in Edmonton is tuning in, they will note with sadness that this game is lousy with ex-Oilers: Charlie Huddy and Jari Kurri and Marty McSorley and Himself all playing for the Kings, Glenn Anderson and Mike Krushelnyski toiling for the Maple Leafs. And they are about to experience a little flashback.

Gilmour is stymied in the Kings' zone and tries to slide a pass back to the point. It never gets there. Kurri intercepts and, in the tradition of the great Edmonton teams, rather than simply icing the puck, begins a short-handed attack. Gretzky and McSorley immediately skate hard to the Toronto net and are rewarded when Kurri's clever pass sets them up on a two-on-one, with Dmitri Mironov the last Leaf defenceman standing. Gretzky skates right at him, creates the perfect passing angle and slips the puck to McSorley, who seems to have Potvin at his mercy. McSorley is having a great night; though he came to the Kings at Gretzky's behest as a security blanket, happy to ride shotgun alongside him, he demonstrates again that he's no simple goon. Right now, he is the second-best player on the ice, though perhaps a bit too deferential: instead of taking the chance offered him, McSorley decides to pass back to Gretzky, who by then is almost to the goal line, ready to watch McSorley tap it in. He is forced to react, takes the pass—awkwardly—off his right skate, and with all of his momentum still carrying him towards the boards, somehow deflects it to his stick and fires the puck past Potvin from the narrowest of angles.

"He had the gaping net and fills it with the puck," Cole says.

"He took it off the skate and then found that he didn't have much of an angle," Neale says. "But he was very cool."

Los Angeles 1, Toronto 0.

Temporarily, the crowd settles. But the fans are back in full voice soon enough. Gilmour, perhaps trying to atone for his mistake, plays as though possessed. There's a wonderful flow to the game, few whistles, plenty of chances. Then, for one glorious shift, Gilmour and his linemates—little bowlegged Borschevsky, and Dave Andreychuk, with his remarkable nose for the net—take over, pin the Kings in their own end and come oh so close to tying it. They make the mistake of staying out a little too long at the end, seeming just a little bit spent, and it costs them dearly. The Kings clear their zone, and suddenly Gretzky, McSorley and Tomas Sandström find all kinds of open space. It's a textbook three-on-two: Gretzky provides the soft pass to Sandström, trailing the play, and he beats Potvin with a wrist shot.

Los Angeles 2, Toronto 0, and the Gardens grows very quiet indeed.

"You'd better watch out for Wayne Gretzky in a big game," Neale says.

In the final seconds of the period, the Kings enjoy another power play. "What a great chance to put it on salt," Cole says. But they can't quite pull the trigger. The home team heads for the dressing room barely breathing.

It wasn't around his hockey team that the first cracks began to show, the first signs that the grand facade Bruce McNall had been constructing for most of his adult life was beginning to crumble. Of all of the elements of his fraudulent, precariously balanced financial empire, the Los Angeles Kings were among the most straightforward and the most legit. The question of where he got the money to fund his excesses, for the private jet, for Gretzky's salary—that was another story, one kept well hidden from those who ran the team day to day. As far as they were concerned, hockey per se was a straight cash-in, cash-out proposition, one that, despite the escalating costs of operating in the NHL, continued to turn a profit. For the longest time, they didn't suspect a thing.

But the bankers were wising up, though many of them were in so deep that they couldn't blow the whistle without incriminating themselves. Some of those ensnared in his rare-coin scams were coming to realize that they had been bilked. On the movie front, things were unravelling fast. And for McNall's other sports property, the Toronto Argonauts, the first flush of success, including a Grey Cup championship in 1991, strangely didn't seem to have positively altered the bottom line. The team's president, Brian Cooper, discovered that it was becoming a one-way street, that money was making its way from Toronto to Los Angeles, but precious little was coming back to keep the team afloat. "We had to pay Rocket Ismail up front, and that wiped out the season's-ticket money that I needed to operate," he remembers. "I called Sue Waks [in McNall's office] and she stalled me and stalled me." Soon afterward, Cooper was out for dinner with his wife and was accosted by a printer who was owed money and hadn't been paid—though Cooper believed the debt had been taken care of by the folks in L.A. In essence, McNall had cut off the Argos' financial lifeline, redirecting whatever cash the team could generate to more pressing concerns, leaving the team to run on fumes.

Meanwhile, McNall's larger master plan for hockey seemed to be proceeding right on schedule. He had rocketed through the ranks to become the chairman of the NHL's board of governors, an owner elected by the other owners to represent their collective interests, usurping the old-guard powers like Bill Wirtz. There had been some brief unpleasantness in 1992 when Gil Stein, who was supposed to be running the league on an interim basis after the ouster of president John Ziegler, decided he wanted to stick around—and then decided that the price of a clean exit would be his entirely undeserved election to the Hockey Hall of Fame. McNall had a hand in that, writing a letter that endorsed Stein's candidacy, but he managed to steer clear of the scandal when, amidst a torrent of bad publicity, Stein was forced to withdraw his nomination. That turned out to be but a small bump in the road. By shuttling Stein aside, McNall was able to clear the deck for his own choice to become the NHL's first commissioner: Gary Bettman, one of the two top lieutenants of National Basketball Association commissioner David Stern. Bettman took the job on February 1, 1993. (McNall actually preferred the other guy, Russ Granik, but Stern had refused to let him go, pushing Bettman to the fore instead.)

Bettman certainly wasn't a hockey guy. It wasn't just that he'd never played the game, but that you couldn't have imagined him ever playing the game. The sport seemed completely alien to him—an impression that, for Canadian fans at least, proved nearly impossible to fully erase. But since real hockey guys tended to be stuck in the past, McNall considered Bettman's lack of shinny bona fides almost an asset. The NBA under Stern had earned a reputation for being on the cutting edge of sports marketing, for packaging its games as entertainment, complete with cheerleaders and non-stop noise, leaving nothing to chance. Bettman was empowered to bring a little bit of that magic to hockey, to drag the game into the present. They wouldn't need it in Toronto or Montreal—in fact, it would run completely against the grain in traditional hockey cities—but they would certainly need it in the many far-flung, non-traditional outposts where Bettman would be expected to take the NHL through aggressive expansion and relocation.

That bandwagon was already rolling. In 1991–92, the Gund brothers were granted an expansion franchise for the Bay Area. After a couple of seasons in San Francisco's Cow Palace, the Sharks would move to a brand new arena in San Jose. (Thus was completed a circle of sorts. In the 1970s, the Gunds had been part owners of the Oakland-based California Golden Seals, who became the Cleveland Barons in 1976, then merged with the failing Minnesota North Stars two years later.) To begin the 1992–93 season, the league added teams in Ottawa (an anomaly, a smallish Canadian market, which got its team in large part because the move allowed the Leafs and Buffalo Sabres to block a franchise from being placed in Hamilton, within their territorial boundaries) and Tampa, Florida, the latter becoming the Kings' first true sunbelt cousin. In both places, the ownership situation seemed a tad vague, and perhaps a tad short on cash, but both groups promised to pay the whole fifty-million-dollar expansion fee up front, and the governors were more than happy to cash the cheques. By the time the Leafs and Kings squared off in the spring of 1993, it had been all but decided that Norm Green, the new owner of the Minnnesota North Stars, would be allowed to move his franchise to Dallas (he had originally hoped to take it to Anaheim, but other interests, as we will see, got in the way). Bettman's mission was crystal clear: keep the expansion ball rolling, enlarge hockey's footprint dramatically in the United States, build franchise equity and secure a lucrative U.S. network television contract.

In 1992–93, in the style of the Kings' own pre-season barnstorming tours, the NHL played "neutral-site" regular-season games in Indianapolis, Milwaukee, Phoenix, Miami, Oklahoma City, Dallas, Sacramento, Atlanta, Peoria, Cincinnati, Providence and Cleveland, hoping to seed hockey interest. (Games were also played in poor old Hamilton, forever destined to be stood up at the altar.) And McNall had just about wrapped up a deal that would kick-start the expansion boom, add two enormously wealthy, high-profile owners to the lodge, and perhaps, as a happy byproduct, save his own skin.

That's how McNall operated. That's how he managed to sleep at night—believing that somehow, despite the impossible situation he had created for himself, the web of deceit, the impossible debt, it would all work out, there would be one big score allowing him to cover his tracks. If he could talk Michael Eisner into buying a franchise and locating it in the new rink in Anaheim, just across the street from Disneyland—the *Mighty Ducks* movie was going to happen, the synergies were just too delicious, they could even use that goofy moniker for the NHL team—the league could ask for fifty million and Disney would happily pay it. If Eisner came in, that would be the hook to land Wayne Huizenga, the Blockbuster Video founder who also owned the Miami Dolphins, and who could establish an NHL beachhead in South Florida for another fifty million dollars. And in eternal gratitude for what he had brought to the table, for upping all of their franchise values, as a kind of super finder's fee, the governors would happily allow McNall to pocket half of the Ducks' franchise fee in return for allowing another team into the Kings' greater Los Angeles market.

That money would go straight from McNall to his bankers. But it wouldn't be nearly enough. The truth, unknown to everyone outside of his most inner circle, unknown even to his wife, was that even before the Kings and Leafs played out the last act of their compelling drama, Bruce McNall was pretty much fucked. He wasn't just going broke. He was going to jail.

"I knew I was in deep trouble," he says. "But I thought as you always do when you're in shit—you always think you can fix things. If you don't feel the ability to fix things and straighten things out, you wouldn't do anything. So I always thought I could fix it. Even at the last moment. . . . I am juggling like crazy. I'm surrounded by the Indians. I'm at Little Big Horn. And although I've got a few little helpers around, they've got popguns compared to the big bullets these guys have got. I felt right in the middle of a mess then, but I had to put on as good a face as I could.

"I've got Michael Eisner at those games too, because I'm trying to get that deal done, which is twenty-five million to me. I had the Ducks going, I had Huizenga going, I was trying to do this giant transaction with Sony Pictures, and here I've got this event going on at the same time. At some ways it was hard to focus on both.

"Very few people knew it. Even Wayne. I protected him from that for the most part. The only thing Wayne would know was that I was trying to do a new arena deal. I remember the seventh game in Toronto, when I was nervous as hell. Wayne said to me, 'What are you nervous about? I've got this. Relax.' Almost like Babe Ruth calling that home run shot. 'What are you nervous about? This is what I get paid for,' he said. I tried to separate things as much as I could. I tried to separate hockey from the things I was dealing with in the outside world. It wasn't until April of '94 that it all came crashing down. In that time I was still very confident that I would get through it. My problem was the same problem that I had when I bought Gretzky: I was under water. And I was juggling, too. I was trying to make all of this stuff work."

"The Toronto Maple Leafs are being manhandled by the ex-Edmonton Oilers," Harry Neale says to start the second period.

So far, he's right about that. But the home side isn't finished. On a power play in the early moments of the second period, Dave Andreychuk swings wide down the right wing and powers his way behind the Los Angeles net. Two Kings defencemen, Charlie Huddy and Rob Blake, fall trying to cut his angle, and when he rounds the far post, Andreychuk is met with an embarrassment of riches. Dave Ellett is cruising in from the blue line, unmarked. But even closer is Wendel Clark, sporting his full, dark playoff beard, standing on the edge of the crease. It's an easy pass, and an easy tap-in past Kelly Hrudey.

Los Angeles 2, Toronto 1.

"That's a big goal for the Toronto Maple Leafs," Cole says.

"Wendel Clark has saved his best moments for the seventh games of these series," Neale says. "And he starts this one off like he's not going to make this one an exception."

They are re-energized now. Gilmour and Clark, magnificent in the game-seven wins over Detroit and St. Louis, seem to be willing the team forward, hearts on sleeves. But it's not just them. It is everyone right down to the bit players. As a collective, in this moment, they are the equal of anyone in hockey, and the minutes that follow are among the finest and most thrilling in modern Toronto Maple Leafs history. The crowd picks up the chant: "Go Leafs, go!" The Kings are forced back on their heels. The equalizer is inevitable: Gilmour goes into a corner after a loose puck, battles one on one against defenceman Corey Millen (who is, of course, much bigger and stronger), finally escapes when Millen drops his stick and reaches to pick it up, then passes to Anderson, who, having watched that struggle play out, streaks to the net the moment he sees Gilmour seize control. He scores.

Los Angeles 2, Toronto 2.

"It . . . is . . . tied!" Cole hollers.

Neale waits for a break in play, as is his wont, and then delivers another of his miniature soliloquies over the replay.

"Doug Gilmour: talent does what it can, genius does what it wants to. That describes Doug Gilmour in these playoffs perfectly."

The Leafs have the emotional advantage now, are one with their fans. Melrose calls a timeout to calm his team down. There's a shot of McNall sitting high above in a private box, his chin in his hands, looking grim. The Kings have only threatened when Gretzky was on the ice, and now even he seems powerless to hold Toronto back.

But then, a single mental error changes the game again. An apparently harmless three-on-three in the Toronto zone, a pass sent back to Gretzky, Kent Manderville right there to check him. But instead of doing it by the book, playing the man, neutralizing him, Manderville tries to get clever, to stick-check Gretzky and maybe set up a rush the other way. Gretzky sidesteps him easily. Manderville is left at sea. Gretzky, untouched in the slot, winds up and fires a slapshot worthy of Bobby Hull. Potvin doesn't have a chance.

Los Angeles 3, Toronto 2. It's a little past the halfway point of the game.

"You don't try to poke-check that guy," Neale says. "Guys that have poke-checked him are sitting at home watching tonight—they're not in the National Hockey League anymore."

The Leafs suddenly seem lost—all of that energy and desire and confidence instantly evaporated. A whistle stops play.

"Well, the L.A. Kings needed that goal to relieve the pressure," Neale says. "And Wayne Gretzky, who has been criticized for not being a leader and not being able to play the way he did in series one and two, came back to life in the sixth game with that over-time goal, and has certainly been a dominant player tonight with two goals.

"The biggest games are always saved for the biggest players."

The period ends with a whimper, but for a flash of passion from Andeychuk in the final minute that draws a Los Angeles penalty. The Kings look like they're cruising to victory now. Neale chimes in with one more tribute.

"Gretzky: 1,044 league games over fourteen seasons. This is his 174th playoff game. Remember the five times that his teams got to the Stanley Cup finals. Remember the four Canada Cups. Don't tell me this guy Gretzky has played fourteen years. He's played eighteen years, and he's dodging Father Time tonight.

"And anybody that worried about Wayne being finished need not worry any longer. He's back."

There was a writer hanging around with McNall on the road trip, a guy from *Vanity Fair*, working on a profile, and the subject was more than happy to cooperate, spinning the now-familiar, semi-fabricated tales of his improbable rise. The Kings were staying at the Hilton on University Avenue, and at the bar there the writer talked to Sue Waks, and she got worried. Bruce was going to get in trouble, she realized. He'd blabbed. He'd told this guy too much. Not about the bank scams, about the loans covering loans, about the phony companies and duplicate sets of books, but about his ancient-coin business, how he'd started as a kid, and how every once in awhile, when required, he'd smuggle stuff into the country, he'd stick a Greek or Roman coin worth thousands upon thousands of dollars into a back pocket, and no one would be the wiser. Bruce just couldn't help himself. Little white lies turned into great big lies. Little enhancements to his biography—did he really graduate from Oxford?—became part of the permanent record. He just wanted to be liked. That's one of things they would say after it all came tumbling down, at least the people who weren't burned directly, who weren't left holding the bag, who chose to remember McNall for the good times he'd engineered—it was all because he just wanted to be liked.

Roy Mlakar heard about the magazine story that might be coming, and it worried him as well. But he also had his own concerns. He was charged with keeping track of Michael Eisner's hockey-loving teenaged sons, who were along for the ride (at one point earlier in the playoffs, he'd had to drag them out of a casino in Calgary before anyone figured out that they were underage). And he was working on a project that he thought might put the Kings over the top, might turn the hockey team into a gold mine. A plan was unfolding to build a new arena on the site of the Hollywood Park racetrack, not far from the Forum, where revenues could be multiplied several times over. The Sony Corporation was coming in as a partner—they'd call it the Sony Centre. Al Davis, the owner of the Raiders of the National Football League, wanted to build a stadium right next door.

To Mlakar's face, McNall was also pushing the Sony deal forward, encouraging him to get it done as soon as possible. Behind his back, McNall was doing something else entirely, with an entirely different set of people, something designed to bring in money, fast. Time was running out.

The Leafs begin the third period on the power play. They know that they have to score the next goal, that this is their chance to push the Kings back on their heels. They don't do anything during the two-minute advantage, but a few seconds after Rob Blake gets out of the box, Gilmour steals the puck behind the Los Angeles net. Wendel Clark has fallen down trying to establish position in front. When he scrambles to his feet, the Kings defenceman seem to have lost interest in him. Gilmour puts a pass on the tape, Clark doesn't hesitate, and once more the two local heroes connect.

"And Clark has tied it for the Maple Leafs!" Cole shouts.

Los Angeles 3, Toronto 3.

Play resumes over the familiar nasal drone of public address announcer Paul Morris. "Toronto goal by Number 17, Wendel Clark . . ." They don't sound like that anymore, anywhere.

The game becomes a bit more tentative now, neither team wanting to make the error that would end its season. And in the old style, Van Hellemond has put away his whistle. There used to be a predictable rhythm to officiating a playoff game, an orthodoxy all but unbending before the league decided to open things up, to encourage referees to call any penalty at any time. They would work by the book in the first period, especially early, to establish a tone of authority. They would loosen up a bit in the second period, and when possible even things up with coincidental minors. Then in the third, barring a homicide, they would let the players decide it for themselves.

The Leafs are the better team right now. When Gretzky's on the ice, the Kings are dangerous, but it's not like in the old days with Edmonton. He can't double- and triple-shift. He needs his rest. And any time he's been on the bench, his team has suffered by his absence.

Eight minutes to go. Hrudey makes a great stop. Seven minutes . . . then six. Potvin snares a Gretzky slapshot.

"The winner of this game goes on to meet the Montreal Canadiens Tuesday night at the Forum in the Stanley Cup final," Cole says. "You might say a pile is riding on this hockey game tonight."

Four minutes, ticking down to three. Gretzky taking a rest.

"The Kings' Donnelly parked at the side of the net!"

There is nothing beautiful about it. Tony Granato cruises into the Toronto zone with the puck, leading a three on two, as the Leafs' forwards skate back desperately, trying to get into the play. He drops the puck to defenceman Alexei Zhitnik, who has jumped into the rush. Bob Rouse, the Toronto defenceman, plays him well, dropping down to block a potential shot, and Zhitnik seems uncertain whether to pass or shoot. What comes off his stick is a bit of a hybrid, a soft wrister that deflects off Rouse's leg. Sylvain Lefebvre, the other Leaf defenceman, is in perfect position, guarding the path to the far post. But when the puck changes direction, he is left flat-footed, unable to react as it slides behind him. Waiting all alone is Mike Donnelly, a bit of a journeyman who is nearing the end of what will be, by far, his best season in the National Hockey League. He puts it behind Potvin.

Los Angeles 4, Toronto 3.

Three minutes and one second remain.

With the Leafs still reeling, the crowd in shock, comes the game's virtuoso moment. Toronto is pressing desperately, trying to tie the score. They're taking chances now. Dave Ellett, the defenceman, is pinching, trying to keep the puck in the Kings' zone. He shoots, the puck is deflected and slides outside the blue line, where Ellett retreats, trying to retrieve it near centre ice.

Gretzky is hovering there, ever the opportunist, waiting for the error, waiting to pounce. With a sweep of his stick, he picks Ellett's pocket, steals the puck and heads up ice.

No teammate heads up ice with him. In other circumstances, they would jump into the attack, but now the other Kings are taking no chances, falling back, protecting their lead. Gretzky is all alone, surrounded by Maple Leafs. Defenceman Todd Gill follows him, pushing him wide as he sweeps behind the net. Ellett is now stationed out front, looking for any King who might be trailing, hoping for a pass. There are none.

All three forwards have retreated into their own zone: Anderson, Borschevsky, Krushelnyski. So it's one-on-six, and Gretzky is just killing time, trying to take a few more seconds off the clock, trying to delay the moment when the Leafs can pull their goaltender and add an extra attacker to push for the tying score.

Gretzky rounds the Leafs' net, and on the backhand flicks the puck into the crease, where it strikes the back of Ellett's skate and bounces into the net.

Anyone else, it's a fluke. Anyone else, it's dumb luck. And maybe it is this time, too. Maybe, as Neale says, "Wayne Gretzky gets a lucky goal." But it's him, and you suspect he meant to do it, that at the very least, with no passing option, he saw the skates and legs in front and figured, what the hell, let's try the bank shot.

Los Angeles 5, Toronto 3.

It is Gretzky's third goal of the game, and it's a jaw-dropper. It ought to be the killing blow, with only 3:14 to play. Up in his box, McNall is pumping his fist, putting on his jacket, getting ready to head downstairs to the dressing room for the celebrations. But the Leafs aren't quite dead yet. With 1:07 to play, the Kings get a little sloppy in their own end. The puck comes to Ellett, and his slapshot beats Hrudey cleanly.

"Don't leave yet!" Cole hollers. "Morning might be dawning again."

Los Angeles 5, Toronto 4.

The Leafs have been prematurely left for dead before in these playoffs. When they lost the first two games to Detroit. When they struggled through seven games against St. Louis.

"Last minute of play in this period," Morris intones.

Bob Cole's call of the tense final seconds is some of his finest work in a long and distinguished career. He uses his voice like a great musician, rising through a crescendo, with the same tinge of desperation felt by everyone who has grown up dreaming in blue and white.

Andreychuk's shot is blocked by Hrudey. Potvin is on the bench, folks. The Leafs pulling out all the stops. Extra man on. Rouse from the blue line. Forty seconds left. In front of the net . . . mad scramble! Right in front! It's cleared to the boards. Kings trying to get it out—they don't. Another shot knocked down. It's still in there. Here's Clark! Can't find it. Anderson kept it in with his leg. It is shot back of the goal. Twenty-three seconds left. Gilmour. Looking for it, fell. And now Anderson will have to hustle. Fifteen seconds left. Ellett shoots it very calmly back of the net. Here's Gilmour coming out. Ten seconds left! The crowd in a frenzy! It is Rouse . . . it will come out over the line . . .

And the L.A. Kings are going to win it—two seconds left—and the Kings have won it. And they go on and meet the Montreal Canadiens in a heartbreaking loss for the Maple Leafs tonight and a big win for the L.A. Kings tonight. Five-four, Los Angeles. They'll meet the Montreal Canadiens in the Stanley Cup finals!

Wayne Gretzky is nearly on top of the hockey world again, the first time he's flown this high since the last Stanley Cup in Edmonton.

"Wouldn't you know it?" Cole says. "The most maligned L.A. King in the L.A. media, Number 99, Wayne Gretzky, comes up with one of his great performances. He was the difference tonight."

It doesn't get any better, and it won't get any better—not for Gretzky, not for the Kings, not for the Maple Leafs.

And by the time the final is complete, not for Canadian hockey.

—

The Montreal Canadiens, like the Toronto Maple Leafs, have a glorious history and a funky old building they call home. One big difference, though. They have actually won a Stanley Cup within recent memory. Like that triumph in 1986, the one about to be completed will in large part be the work of a single player—goaltender Patrick Roy—and a coach who knows just how to handle his enormous talent and titanic ego, Jacques Demers. But that's not what anyone is talking about in the hours leading up to game five of the 1993 final against the Los Angeles Kings. What they're talking about is the series' apparent turning point—one of the great, clever coaching moments in NHL history.

The Kings had come out flying following the seventh-game win in Toronto, dispatching the Habs 4–1 at the Forum in game one, a victory that suggested in every way that their moment had indeed arrived. Wayne Gretzky was nothing if not a closer. He could smell that fifth Stanley Cup. He could taste it now.

The second game, still in Montreal, was a much tighter affair, with the Kings clinging to a 2–1 lead heading into the final two minutes. Teams that lose the first two at home in any best-of-seven series rarely come back to win, a fact not lost on Demers. So he opted to roll the dice. It was an audacious gamble. Summoning the referee to the Montreal bench during a stop in play, Demers requested a measurement on the blade of Marty McSorley's stick. Way back when, in the early 1960s, when players first started curving their sticks to make the puck dance, there had been no restrictions at all, and some wound up bent like a banana. Eventually, in fairness to the poor goalies, the NHL instituted a rule limiting the curvature, assessing a two-minute penalty to those who went too far. But it was rarely called because the opposing team had to request a measurement, taking the risk of being penalized itself for delay of game should the stick in fact be legal.

In other words, if McSorley's blade had passed the test, the Canadiens would have been left down a goal, and down a man, with 1:45 to play in a game that they absolutely believed they had to win—and Demers would have been run out of town by the never-forgiving Montreal fans. It turned out that he knew exactly what he was doing—perhaps a little home-rink intelligence had helped him along—and McSorley was sent to the box (becoming the cautionary tale ever after: before playoff games, sticks are now routinely checked by teams to prevent any more McSorley moments). The Habs would enjoy a power play to the end of the game—or until they scored. That wasn't enough for Demers, though. He pulled Roy as well: it would be six-on-four with the Montreal net empty, for all the marbles.

A generation of Montreal schoolchildren would soon enough be able to recite, chapter and verse, what came next. The least likely of scorers, defenceman Eric Desjardins, tying the game with a slap-shot, sending the game to overtime. Desjardins scoring again in the extra period—his third goal of the game, a softie that Hrudey mis-played—to send the series to California all even. It was the Habs' eighth overtime win without a loss in the 1993 playoffs, tying a league record, which would be followed, remarkably, by two more overtime wins in Los Angeles, to put the Kings on the brink of elimination.

So it is game five back at the Forum, the scene set for a moment suggestive of so many others in the past, which has yet to be repeated: Montreal's twenty-fourth championship, the most by any franchise, and their last to date; a Stanley Cup awarded to a Canadian team, and, as a bonus, on Canadian soil.

It hasn't happened since.

In the nervous moments before the opening face-off, Roy Mlakar's head was filled with bad omens. He was still in charge of the young Eisners. He was doing his best to steer clear of McNall's entourage, the planeload of the famous and near-famous and mere hangers-on that he had flown to Montreal on the team's private jet. He was try-ing not to get between Melrose and the Kings' general manager, Nick Beverley, who were feuding. Mlakar slipped away and found an exercise bike, spinning a few miles while trying to find a little peace. That's where he was when McNall found him and casually passed on a little news—that he was on the verge of making a deal with a couple of guys named Jeffrey Sudikoff and Joe Cohen, that he didn't think the Sony deal was going to happen, that he was planning to move in a different direction.

"I think that they're a better option to buy the team," McNall said.

"Buy the team, Bruce?" Mlakar asked, incredulous. "Who said anything about buying the team?"

Montreal won the game easily, 4–1. Celebratory riots broke out on Ste. Catherine Street. The defeated Kings made their way to the airport, to their private plane, and took off for the long flight back to Los Angeles. No one was talking much. There wasn't much to say.

But Luc Robitaille vividly remembers a scene that has stuck with him all of these years. It was the owner and the star player, off by themselves, in quiet intense conversation, serious, grim even, as though some very bad news was being delivered.

Chapter Fourteen

MIRAGE

ALMOST EXACTLY ONE YEAR later came the glorious, ecstatic peak, the single greatest moment in terms of visibility, marketability and relevance in the history of the National Hockey League, at least where the United States was concerned. By kismet and by design, the game was, for the first time, truly in the mainstream of American sport, pushing even into the realm of pure popular culture, just as Bruce McNall had dreamed it would.

The New York Rangers hadn't won the Stanley Cup since 1940, by far the longest dry spell of any of the Original Six franchises, and though they enjoyed a devoted local following, though Madison Square Garden was nearly always full and their television audience was strong, there was also a deep well of unrewarded devotion to be tapped in what was still the most important market in the country. In the spring of 1994 came deliverance, finally, thanks in large part to the ghosts of the Edmonton Oilers, to players who had left in the wake of the Gretzky trade.

Mark Messier, who until the 1990 Cup win was second banana to Gretzky, had come to embody the perfect, inspirational dressing room leader with the Rangers, his shaved head and intense gaze suggestive of just the right amount of menace, edginess and intimidation. That spring, when the Rangers struggled against their cross-river rivals, the New Jersey Devils, in the Eastern Conference final, Messier stepped up like Joe Namath before Super Bowl III and guaranteed a victory in the New York press. Truth was, there had been plenty of guarantees since Broadway Joe made his famous boast: conveniently, no one remembered the ones that weren't quite backed up by the results. But this time, Messier and his teammates, including ex-Oilers Kevin Lowe, Adam Graves, Craig MacTavish, Glenn Anderson and Esa Tikkanen, delivered by beating the Devils in double overtime, then did it again in a memorable Stanley Cup final, besting the Vancouver Canucks in game seven at Madison Square Garden. The victory transformed Messier into a New York sports icon, and the city that never sleeps temporarily became the hockey capital of the world.

It was more than that, though, more than just a championship won in the right place at the right time in front of a whole lot of people who would stand up and take notice. It was also the larger sense of creeping hipness around the game. The pendulum had swung somehow. The whole Gretzky phenomenon had begun the process of casting hockey in a different light. American kids were playing in ever-greater numbers, hauled to the rink in minivans by their hockey moms; characters on the number one television show of the moment, *Friends,* were shown attending a Rangers game in one episode, something previously unimaginable; Gretzky and Messier were frequent guests on late-night talk shows, and Gretzky hosted *Saturday Night Live* (he even appeared for awhile in animated form on the Saturday morning cartoon *ProStars,* fighting crime, protecting the environment and being kind to small children as part of a heroic trio with fellow icons Michael Jordan and Bo Jackson); hockey players, in all their aw-shucks humility (which could be read by some as their "whiteness"), were viewed by some as an antidote to the selfish, self-aggrandizing, vaguely menacing (qualities that could be read by some as reflective of their "blackness") players in other sports. Specifically, the National Basketball Association, which had been hailed far and wide for its marketing savvy, which had ridden the genius of Larry Bird and Magic Johnson, and then Jordan, to unprecedented heights, could now be portrayed as a game in decline, in its late decadent phase, in contrast to the NHL, a fresh-faced sport in ascendancy. The pupil, Gary Bettman, might well be outstripping the master, David Stern, at least according to *Sports Illustrated,* arbiter of American sporting tastes. On June 20, 1994, the magazine pronounced on the subject with a story that could have run under McNall's byline. It echoes—though ironically—to this day.

Hot Not
While the NBA's image has cooled, the NHL
has ignited surprising new interest in hockey
by E.M. Swift

Let's see if we've got this straight. NBA basketball, as played by the Eastern Conference champions, the New York Knicks, is called "butt-ugly" and "thuggish" by USA Today, while the erstwhile black sheep of professional team sports, the National Hockey League, appears in the "Styles of the Times" section of The New York Times, where it is described as "hip," "sexy" and "cutting edge."

The Los Angeles Times, citing a 30% drop in prime-time television ratings during the conference finals, denounces the NBA playoffs as "a game of mud wrestling" and host to "the occasional near riot," while the trade magazine Sports Licensing International gushes that "the convergence of an exciting sport, a new executive team at the NHL itself and a renewed marketing emphasis at NHL Enterprises has made hockey the place to be."

Basketball, thuggish? Hockey, the place to be? Talk about your role reversals. When former NBA executive Gary Bettman took over as commissioner of the NHL last year, everyone predicted hockey would assume the NBA look: hip music in the stadiums; an influx of young, energetic marketing whizzes in the league offices; zippy new promotions. What no one foresaw, however, was the simultaneous and inexplicable NHL-ing of the NBA: on-court brawls spreading into the stands; a sudden and embarrassing franchise shift;

bizarre, pugnacious behavior by out-of-control owners; outrageous refereeing gaffes; and spin-doctoring denials from the league.

Gone is the image of the NHL player as a toothless face-buster. Fighting in the playoffs, this year and last, has been practically non-existent (though it remained a problem during the regular season). Brawling was almost entirely eliminated. Even the fans' image has changed: Pre-Bettman, when the NHL was the boil on the pro sports boom of the 1970s and '80s, hockey's spectators looked like the spillover from Wrestlemania. This year elegant couples like John F. Kennedy Jr. and Daryl Hannah (also Knick attendees) and Farrah Fawcett and Ryan O'Neal were spotted at NHL games. Big Apple mayor Rudy Giuliani has confessed to having a hockey goal set up in the backyard of Gracie Mansion, the mayoral digs, for his eight-year-old son, Andrew.

But the real news was not that the Rangers generated tremendous excitement in New York, long a great hockey town. No, it was that hockey began making strides in the Sun Belt. It started last year when Wayne Gretzky led the Los Angeles Kings into the Stanley Cup finals. Then, for once, the NHL did expansion the right way, allowing the Florida Panthers and the Mighty Ducks of Anaheim to field competitive teams in their first season. Both sold out nearly half their games. The Sharks were the surprise team of this season's playoffs and, as the most improved team in the history of hockey from one year to the next, won the hearts of the Bay Area. And the second-year Tampa Bay Lightning averaged more than 21,000 fans a game. "We're not just a cold-weather sport," says Bettman. "We're getting a national footprint."

That last quote would stick to Bettman like glue.

Sometimes, it's all about the timing. Anaheim and Florida had entered the league the year of the Rangers' resonant victory. Quebec City was about to move to Denver, as the NHL evolved away from smaller Canadian markets, a process seen as sad but inevitable, and the Sharks were finally settling in to shiny new permanent digs in San Jose. The bright minds behind the Fox television network, then very much the brash, hip counterpoint to the staid Big Three, decided to embrace hockey, to make it their own, committing to the league's first true U.S. national television deal since 1975. To the broadcasts, Fox would add animated hockey-playing robots and pucks with computer-generated flaming tails (to make them easier for hockey neophytes to see), absurd in hindsight, but imagine now the idea of such a huge media company trying so hard to make the sport palatable to a mass audience.

So naturally it was time for the NHL to ride that wave, ride that attention, ride those good feelings, to give no one a moment to forget why they had temporarily been swept away the previous spring.

Instead, the owners shut the doors. They turned out the lights. They decided to provoke a war they didn't really have the stomach to fight, let alone win. After having gone through the 1993–94 season without a collective-bargaining agreement, they decided that now was the time play hardball with the National Hockey League Players' Association, the not-quite union that had been founded, with Alan Eagleson as its head, at the very dawn of the sports labour movement in the 1960s. The players' current leader was Bob Goodenow, smart, edgy, confrontational, a guy certainly spoiling for a scrap. When the owners decided that the future of the game rested on imposing a hard salary cap to limit spending, Goodenow's players held firm, just as baseball players had when faced with a similar ultimatum. The owners responded by locking them out.

So the 1994–95 season didn't start on time. Arenas remained dark. Autumn turned to winter, and there was still no NHL hockey, and the memories of those magical nights in Manhattan inevitably faded. One hundred and six days after it began, the lockout ended—just in time, everyone agreed, to save enough of the season so it might still seem legitimate. There was still no salary cap. The owners of the wealthier franchises apparently didn't want one badly enough to sacrifice an entire year's revenues, and so the management side crumbled without being able to claim even a pyrrhic victory. A new contract was struck that still allowed the owners a tremendous degree of control over players from their drafting at age eighteen to their eligibility for full free agency at age thirty-one.

But over the next ten years, the deal would be probed for loopholes and exploited by the union, exploited by agents, allowing player salaries to escalate to unimagined heights. Of course, the owners were willing accomplices (they renewed the contract twice), and the money had to come from somewhere. Along with all of the new revenue streams that were being added at that point in professional sports history—private boxes, arena naming rights, signage here, there and everywhere—the NHL owners also benefited from the league's expansion pyramid scheme. New teams continued to be added, increasing the "footprint," whatever the strengths or weaknesses of the new markets, whatever the real financial wherewithal of those willing to pay. In addition to the expansion money, the price charged for those teams artificially increased everyone else's equity, creating new opportunities to borrow against perceived value and providing fresh cash that could in turn be used to pay the players. The artificial growth wasn't sustainable, but anyone who dared suggest that in the moment would have been branded an out-of-touch pessimist.

The NHL season resumed early in 1995, and that spring the New Jersey Devils won the first Stanley Cup in their franchise's history (one that stretched back to 1974 and was marked by unsuccessful residencies in Kansas City and Denver), employing a team built to play a defensive, "trapping" style that negated the natural flow of the game (the antithesis of the "firewagon" hockey made famous by the Montreal Canadiens, and arguably perfected by the Oilers) and relying on the spectacular goaltending of Martin Brodeur. In a league in which the talent was being spread ever more thinly because of expansion, weaker teams would naturally emulate that grim but effective style, since it allowed them to become competitive quickly against better opposition. Coaches bent on preserving their jobs were more than happy to give up a few style points and win ugly rather than lose with élan, since losing was what got you fired. Not only had the lockout killed much of the NHL's marketing momentum, it also ushered in an aesthetic Dark Age, causing loyal fans to despair and potential new fans to wonder what the fuss was all about—where was this "fastest game on ice"?

By 2004, the after-effects of the 1995 CBA—and more significantly, the imminent collapse of the NHL's phony economy—set the stage for a far more devastating labour war, in which the league became the first in professional sports history to sacrifice an entire season at the altar of "cost certainty." The owners, now willing to stay the course no matter what the consequences, finally got their salary cap, got Goodenow fired, and came close to breaking the players' association—but at a horrific cost. Big-league hockey disappeared for a calendar year, and though it eventually came back in Canada stronger than ever, though rules changes were enacted to bring back its speed and excitement, in many of the non-traditional markets populated during the expansion binge, the game never really recovered.

By then, Bruce McNall, the league's little embarrassment, had been all but erased from the NHL's history, the hockey equivalent of de-Stalinization. Even ten years earlier, during that brief shining moment of hipness that he had done so much to engineer, McNall was too preoccupied with his own troubles to really appreciate what he had wrought. Through late 1993 and into 1994, stories began to trickle out suggesting that McNall was experiencing financial difficulties—and just as soon as they popped up, the master thespian, aided by gullible journalists, moved to tamp the rumours down. Not to single anyone out—just about everybody fell for it, since McNall was among other things a virtuoso liar who kept his tracks well covered, and of course it wasn't sportswriters but bankers who were the real dupes—but a Bob McKenzie column from the *Toronto Star* written towards the tail end of the 1992–93 season stands as a classic document of the moment. Under a breathless headline—"Is Bruce McNall feeling the pinch? Let's get serious!"—McKenzie wrote:

> Little whispers suggest Bruce McNall is in some kind of trouble.
> The buzz is that the owner of the Toronto Argonauts and Los Angeles Kings, in time, won't have two Athens Decadrachms to rub together.

Not so, says the man who should know.

"The curious thing is, where does stuff like this get started?" said an incredulous McNall, the collector of ancient coins who amassed a personal fortune that has been used to start enterprises in sports, entertainment and art.

"It's just not true. I own a lot of companies. Some do well. Some not so well. But none of them, good or bad, have a lot to do with me or my personal wealth." . . .

McNall admits the ancient coin business is a little flat these days, but even if the bottom were to fall out of it, he added, it wouldn't pose a problem.

"You have to understand how I operate," McNall said. "Each business venture operates independently. There is no universal supply of money that they can draw on to keep things going.

"It's the easiest thing in the world that when you're strapped for cash, you go to Daddy and ask for money. Well, I am not Big Daddy and if I have a business that is continually coming back to me and asking for financial help, I have to take a long hard look at that business."

In fact, all of McNall's business ventures were linked by the fraudulent financing on which they were built, and so, when that foundation of charm and smarts and shamelessness and deceit and confidence-building and bright ideas and big lies began to crumble, it all came tumbling down—and remarkably fast.

In one 1993 financial statement, McNall claimed a net worth of $433,018,496. He had a six-million-dollar house in the posh Holmby Hills neighbourhood of Los Angeles, right up the street from the Playboy Mansion, and other homes in Malibu; Studio City; Rancho Mirage; Park City, Utah; Kauai, Hawaii; and in the Trump Towers in New York City. He owned a Rolls Royce, a Range Rover, an Aston Martin and a Maserati. He had the Kings, with a value he estimated at $100 million—and of course there were still the coins, the racehorses, the sports memorabilia, the movie deals.

McNall was, by all appearances, loaded—and he was, in reality, way beyond broke. The assets were overvalued and the debts that secured them, built on empty promises and phony collateral, were massive. McNall and his companies owed the Bank of America and the French bank Crédit Lyonnais a hundred million each, much of it procured under false pretences, employing elaborate circular-accounting schemes involving shell companies and double sets of books. (In one infamous case, when the Bank of America got nervous and wondered about a fifteen-million-dollar coin collection pledged as collateral—and which, unbeknownst to them, didn't actually exist—McNall played out an elaborate bit of theatre. He told the bankers that he had traded the coins for sports memorabilia worth far more, then showed them what was in fact an extremely impressive collection. The problem was, it had been hastily assembled on consignment—McNall didn't own any of it. But the bankers were temporarily fooled.)

"The banks were telling us what to do," McNall says. "The bankers didn't want to lose their jobs. They didn't want to have a bad loan. They were exposed. They said 'Don't worry about it.' I was always thinking that I would be able to fix these problems. Always assuming that I would do that. So in a weird way, although I knew that what was going on was wrong, I didn't see the victims here. This wasn't like me running around taking money from old ladies—or from friends, which is why I had them all. It wasn't like me taking money from this account or that account. This was institutions who were saying, 'We have a problem, we don't want to know about this, you fix it, we're cool.' I didn't feel at that moment that what we were doing was that wrong."

The *Vanity Fair* story was the beginning of the end. McNall's bragging about his coin-smuggling exploits inspired investors in one of his coin-based funds to launch a class-action suit against him. There was also an aggrieved former employee, as is so often the case, who went to the feds and explained to them exactly how the books had been cooked. Early in 1994, McNall resigned as chairman of the NHL's board of governors after learning that he was under criminal investigation. He had already looked after Gretzky with a new three-year contract the fall before, which would pay him $25.5 million (and when Gretzky broke Gordie Howe's career goal-scoring record in March 1994, McNall still was able to raise the money to buy Gretzky a present. At Janet's suggestion, McNall says, he gave Gretzky a $300,000 Rolls Royce Corniche). On April 20, 1994, the FBI arrived at McNall's offices to go through the files and interview the staff. On May 16, less than a year after the Kings were in the Stanley Cup final, with the Bank of America breathing down his neck, McNall finally completed the sale of the team to Joseph Cohen and Jeffrey Sudikoff (and cut a nice little side deal for himself, a $487,500-a-year consulting fee) just minutes ahead of being forced into bankruptcy and losing control of his assets. The Toronto Argonauts were sold to the Labatt brewery, the coin company and film company disappeared, the horses, the memorabilia, gone so quickly it was though it had all been a mirage. And, of course, Bruce himself was about to disappear as well.

On December 14, 1994, McNall pleaded guilty to multiple counts of bank fraud. Sentencing was delayed while he assisted the authorities in unpicking the enormous scam that he and his cohorts had created. "I didn't do what a lot of the Enron guys did, which was blame somebody else," he says in his own defence. It wasn't until almost two years later that McNall was sentenced to seventy months in prison, the minimum allowable for his crimes under sentencing guidelines (it was eventually reduced to a straight five years). His would be no easy, white-collar, country club prison stretch. McNall did hard time, in tough places, including periods in the "hole" for disciplinary reasons. In his biography, he makes it clear that he believes he was persecuted by prison authorities because of his celebrity, but thinking back to that Alan Thicke anecdote about ordering fast food through the guards, it's worth wondering whether the old sense of entitlement persisted, whether Bruce McNall got in trouble at least in part for trying to still be Bruce McNall behind bars.

Certain people, he says, stuck by him from beginning to end, staying in contact, visiting when they could: Thicke; Luc Robitaille; the celebrity architect Frank Gehry; and especially, Wayne Gretzky. "Everybody has their ups and downs," McNall says. "Everybody has their issues. Ultimately, [Wayne] looks at where your heart is. Is your heart in the right place? If you go out to rob a bank and your intent is to rob a bank and take some money—well, that's a certain intent. If your intent is to try to fix problems, you may end up doing the same thing, but it's a different mechanism. Wayne looks at where your heart is. He's not one to like bad guys. He's known a few of those that we've come across over the years who were not good guys. It's where's your heart at and how do you treat other people that's important to him.

"When all of this hit the fan, he was the first guy to say, 'Who's going to pay the legal bills?' He wrote a cheque for a half a million or a million dollars right away. I told him what had happened. I told him everything I knew. He said, 'Okay, how can I help you?'"

When Gretzky announced his retirement from the National Hockey League, McNall was stuck in solitary confinement and missed the news. He says that Gretzky sent him a note afterward.

"I'm retiring," it read. "They want me to retire my [Kings] jersey. I won't do it until you're there to see it."

He kept his word. McNall was released from prison in March 2001. The jersey retirement took place in 2002, with McNall in attendance. Since regaining his freedom, McNall has tried to work his way back into the deal-making side of the movie business. You can find his name as a producer or executive producer on a handful of low-budget films as he works to pay back the five million dollars the courts ordered him to return to those he bilked.

"Of all the things I've done in my life, the Gretzky deal is what I'm certainly most proud of—not just the Gretzky deal itself, but this whole momentum-shifting of hockey into the twenty-first century," he says. "I'm disappointed that there was no follow-up. The Gretzky deal was a start. It wasn't a finish."

More than twenty years later, most of the others involved in the trade of the century, directly or peripherally, can still be found in and around the sports world. In Los Angeles, Jerry Buss, who turned seventy-five in June 2009, remains the owner of the wildly successful Lakers, now based (along with the Kings and the NBA

Clippers) in the downtown Staples Centre. He sold the Fabulous Forum to the Faithful Central Bible Church, which uses it for huge services, as well as renting it out for the occasional concert. Luc Robitaille went from the playing ranks to the front office, and is the current president of the Kings, who have never again come close to winning a Stanley Cup—who in fact have made only four playoff appearances and won only ten playoff games, total, since that run to the final in 1993. But the other Southern California–based NHL team, the Anaheim Ducks (né the Mighty Ducks of Anaheim—the name was changed in 2005), did finally bring a hockey championship to Lotus Land in 2007, setting off spontaneous celebrations in . . . well, in their arena parking lot, and not really anywhere else. By then, the movie tie-in, the Disney ownership and Michael Eisner were but memories. Despite that triumph, the NHL is nearly back where it started, far down the food chain in the Los Angeles market, behind just about every other sport, including college football and basketball, and arguably even behind soccer during the brief time that David Beckham called the city home. Those great nights at the Forum when hockey was front-page news and the building was packed with movie stars dying for a glimpse of Gretzky ended the moment he left town.

Roy Mlakar escaped the McNall collapse with his reputation intact. (It is worth pointing out that when the feds rolled in and started charging people, Mlakar was never implicated in any wrongdoing.) He remembers McNall coming to him early in 1994 after a board of governors meeting and telling him that the team was about to be sold, that one of the new owners would be moving into his office at the end of the week, that he'd talked to a couple of other franchises who might be able to offer Mlakar a job. "Then he broke down and told me what happened," Mlakar remembers. "He told me that he owed a lot of money to several banks. He said he was sorry. 'Bruce, you're sorry? You're in deep trouble and you're telling me you're sorry?' He was pretty emotional. He wasn't his gregarious self. It was the only time I saw the wall of confidence come down. It never came down in any of the jails I saw him in, either."

Today Mlakar is the president of the Ottawa Senators—an anomaly from the expansion era, a new franchise that wound up not in an American sunbelt market, but in just the kind of mid-sized Canadian city that the NHL seemed all too anxious to abandon. The Sens certainly struggled throughout their early history, at one point falling into bankruptcy, but under the ownership of Eugene Melnyk they have achieved stability on and off the ice. Mlakar enjoyed his second trip to the Stanley Cup finals in 2007, when the Sens played the Ducks, though alas, he again ended it without the silverware.

In Edmonton, the Oilers survived a series of near-death experiences of their own in the waning days of the Pocklington era, as the owner's failing finances, combined with a weak Canadian dollar and spiralling player salaries, made it seem like the franchise's days in Alberta were numbered. In 2000, with the Alberta Treasury Board in hot pursuit of an unsettled hundred-million-dollar loan, Pocklington finally sold out to a local ownership group. That was Glen Sather's cue to exit, stage left. He opted for greener pastures, leaving the franchise where he had been player, coach, general manager and president to take over the hockey operations of the New York Rangers, the highest-spending team in the pre–salary cap NHL. It seemed a potent match—Sather's unassailable hockey smarts coupled with an all-but-unlimited payroll—but it didn't play out as most expected. His Ranger teams, with their enormous financial advantage, with rosters stacked with big-name players, failed to even make the playoffs during the first five years of his tenure (in fact, the team missed the postseason for seven years in a row leading up to the 2004–05 lockout). Ironically, it was only under the new cap system, in which their spending on player salaries was limited, that the Rangers finally found their way back to the postseason. So far, there has been no repeat of 1994—not even close. In fact, it's the Oilers who have come within a hair of winning another championship. In 2006, they made an underdog run to the Stanley Cup final, where they lost to the Carolina Hurricanes in a seventh-game heartbreaker. Under a new owner, drugstore magnate Daryl Katz, with plans for a new arena in the works, the team's future in Edmonton appears to be more secure than it has been since the glory years.

Unlike the tearful day he left Edmonton, Wayne Gretzky's parting from the Los Angeles Kings seemed cold, rational, and in the best interests of all concerned. There were still hockey fans in California—certainly more than when he arrived—and the most committed core of the Hollywood crowd still turned out for Kings games. But by 1996, McNall was finally on his way to jail after the legal system had finished with him, and the happy glow that had engulfed the franchise since the moment Gretzky arrived nearly eight years earlier had unquestionably faded. The Kings had missed the playoffs for the previous two seasons, the first times in Gretzky's career that he'd ever spent the entire spring on the side-lines. During his final weeks with the franchise, it had become obvious that the team was going to miss out once again, and there were also extenuating circumstances that influenced the team's ownership. Gretzky was in the last year of his contract, and the new proprietor was disinclined to pay him market value, especially at this late stage of his career, especially in a city where it was dead obvious that his star power had pretty much played out.

Once more, Gretzky was a diminishing asset—and once more, he wasn't entirely heartbroken to be leaving a team behind. It wasn't like the McNall days. Losing wasn't much fun. His brand was tak-ing a beating. And so, though the parting was a touch bittersweet, Gretzky was happy to be traded to the St. Louis Blues for the final eighteen games of the regular season, where he would be paired with Bret Hull, one of the game's most prolific scorers. (Plus, per-haps he could comfort himself with the notion that, once upon a time, the Midwestern city had been home to Janet Jones—though there was certainly no suggestion the Gretzky clan would be pack-ing up the house in L.A.) "This is easier than it was leaving Edmonton," Gretzky said. "I was leaving a winning team, not a floundering team. This is the opposite situation. This is a chance to play for a championship again. This is what it's all about. That what I'm excited about." The Blues' championship dreams went unrealized, and though Gretzky played well, with sixteen points in thirteen playoff games, in his nineteenth season as a professional hockey player he was no longer at a stage when he could deliver miracles all by himself.

Next stop, New York. After his short stay in St. Louis, Gretzky signed with the Rangers as a free agent, and the town was abuzz about the possibility of the most famous hockey player in the world again being teamed with Mark Messier—one last, great Oilers reunion, and perhaps one more Stanley Cup. But though they enjoyed a few flashback moments, though Gretzky had ninety-seven points in his first season with the team, and though there moments when it seemed as though the old magic was recaptured, a return to glory wasn't in the cards. That first season in New York was by far the best. The next year, Messier was gone, bound for his ill-fated stint in Vancouver, and the remainder of Gretzky's NHL days seemed destined to peter out with a team not good enough to win.

Perhaps that last stab at glory would come in a different theatre. Perhaps Gretzky could end his career with an Olympic gold medal, delivering for Canada what had been denied since 1952. Taking its cue from the NBA, which had received a huge boost in 1992 when an all-star "Dream Team" led by Michael Jordan won the gold medal for the United States in Barcelona, the NHL followed suit in 1998, temporarily shutting down in midseason so that the best of its players could make the long journey to the Olympic Games in Nagano, Japan. Though he was no longer the best player in the world, or even the best Canadian, Gretzky was naturally selected for the Olympic team, but, controversially, was not named its captain—that honour went to rising star Eric Lindros.

Canada and the United States were the gold medal favourites going in, having met in the finals of the first hockey World Cup in 1996 (in which the United States prevailed), which was exactly the outcome the NHL desired, given how it might pique interest in the professional game back home. Unfortunately, the rest of the hockey world declined to follow that script. Canada did its bit through the preliminary round, winning all three games by a cumulative score of 12–3, but the Yanks flamed out in the quarterfinals—

after which some of the American players embarrassed the league by trashing their rooms in the athletes' village. With their great rivals gone, Canada needed only to overcome the Czech Republic to reach the final for the gold medal, but the great Dominik Hašek had other plans. That traumatic loss for Canadians would overshadow everything else that happened at those Games, and among the great debating points afterwards would be coach Marc Crawford's decision to leave Gretzky on the bench for the decisive shootout. (Hardly remembered is the bronze medal game that followed, in which Canada lost 3–2 to Finland, forfeiting any chance at a medal.)

Gretzky went back to the Rangers for one final season after the Olympic year. He scored only nine goals in seventy games, his lowest total since his first year of minor hockey. When the story broke that he planned to retire at season's end, his final days in uniform set off a remarkable display of affection from fans—in the United States, to be sure, but especially in Canada. It had been more than ten years since he'd left the country for good, to live and to play full time in the U.S., and yet it was as though he was still the kid from Brantford. The golden child, the shinny god—they could market him and sell him, and in real life he could live an American's life, with an American wife and American-born children, but still the myth persisted. Gretzky's last game in Canada, against the Ottawa Senators, was the occasion of a national love-in, and the grand finale at Madison Square Garden was the most important hockey game that year. At one of his many pre-retirement press conferences, Gretzky was asked if he would be moving back to the country of his birth—as though, given his druthers, he and Janet and the kids would surely turn their backs on Manhattan, on Los Angeles, on all of those places that were too glitzy, too inauthentic, too far removed from the true organic hockey culture, too un-Canadian, and find themselves a nice little house up the street from Walter and Phyllis in Brantford, where they could raise their family right, where they could have their own backyard rink. Of course, Gretzky was polite about it when he said no.

—

That same impulse, that same belief in Gretzky's pure Canadian heart, had the country all but begging him to return and assemble the Olympic team heading into the 2002 Olympics in Salt Lake City. Having been away from hockey, having seen his brand power diminished for the first time in years, it was an attractive job for Gretzky the businessman, along with a call to duty. What's most remembered, aside from the final, glorious victory itself, aside from that first Canadian gold medal in fifty years, is a speech Gretzky made, unprovoked, out of the blue, after one of Canada's disappointing performances early in the Olympic competition. He sat down at the post-game press conference and, before even being asked a question, wrapped himself in the flag, cited historic grievances real or imagined, and suggested that Canada was all alone, that the rest of Planet Hockey wanted it to fail, that it was us against the world. Standing in the room listening to him that day, it was difficult to tell how much was honest emotion, how much was a contrived attempt to inspire his team. But, as with the "lucky loonie" buried at centre ice, the proof was in the final result, and with the gold medal victory over the Americans, Wayne Gretzky seemed infallible again.

But he pushed his luck. Four years later in Turin, the country demanded a sequel, and Gretzky was again in charge, but the magic was gone. He and Janet had become embroiled in an embarrassing, though in the end trivial, gambling scandal, which provided an unwelcome distraction, and the Canadian team he had a huge hand in selecting proved to be nowhere near up to the task. That flop seemed in some ways an extension of Gretzky's return to the National Hockey League the year before, and for anyone who had traced the story arc of his career, there were familiar elements in play.

In 2001, a flashy real estate developer from Phoenix named Steve Ellman purchased the Phoenix Coyotes—the former Winnipeg Jets—a hockey franchise that had never really found a comfortable home in the desert and had certainly never earned a penny in profit. What Ellman had in mind had precious little to do with the sport itself: his plan was to build a new arena in the wealthy enclave of Scottsdale, on the eastern fringes of the city, and then spin off development around it. Ellman needed to put a face to his scheme, needed someone involved who might turn the heads of local politicians and attract potential investors. Enter Gretzky, once again playing the role of flashy bauble for a rich hustler, an unbroken line that extended all the way back to Nelson Skalbania. Ellman gave Gretzky equity in the franchise without requiring any actual investment, gave him a fancy title and started to beat the drums.

The Scottsdale deal eventually fell through, but Ellman found a new location for his arena—Glendale, Arizona, less wealthy, certainly less glamorous, on the far western fringes of Phoenix, where local politicians were intent on spending money on sports facilities to put their town on the map. They helped build a new stadium for the Arizona Cardinals of the National Football League, and they kicked in $180 million towards the $220 million cost of the Coyotes' new arena, in the belief that they would reap a bonanza in future sales taxes. Bad economics that, and a misplaced faith in the spin-off power of professional hockey. The arena was built, but the fans didn't come, and the Coyotes stumbled on.

After the lost lockout season of 2004–05, Gretzky agreed to step behind the bench as head coach, for an additional million dollars in salary, a sum he would later negotiate upwards to somewhere between $4 million and $8 million, depending on who you believed (no other coach in the league made nearly that much) after the cash-strapped Ellman was forced to sell out to his minority partner, trucking magnate Jerry Moyes. There he remains today: four seasons as head coach, four seasons out of the playoffs, the uncomfortable public face of a franchise on the fast track to financial disaster. During the winter of 2008–09, in the teeth of the worst economic downturn since the Great Depression, there were reports that the Coyotes had lost $35 million the season before, that they stood to lose $45 million more in the current season, that Moyes was willing to sell the franchise for a dollar to anyone willing to take on its liabilities, but that prospective owners were few and far between because the team's lease locked it into the arena in Glendale.

Other franchises emblematic of the great expansion dream inspired by the Gretzky trade—in Miami and Tampa, in Atlanta and Nashville and Columbus and Carolina—were also facing very tough times, all but giving tickets away in order to lure fans into what remained half-empty buildings. The economy was part of it, but part of it also was the fact that hockey had simply failed to take root in those cities. Maybe it wasn't transferable after all. Maybe it wasn't as McNall had imagined way back when. Maybe its many virtues weren't self-evident to those with no personal history tied up in the game. With Wayne Gretzky playing, with Wayne Gretzky headlining, with Wayne Gretzky bringing out the celebrities, appearing on the cover of magazines and all over television, that simple fact had been obscured. But without Gretzky the player, the spell had worn off. It was hockey before, and to hockey it had returned.

From a distance, it wasn't so difficult to sense the poetry there, to see in the messy death throes of a franchise in a place so distant from any organic hockey culture a great circle becoming complete. Here were the former Jets, a vestige of the World Hockey Association, the league that once had dared go where the NHL feared to tread. Wayne Gretzky knew the WHA. He and his family had opted for the quick, immediate money, had accepted a pitch from a fast-buck operator, shunning tradition, shunning the sport's powers, thumbing their noses at the great god NHL. Not so long afterwards, he had boarded a plane in Indianapolis, fuelled up courtesy of Eddie Mio's credit card, and might well have landed in Winnipeg, home of the WHA champions, might well have been a Jet himself had Skalbania not found a more willing dance partner in Peter Pocklington. As an Oiler, Gretzky had tortured Jets fans in the old Winnipeg Arena, where the Queen glared down from that odd portrait that dominated one end of the rink. The Oilers were the model franchise, the success story, the dynasty, while the Jets could never get by them, were never quite good enough.

The day Gretzky was sold to the Los Angeles Kings was a joyous one for fans in Winnipeg. Little did they know it was also the beginning of the end of their team. The market forces unleashed by the grand plans of Bruce McNall didn't leave any room for franchises playing in outmoded buildings in small Canadian cities. Winnipeggers tried their best to save the Jets, they rallied in the streets, they shed a million tears, but it didn't make any financial sense, and it didn't make any more difference than standing in front of an onrushing train, pleading with it to stop.

And now here was Wayne Gretzky, his face broadened in middle age, his hair darker, his frustration, his embarrassment palpable, doing a job for which he seemed distinctly ill suited, the effortless genius of his on-ice artistry now turned to the drudgery of coaching a dead-end team, of practices and road trips and precious little joy, not even one of the boys anymore. In a nearly empty rink, with no movie stars, no bright lights, and outside lay a flat, brown, arid landscape, with not a flake of snow, not a backyard rink in sight. Selling a game that they didn't want, that they'd never asked for, selling a vision that no one really believed in anymore. Inadvertently, he had helped kill the Jets, and now he was desperately, fruitlessly fighting to keep them alive, in bastardized form, in a place far away, where they just didn't belong, where they just couldn't understand.

EPILOGUE

On May 5, 2009, Jerry Moyes surprised the National Hockey League by taking the Phoenix Coyotes into Chapter 11 bankruptcy. He had waited patiently for the league to find a buyer for the team, his pain dulled considerably by the fact that his fellow owners had been paying his bills for months, while publicly denying that they were doing exactly that. But as summer approached, Moyes sensed, correctly, that whatever solution was coming would be extremely unpalatable, that he was about to be thrown under the bus.

After months of desperate searching, commissioner Gary Bettman had finally managed to persuade Jerry Reinsdorf, owner of the Chicago Bulls of the National Basketball Association, to make an offer for the Coyotes. But Reinsdorf was no patsy. He understood the franchise's history all too well, and would go only so far, leaving Moyes to swallow a huge loss, not just in evaporating equity but also in the millions of dollars he had personally loaned the team to keep it afloat.

With Reinsdorf and Bettman poised to present their take-it-or-leave-it proposition, out of the mists appeared a white knight, who offered deliverance for the beleaguered Moyes.

Jim Balsillie, one of the brains behind Research In Motion, creator of the ubiquitous BlackBerry, had long had the singular goal of setting up an NHL franchise in downtown Hamilton, Ontario. Problem was, the league had no interest in him doing that—it would set off a legal firestorm for a start, given that both the Toronto Maple Leafs and the Buffalo Sabres laid territorial claim to the market. And, in any case, if they were ever to put a second team in southern Ontario, it would be intended as a mass cash grab for all thirty owners, revenue that couldn't be generated by a team in the working-class Steel City. Bettman had gone to remarkable lengths to thwart Balsillie's previous attempts to buy both the Pittsburgh Penguins and the Nashville Predators, leaving Balsillie with the distinct impression that there was no front door open to him, that his only way to get a team in Hamilton was through the courts, specifically bankruptcy, where a judge might well overrule the NHL's objections in the interest of satisfying creditors.

Balsillie offered $212.5 million for the bankrupt Coyotes, enough to satisfy everyone owed money by the team, on the condition that he be allowed to relocate them. The NHL and its band of lawyers naturally jumped in to fight him on that point, citing the sanctity of its own rules. Meanwhile, thanks to the transparency of the court proceedings, it became clear to all just how empty the dream of sunbelt hockey had become. Since moving from Winnipeg to Phoenix thirteen years earlier, the franchise hadn't once posted a profit, and in the four seasons before the bankruptcy it had incurred losses totalling close to $100 million—losses that under a salary cap system Bettman and the NHL owners had sacrificed an entire season to impose.

Wayne Gretzky was hardly a disinterested bystander. In addition to his coaching salary, which as the court revealed was at the high end of what anyone had imagined—$8 million a season, or approximately eight times what the next highest paid coach in the league was making—he had a small ownership stake in the franchise. Balsillie, in his offer for the team, promised to honour Gretzky's contract in full.

Anyone else who might buy the team would make no such pledge. In fact, a lawyer for the City of Glendale, the Phoenix suburb where the team actually played and which had much to lose in the proceedings, argued that getting rid of the Gretzky obligation in part or entirely would be step one towards financial sanity. For Gretzky, who had so carefully protected his image for so long, it had to be wildly embarrassing, an open discussion of just how little his presence had done to secure hockey's future in Phoenix, or even to make the Coyotes more competitive on the ice.

Hockey fans waited for Gretzky to speak. Would he endorse the interloper, Balsillie, who along with his legal manoeuvring had wrapped his cause in the Canadian flag, launching a public relations campaign under the banner "Make It Seven," stirring anti-NHL and especially anti-Bettman sentiment under the cover of Canadian nationalism? Brantford, his old home, where Wally still lived, was just a twenty-minute drive from Hamilton. Surely that was where his heart still lay.

Or would he be the company man, siding with the league, standing beside the commissioner and the owners? In his hockey life, Gretzky had both end-run the rules when it suited him—signing with the World Hockey Association and in the end entirely avoiding the NHL draft—and had toed the party line, steering clear of controversy, not taking a stand on just about anything that might be deemed controversial.

They waited. And they waited. As the court proceedings dragged on, Balsillie's legal options seemed to narrow, and his chances of winning through the courts seemed a long shot, the idea of a hockey team in Hamilton a pipe dream. But still nothing from Gretzky, until late in June when, with the Coyotes still in limbo, he was cornered by a group of reporters in Vancouver during a public appearance, and was forced to speak.

"In my heart of hearts, I hope one day Hamilton will have a franchise," he said. "They could definitely support a franchise. Everyone knows that. I don't think anybody could question that. . . . Eventually, I'm sure Mr. Balsillie is going to acquire a franchise and live out his dream of putting a team in Hamilton. We just don't know when that's going to be."

But no, that wasn't really an endorsement of Balsillie, or of Hamilton, or of Canada. Gretzky wanted that made clear.

"It's not my fight," he said. "It's between Mr. Balsillie and Jerry Moyes, and the National Hockey League and the commissioner and their office. . . . I'm not involved. I'm just like everyone else, sitting back, waiting to find out what's going to happen, and what will be the direction of our hockey club. . . . It's like anything else. It takes time, and Phoenix is a great city and a great sports town. Obviously there's some turmoil right now, but it looks like things are going to get worked out."

Gretzky had single-handedly changed the direction of professional hockey in North America. He had made the game relevant where it had never mattered before. He had remained an icon in his homeland, despite a two-decade absence, hailed again as a hero for the 2002 Team Canada Olympic gold medal. But now he seemed impotent, had been humiliated, was being badgered by reporters, asked whether he'd accept a pay cut to keep his coaching job in Phoenix, if the team was in fact still there and still in business.

"Yeah," Gretzky said.

By staying out of the debate—or at least by refusing to endorse Balsillie's bid to bring the Coyotes to Hamilton—Gretzky played the good soldier for the league he had done so much to build. In doing so, his carefully cultivated brand took a hit where it was still extremely potent more than twenty years after his departure—in Canada. Balsillie had cleverly framed the debate, at least outside of the courtroom, as being between those who wanted to repatriate the game to its homeland as an act of nationalism and those who resisted, puppets of anti-hockey American interests. By remaining on the sidelines, Gretzky had aligned himself in the public mind with Bettman, a cartoon villain for many Canadian hockey fans long before the Coyotes debacle began.

He might rightly have felt the league owed him something for that—and for the fact that he had deferred some of his compensation for the Coyotes when cash began to run short. But the NHL felt differently. When Balsillie's bid finally hit an insurmountable roadblock (the bankruptcy judge Redfield T. Baum refused to enter the realm of antitrust law, which might have forced the league to allow Balsillie to purchase and move the franchise to Copps Coliseum), and the league was left as the final bidder for the team (Reinsdorf having decided in the end he wanted no part of it), Gretzky was left high and dry, just another unsecured creditor. They didn't have to pay him—so they didn't. They didn't think it was worth a few million dollars, at a time of extreme distress, to make the game's great icon whole.

Of course Gretzky didn't say anything, at least for general consumption. That had never been his style. Instead, as the 2009–10 season began, with Dave Tippett now behind the Coyotes' bench, Gretzky fell silent. He was sighted occasionally at his son's high-school football games in California, and consented to one appearance for the broadcast consortium that would carry the Vancouver 2010 Winter Olympics in Canada, reminiscing about the glorious gold medal run in 2002, and lamenting Canada's abysmal failure in 2006 (strangely enough, given the sensitivities surrounding the Rick Tocchet gambling scandal, he chose to give his interview at the MGM Grand Hotel & Casino in Las Vegas). Gretzky would have no role with the 2010 Canadian Olympic team, other than in a vague advisory capacity. Otherwise, for the first time since early childhood, he would have nothing to do with hockey on a personal level, on a professional level, and for the first time since those squeaky-voiced preadolescent radio interviews, he would effectively disappear from the public eye.

The Coyotes would improve dramatically on ice, but the only potential owners to appear were an underfunded group who planned to play five regular games a season in Saskatoon, of all places. Though Bettman still stood four-square behind other struggling teams in sunbelt locales, it had become clear to all that it was now only a matter of time, that the forces unleashed in 1988, when Gretzky was sold to the Kings, were all played out. In the first days of 2010, credible sources began to suggest that one of those failing franchises was headed back to Winnipeg. In Quebec City, powerful political and business forces were collaborating to return a team there. And though Hamilton seemed destined to forever be left at the altar, there was plenty of money available if someone could find a way to squeeze a second franchise into the Toronto market, which had been monopolized so profitably for so long by the sad-sack Maple Leafs.

But unlike the winter before, Canadians weren't paying much attention to the NHL's travails. Instead, the first Olympic Games staged on home soil since 1988–and the possibility of a Canadian winning the first gold medal, ever, in Canada–dominated the national conversation, beginning with the question of which national sports hero should be chosen to light the cauldron at the Opening Ceremonies.

Under the rules of the International Olympic Committee, the final torchbearer had to be a past, present or "future" Olympian (which ruled out an homage to Terry Fox, one of the most popular options, but didn't rule out Rick Hansen, famous for his round-the-world Man In Motion tour, and also a former Paralympian). Tradition suggested that it was most often a medal winner, and someone with local ties, which pointed towards Nancy Greene-Raine, the BC skier who had been named Canada's greatest female athlete of the twentieth century.

But nearly every time the public was asked, every time a poll was conducted, the name at the top of the list was Wayne Gretzky's. In the coming weeks, Canadians would embrace athletes in a whole host of sports, but in the end, hockey still trumped all, and in the end, if one person was going to be selected for that great honour, it would have to be a hockey player. Who else but Gretzky, then, who had played in the 1998 Winter Olympics in Nagano, who had been part of that first gold medal in fifty years in 2002? Olympic purists might have objected, since the appearance of professionals from team sports had been a late (and in some circles, lamented) addition to the Games, but for John Furlong and a small circle of his colleagues charged with running the Vancouver 2010 Winter Olympics, there was no ignoring the *vox populi*.

Not that they didn't do their best to camouflage those intentions. In the days before the Games began, reports began to circulate that

Gretzky was indeed in Vancouver. Wally was chosen to run one of the last legs of the torch relay, but if he knew what was to come, he certainly wasn't letting on. On the eve of the Opening Ceremonies, Furlong was asked directly if Gretzky was the guy. He tried to deflect the question, suggesting that what was about to happen would be a huge surprise that no one could anticipate. Reports began to filter out from Opening Ceremonies rehearsals of multiple torchbearers, and until the actual moment—really, until after the actual moment—everyone had their suspicions, but no one was quite sure.

On the night in question, in the domed football stadium that normally housed the BC Lions, now magically converted for the occasion, perhaps it should have come as a clue when one of those given the honour of carrying the Olympic flag was another Canadian hockey icon who had left as a young man to ply his trade in the United States, never to really return, the face of the game during another bold expansion: Bobby Orr. The four final torchbearers were gradually revealed to the crowd: Greene-Raine; speed skater Catriona Le May Doan; basketball star Rick Nash, a BC native who played for Canada in the 2000 Summer Olympic Games in Sydney; and yes, Wayne Gretzky (with Hansen off to one side, in a slightly awkward supporting role). The cauldron would rise from the floor, and in the appointed hour, all four would light it together, which seemed a classic Canadian compromise.

Alas, Le May Doan was denied her chance when one of the four arms of the cauldron malfunctioned. After an awkward pause, the other three stepped forward, the great flame erupted, and an Olympic Games which would go on to become a Canadian cultural touchstone had officially begun.

But then, a surprise coda. Gretzky alone, with his torch still burning, ran out of the building, made a slightly awkward exit through the airlock doors designed to make sure the inflatable roof remained aloft, and clambered into the back of a pickup truck. What followed, in the midst of an event that was planned and choreographed to the second, was something like happy, glorious, unscripted chaos. As the rain poured down, the truck moved along the streets of downtown Vancouver, while people poured out of their houses, out of the bars and restaurants, gradually understanding what was going on. A secret, second cauldron—though it wasn't that much of a secret to some—had been constructed by the harbour, where unlike the indoor flame it could burn all day and night. It would be lit by one man alone. They were chanting, "Gretzky, Gretzky" now—and Lord knows, when he was playing against the Canucks, he was never so beloved—following in the truck's wake, nearly surrounding it at times. In his pure white torchbearer's uniform, his face older but still so familiar, Gretzky clambered down at the destination, jogged to the base of the second cauldron, and again the flame erupted.

In that moment, he was what Canadians had always wanted, always imagined, always believed him to be: the embodiment of a place, of a game, of a people. He had left, he had been sold, he had chosen to never come back, and just months before he seemed to have turned his back on a chance to help bring an NHL team back to Canada. None of that mattered. It didn't matter at all.

ACKNOWLEDGMENTS

F OR A BOOK ENVISIONED – at least in my own mind – as a sequel to *Searching for Bobby Orr*, I feel blessed to have again worked with those who had so much to do with its success. This is in fact my fourth book with Knopf Canada, which has been a dream publisher. As always, I would especially like to thank the trio who lured me back into the wonderful world of books: Matthew Sibiga; my friend and music guide Scott Sellers; and my editor and Newfoundland neighbour Diane Martin, who at this stage understands my idiosyncrasies as a writer (and perhaps as a person) better than I do.

I was again aided in my research efforts by Elizabeth Klinck, and by Paul Patskou, who along with digging up archival video and keeping me on the straight and narrow when it came to hockey history also located the photographs that appear in the book. Deft copy editing was provided by Lloyd Davis. My friend, the poet Randall Maggs, was an early reader of the manuscript.

Only two of the principals in the story of the Gretzky trade declined to participate in this project. Wayne Gretzky himself let it be known that he had said everything he had to say on the subject – which left me to rely on the extensive public record. I would especially like to thank his brother Glen and his dad, Walter, for their help in filling in the family's side of the story, and his former agent Michael Barnett, who provided a unique perspective.

Peter Pocklington chose not to be interviewed because he was writing his own book, which presumably will contain his own version of events. Special thanks to Don Metz and everyone at Aquila Productions, who among many other favours (including providing raw video from the famous press conference) showed me an unedited copy of an interview Pocklington conducted on the twentieth anniversary of the trade. Among those who spoke to me for this book, I would especially like to thank Mike Altieri, Ian Barrigan, Dr. Jerry Buss, Brian Cooper, Dan Craig, Al Eagleson, Jeffrey Goodman, Kim Hartley, John Iaboni, Terry Jones, Bill Kenney, Kevin Lowe, Jim Matheson, Bruce McNall, Ralph Mellanby, Roy Mlakar, Marc Nathan, Luc Robitaille, Glen Sather, Nelson Skalbania and Alan Thicke.

Along with archival material from the *Globe and Mail*, the *Los Angeles Times*, the *Edmonton Sun*, the *Edmonton Journal*, the *Brantford Expositor*, *Sports Illustrated* and a selection of other publications, I would especially like to acknowledge the following books that I turned to during my research.

Gretzky: An Autobiography by Wayne Gretzky with Rick Reilly (HarperCollins, 1990)

The Game of Our Lives by Peter Gzowski (McClelland & Stewart Ltd., 1981)

The Glory Barons: The Saga of the Edmonton Oilers by Douglas Hunter (Viking, 1999)

Wayne Gretzky: An Oiler Forever by Terry Jones (published by the *Edmonton Sun*, 1999)

Fun While It Lasted: My Rise and Fall in the Land of Fame and Fortune by Bruce McNall with Michael D'Antonio (Hyperion, 2003)

Bob Miller's Tales From the Los Angeles Kings by Bob Miller with Randy Schultz (Sports Publishing L.L.C, 2006)

The Acquisitors: The Canadian Establishment Volume II by Peter C. Newman (McClelland & Stewart Ltd., 1981)

The Rebel League: The Short and Unruly Life of the World Hockey Association by Ed Willes (McClelland & Stewart Ltd., 2004)

John B. Lee's poem "The Trade that Shook the Hockey World"

appears in the collection *The Hockey Player Sonnets* (Penumbra Press, 2003)

The paper "Gretzky Nation: Canada, Crisis and Americanization" by Steven J. Jackson can be found in *Sports Stars: The Cultural Politics of Sporting Celebrity* (Routledge, 2001)

Finally, I would like to thank my family—my kids Nat, Jake and Holly, and my wife, Jeanie MacFarlane, to whom this book is dedicated—for their support, their patience, their general goodwill, and their sense of fun.

Stephen Brunt has been the lead sports columnist at the *Globe and Mail* since 1989. In addition to *Searching for Bobby Orr*, Brunt is also the author of, to name but one, *Facing Ali: The Opposition Weighs In*, which was made into a feature-length documentary by Pete McCormack. Brunt lives in Hamilton, Ontario, and Winterhouse Brook, Newfoundland.